PEACE AS A
GLOBAL LANGUAGE

PEACE AS A GLOBAL LANGUAGE

Peace and Welfare in the Global and Local Community

EDITORS:
TINA OTTMAN, ZANE RITCHIE,
HUGH PALMER AND DANIEL WARCHULSKI

PEACE AS A GLOBAL LANGUAGE
PEACE AND WELFARE IN THE GLOBAL AND LOCAL COMMUNITY

iUniverse books may be ordered through booksellers or by contacting:

iUniverse
1663 Liberty Drive
Bloomington, IN 47403
www.iuniverse.com
1-800-Authors (1-800-288-4677)

Because of the dynamic nature of the Internet, any web addresses or links contained in this book may have changed since publication and may no longer be valid. The views expressed in this work are solely those of the author and do not necessarily reflect the views of the publisher, and the publisher hereby disclaims any responsibility for them.

Any people depicted in stock imagery provided by Thinkstock are models, and such images are being used for illustrative purposes only. Certain stock imagery © Thinkstock.

ISBN: 978-1-4917-9944-4 (sc)
ISBN: 978-1-4917-9945-1 (e)

Library of Congress Control Number: 2016909241

Print information available on the last page.

iUniverse rev. date: 07/19/2016

CONTENTS

FOREWORD

This book, too long in coming, is the outcome of the work of a group of authors and socially-engaged professionals who took part in the 2013 conference of the interdisciplinary international conference series, *Peace as a Global Language* (PGL).

PGL was conceived in the anxious year following 911 by activists of the Gender Awareness in Language Education group in Japan, "Wanting to emphasize peace, feeling very sad and worried". The founders envisioned, "a healing conference devoted entirely to social awareness and socially aware teaching". Meanwhile the times have become even less peaceful; with this driving imperative in mind, the conference has been attended annually by activists, aid professionals, academics and students, from inside and outside of Japan since 2002, and has been held in a variety of locations throughout the Japanese archipelago.

This current volume represents the third in the projected series, and is divided into two parts, *Part 1 - Peace education and praxis* and *Part 2 – Peace and conflicts*.

Part 1 - Peace education and praxis

As Japan prepares to move away from its critical 'peace article', Article 9 of the Japanese Constitution, *Part 1* opens with the timely chapter, **How do Japanese elementary school children perceive peace and war?** from **Motoko Abe,** an associate professor of Tokyo Gakugei University. Via comprehensive research including questionnaires, semi-structured interviews, classroom observation, and students' portfolios at Minami-Alps Children's Village Elementary School in Yamanashi, Japan, Abe measured changes in children's perceptions of peace and war. Utilizing a case study of English lessons with a theme of "Land Mines and Peace" for fourth and fifth graders in Japan (designed to cultivate children's motivation to learn English as well as to take action for peace) Abe found that for the students, peace does not merely mean absence of war, but a condition for which individuals should work towards, wherein "everyone can keep smiling". Concern for issues faced by children in other regions of the world, sensitivity towards land mine victims, and showing willingness to support the victims were outcomes of these lessons, indicating the possibility of sensitizing students on global issues through integrated and themed English language lessons.

In a climate of 'media muzzling' and self-censorship in Japan, the second chapter, **The media literacy deficit in Japan: Exploring the link between digital citizenship, cultural diversity and critical thinking**, also examines the roots of growing Japanese unease. Lisa Friedli explores the link between digital citizenship, cultural diversity and critical thinking, by examining the significance of the removal of the critical thinking component from media literacy curricula in Japan. Considering critical thinking essential to media literacy, Friedli describes an almost exclusive focus on pragmatic, vocational use of technology in Japanese curricula, contrasts this with media studies curricula in the west, and argues that guiding Japanese students to acquire critical thinking skills not only does not threaten cultural heritage or incite non-conformity, but in fact has the potential to safeguard tradition by reinforcing the recognition and distinction of Japanese culture.

Chapter 3 takes a wider theoretical approach. In **Toward a utopian peace education,** Nick Kasparek closely examines various theoretical frameworks and current conceptions of Peace Education, outlining some of the imminent concerns and trends within the field, as related to the notion of postmodernity. Within this context, the author questions and challenges a number of fundamental views and current premises. In addressing these issues, the chapter goes on to detail and outline the transformative potential of utopian studies in opening up new possibilities to engage with, affect, and positively change Peace Education.

Returning once more to the Japanese context, and to its endangered indigenous minority, the Ainu of the northern island of Hokkaido, renowned Ainu activist Akemi Shimada, together with co-authors Jennifer Louise Teeter and Takayuki Okazaki discuss **Education and spaces of, for, and by Ainu: Lessons from the 2013 New Zealand Ainumosir Exchange Program**. They describe the origins of the Aotearoa Ainumosir Exchange Program, in which a group of Ainu youth took part in a five-week cultural exchange program with Maori in New Zealand in 2013 to learn about endeavors for cultural survival. They also discuss two initiatives that were introduced into Japan upon the groups' return: the *Te Ataarangi* method of language revitalization and the *cas ankar* movement to establish a Tokyo Ainu community center.

In Chapter 5, towards the creation of a dynamic learning environment to promote learning for peace, James Short considers lessons learned from the experience of the creation and delivery of a new course in peace studies at the Law Faculty of Toyo University, Tokyo. To illustrate his belief in the importance of specifically-targeted learning for peace, ways in which students and young people are bombarded with information from various sources are discussed. Short documents the progress of the course, describes how difficulties were encountered and handled, and discusses future prospects for the development of the course in this chapter.

Chapter 6, **The World through music: Using the Putumayo World Music site to enhance cultural awareness and linguistic use in an EMI classroom by** Susan Sullivan, discusses some of the linguistic, pedagogic and cultural benefits of exploring non-mainstream music in a Japanese classroom setting, using English as the means of instruction. Is empathy a necessary part of communicative competence? Can exercises be developed to encourage the connection that can lead to empathy, and is it necessary for healthy global interaction? Sullivan explores these questions through a study of first-year comparative culture students at Aichi University in Aichi, Japan and the use of the Putumayo World Music website as a resource for learning both research and presentation skills.

Part 2 – Peace and conflicts

Part 2 of **Peace as a global language: Peace and welfare in the global and local community** engages with many issues relevant to the authors' Japanese context, but also moves farther afield, taking in a range of contexts and global conflicts.

After the fall of the dictator, former President Ferdinand Marcos, the Southern Philippines continued to struggle with Muslim separatists, particularly the Moro National Liberation Front (MNLF). Filipino government worker and scholar **Travis Ryan Delos Reyes** re-examines socio-economic, political and religious aspects as the major causes of armed conflict, with particular reference to the richly-resourced island of Mindanao, in Chapter 7, **Natural resource and topography: Rethinking the cause of conflict in Mindanao**. Using greed and viability approaches, the chapter examines the relationship of natural resources and integration of resources to finance such an armed conflict. Combinations of geographical locations, which provide secure sanctuary and an ineffective state, were additionally considered, using a combination of qualitative and content analysis. While concurring with Amartya Sen's argument that poverty alone cannot cause a conflict, Delos Reyes maintains that other factors are needed to elevate the struggle leading to violence: certain indicators do in fact have a hold on the conflict and could trigger another uprising if not given due investigation and taken into account in collective bargaining in the future. Most conflict analyses focus solely on ethno-religious or ethno-nationalistic factors, but other factors, like national resources and topography, are, according to Delos Reyes, the glue that binds these factors together in inflicting a long struggle and may thrust or elevate any uprising to the next level. Hence, they too are worthy of serious consideration, claiming their place alongside other leading conflict-causing factors.

In Chapter 8, **The sun also rises: A nationalist turn in Japanese foreign policy?** Steven Green returns to topical regional matters, and assesses Japan's role in preserving peace in Northeast Asia. He queries whether a hardening of attitudes in the region reveals a nationalistic or militaristic propensity in Japan's foreign policy. Analysing the influence of public views about Japan's constitution on the nation's defense policies, the development of Japan's Self-Defense Forces into a powerful armed force and attitudes around current tensions between Japan and South Korea and China over territorial claims, Green reveals that the public remains opposed to the use of force and that the popularity of Japan's "peace constitution" remains.

Chapter 9 moves from the Far East to the Near East of the Asian continent. **The Israeli-Palestinian conflict: simulacra of peacemaking** by Tina Ottman, engages with the manner in which the search for peace in the Israel-Palestine conflict focuses on facsimiles of peacemaking. Despite the fact that over 30 years have passed since 'the end of the peace process' the 1983 Declaration of Principles on Interim Self-Government Arrangements (the 'Oslo' Accords), as far as Israelis and Palestinians are concerned, since then there has been a great deal of process and even less peace, suggesting that answers are likely to lie elsewhere, beneath the layers of official elite peacemaking tracks. This chapter considers critically the major processes and initiatives that have taken place since 1991, when the parties commenced an official process of recognition and negotiation, and argues that narratives of collective trauma and willful historical amnesia underpin the conflict; without recognition and treatment of these deep underlying sociological seams and fissures, no resolution is possible.

In Chapter 10, **The Yamba Dam: Conflict and consequences for a rural community,** Hugh Palmer examines the use of state power and its effect on the community of Naganohara in Gunma, during the planning and construction of the Yamba dam, the most expensive and divisive such project ever built in Japan. The contentious 60 year history of the project is examined, along with a critique of the relationship between politicians and the bureaucrats of the Ministry of Construction, and of how the dam, which was initially opposed by 80% of the affected residents, eventually came to be approved, planned and forced towards completion, leading to the relocation of over 1000 citizens and the transformation of the economy and social structure of the towns affected.

One of the book's most topical chapters is Chapter 11: **Language choice and political preferences in Ukraine: Can language unite the nation?** Bogdan Pavliy considers the electoral situation in his native Ukraine and compares it to the electoral choices of individuals and communities. Recognizing that language is one of the principal ways people recognize and realize their belonging to a community, the author analyzes voter choices by region and concludes that language division in the Ukraine is diminishing, and that therefore any attempt to push for one language choice at the expense of another is likely to be at the expense of political unity.

Finally, in **Chapter 12: Multiculturalism: Misconceptions, Misunderstandings and the Current State of Affairs,** Warchulski and Ritchie examine the theme of multiculturalism with a focus on the Canadian model of multicultural policies. They discuss the ways that this issue has been viewed in the media, assess the available research, and conclude that there is much to learn from the Canadian experience and that it offers valid solutions to the challenge of creating culturally plural societies into which all citizens are able to harmoniously coexist.

PART 1

Peace education and praxis

CHAPTER 1

How do Japanese elementary school children perceive peace and war? Changes in children's perceptions through English lessons on land mines and peace

Motoko Abe

An anecdote from the classroom: When I showed a picture of a boy who had lost his leg sitting up on a bald wooden bed without anything to keep him warm, my students gazed at him and one asked, "Who is this boy?" Then another student answered, "I know, he lost his leg by a landmine, right?" "Yes, you're right." I answered. But I wondered if the students could understand how sad he felt on the bed, how scared he was when it happened, and how desperately he longed for peace. (Journal entry, September 19, 2014)

Introduction

Themes of international education including peace, multiculturalism, human rights, and environmental issues have been found in English textbooks in Japanese secondary education since 1981 (Murakami, 2007). However, there are not a large number of studies that have been conducted on students' perception of the issues through English lessons at secondary education (i.e. Iino, 1994; Ishimori, 2008). Needless to say, at elementary school level, since compulsory English education was only introduced in 2011, limited results have been obtained (Yoshimura, 2005).[1] This trend can be found worldwide. There have been no more than about 30 empirical studies on children's or adolescents' perceptions of peace or war since the 1960s (Deng, 2010). Considering these facts, it is deemed to be worth investigating children's perception of peace and war through English language lessons at elementary school in Japan, especially when English is expected to be a compulsory subject for fifth and sixth graders.[2]

Moreover, shifting our ground to peace education in Japan, it is said that peace education in Japan has often focused on the inhuman cruelty of war for cultivating students' emotional sympathy to "precious peace" but had less emphasis on practical aspects for them to take action to realize a peaceful world (Nishio, 2011). This may suggest that it is now necessary to raise students' willingness or motivation to take action for realizing peace in their local and global communities through education in the Japanese context.

The author has been teaching English with global issues at Minami-Alps Children's Village Elementary School, a private Japanese elementary school in Yamanashi, since 2009. In this article, with the aforementioned background in mind, a case study of the author's English lessons with a theme of "Land Mines and Peace" for fourth and fifth graders is discussed, featuring changes in the children's perception toward peace and war through English lessons by cultivating their motivation to learn English as well as taking action for peace. The discussion is based on the results of questionnaires, semi-structured interviews, classroom observation, and students' portfolios. Pedagogical suggestions for further practice are discussed as well.

Factors that influence children's perception of war and peace

As mentioned previously, the number of empirical studies that investigate children's and adolescents' perceptions of war and peace is limited (Deng, 2010). These studies, however, provide profound insights into factors that influence children's perceptions of war and peace such as age, gender, and socio-cultural context. First, let's take a look at the age factor. An assumption that children develop a concept of peace and war at a young age is supported by many studies, but still answers for the question "How young should a child be?" may vary depending on the impact of the children's socio-cultural contexts (parents, school, friends, religion, media and social experiences) (Deng, 2010). Nevertheless, most studies suggest that fourth or fifth graders, the same age group as the target students in this study, are old enough to develop concepts of war and peace and show basic understanding of social dimensions of war (Alvik, 1968; Cooper, 1965; Hall, 1993; Myers-Bowmans *et al.*, 2003; etc.). This may be explained by Piaget's developmental theory, which suggests that children develop a capacity for reciprocal reasoning when they reach the formal operational stage (11–12 years old), which enables them to perceive a conflict behind war.

Moreover, children at this stage may show gender-related differences. Vrien's (1999) review of research during the 1980s under "nuclear fear" suggests the following tendency between boys and girls: Generally boys may have a positive attitude toward war from the age of seven onward, and they tend to identify war with soldiers and war technology such as weapons, although they try to reconsider this positive attitude toward war and even become critical from the age of about 11 onward. On the other hand, girls are clearly against war and in favor of peace from an early age, and they have a tendency to feature victims and caring aspects of life in war. Vrien also points out that these gender differences create totally separated worlds between the two groups that should be more recognized in peace education practice. In this study, a tendency of boys to identify war with war technology such as war tanks or weapons was found. However, their perception of peace and judgment of war seemed similar to that of the girls, who were in favor of peace and showed sympathy to war victims as well as belief against war. It should be noted that both groups mentioned that peace must be achieved by all participants in a society, which may show understanding of their roles for a peaceful society.

This fact leads to the third topic: socio-cultural factors that influence students' perception of war and peace. Since the target school in this study has a unique school system, schools as a social system needs to be addressed. Raviv *et al.* (1999) point out that there are four approaches in the development of the social knowledge of students, one of which is closely related to this discussion: the ecological approach. The ecological approach emphasizes the importance of understanding the relationships between a child and his/her environmental systems such as the family, school, community, and culture. In this model, "development involves the interplay between changing children and their changing relationships with different ecological (societal) systems" (Valsiner, 1979, 1988; Valsiner, 1988; Vygotsky, 1978).[3] Moreover, schools play an important role for the socialization of children's understanding of political knowledge (Löfgren, 1995).[4] The unique features of the school and discussion of its influence on the students' perception are discussed later in this article.

Peace education in Japan

Nishio (2011, p. 9) claims that there have been three main objectives of peace education in Japan: (1) to teach the inhuman cruelty of war, to raise sympathy for anti-war awareness, and to value peace and life (= to promote emotional sympathy); (2) to understand the causes and power structure of war scientifically (= to promote scientific recognition); and (3) to clarify practical processes for preventing war and maintaining peace (= to promote practical perspectives). He then offers the criticism that the first objective has been mainly focused on in peace education in Japan, while the other two have not been valued to raise students' social awareness to prevent war. This discussion may pose a challenge to promote students' social awareness, including their willingness to take action for peace through English language lessons. Therefore, the author considers that this challenge should be addressed in this study.

The school

Minami-Alps Children's Village Elementary School was opened in 2009 in Minami-Alps City in Yamanashi as one of eight children's village schools in Japan. The school started with only 18 students in 2009, but as of 2014 over 150 students are enrolled in the elementary and junior high schools. The first children's village school in Japan, Kinokuni Children's Village was founded in Wakayama. The founder of the Kinokuni Children's Village, Shinichiro Hori, was inspired by the works of John Dewey (learning by doing) and A. S. Neill who advocated "free education" for children. The basic philosophy of free education can be defined as education that secures an environment where children can "have the right to choose freely what they want to do with their lives" because "they have the ability to govern themselves effectively in a working democratic community" (Neill, 1992, p. 25). This philosophy makes the school exceptional in the sense that the school aims for establishing a learning community that consists of students, teachers, and staff members. Most school decisions are made in meetings where all community members have an equal right.

There are three basic principles of the children's village school. The first principle is self-determination. In the children's village school, children's initiative is highly respected. Their thinking processes, such as generating ideas, processing information, testing a hypothesis and evaluating the results, are valued, and students are encouraged to spend a lot of time exploring all these processes. Moreover, in a teacher-centered approach, adults make the majority of school decisions, even those that are closely related to children's lives. In the children's village school, however, teachers simply prepare the most suitable environment and conditions that enable the students to make their own decisions. Children should be allowed to make mistakes as a basic human right. In addition, in order to remove the teachers' authority thoroughly, teachers are called by their nicknames, not by their family names. The second principle is project-based learning (learning by doing). Children learn by taking an active part in a project planned and organized by themselves. This approach can provide useful and sustainable knowledge for the life of each child. Lastly, the principle focuses on individualization. Each child is considered to have his/her own learning style, aptitude, and developmental difference as an independently thinking individual. Flexibility of grouping, diversification of learning styles, and the use of a wide range of learning materials support the individualization of learning.

The school curriculum is very unique. Projects are their main activity, and the classes are organized according to the projects. Children can choose their own class, which is mixed-aged, according to their interest in the project. There were five projects in 2014: "Craft class," making craft arts and wooden school equipment like a jungle gym; "Food class," processing food and cooking with ingredients that they have grown; "Performing Arts class," creating and staging musicals; "History class," exploring and experiencing traditional ways of life in the area; "Newspaper class," reporting current issues of the school and the local area; and "Farming class," growing fruits in the school fruit farms. "Basic Study" means that the students study so-called school subjects such as math, language, science or social studies to gain basic knowledge or skills closely related to each project. "School Meeting (=assembly)" is highly valued in this school where every participant of the school including the students, staff, teachers, and even the principal has an equal right to make school decisions. The discussion agendas include school events, troubles among students, school etiquette, or suggestions by each project team that may influence other teams or the entire school. Finally, this article focuses on the "English class", 45 minutes on Thursday afternoons to fourth and fifth graders with a content-based approach.[5]

The English curriculum and the students

The author has been trying to integrate international education into English language instruction. There are four basic areas in international education suggested by Globe International Teachers Circle (2005). They include human rights education, peace education, intercultural communication, and area studies. Partly because this school highly values democratic management by the children, human rights and peace education are considered as important elements of the school curricula. Thus these two content areas are essential in our English curriculum as well. There are 24 students in this class, six of whom are female students while 18 are boys. There are 18 students in the fourth grade and six students in the fifth grade. Since this school has a sister school in Scotland and provides three-week or two-month programs in Scotland every year, more than half of the students have an experience of staying abroad.

The English lessons of "Land Mines and Peace" and the children's reaction in class

The author referred to *Theme-Based Approach for Elementary School English Activities: Book 2* (Machida and Takiguchi, 2010)to develop this unit. Table 1 shows the unit plan of "Land Mines and Peace." The lessons were given from September 5 through October 10, 2013. The author intentionally did not start this unit with a land mine victim because she wanted the students to consider the victim as one of their friends in the world whom they might meet in the future. Therefore, the unit was started by introducing the victim with other children around the world and phrases such as "Where is s/he from?" and "What's his/her name?" were taught.

Table 1: Unit Plan of "Land Mines and Peace"

	Topics	Activity	Language Focus
1	Children around the world	Listen to voices of children around the world. Introduction of action verbs	Where is s/he from? What's his/her name?: sing, play soccer, eat, talk, etc.
2	Let's do something together	Think what you want to do together with the children around the world.	What do you want to do with —? I want to play soccer with —.
3	The land mine victim: Yan Chai	Guess what happened to Yan Chai and think how to communicate with him.	What's your name? What happened? I want to – with Yan Chai.
4	Our messages	Write messages about what they want to stop and what they need.	No more — (i.e. wars). We need —(i.e. peace).
5	Meet Craig Kielburger	Learn "Free the Children" activities, things that one child can start.	Please stop— (child labor). Let's start —(smiling).
6	Peace poster	Make "MY PEACE POSTER"	What is peace? smiles, no wars, happiness, and etc.

In the second lesson, the children interviewed each other, asking, "What do you want to do with (John from Canada)?" "I want to play soccer with (him)." In the third lesson, the focus shifted to the land mine victim, Yan Chai. A picture of Yan Chai in a Japanese newspaper was shown, and the students were asked to guess what happened and to think what they wanted to ask the child. The students noticed that he had lost his left leg, he seemed very sad, there was another child who had lost one's leg behind him, and the like. The students' answers for the question "What do you want to ask the child?" include "What happened?" "Where are your family?" "Do you go to school?" "Don't you feel cold?" and so on. To answer their questions, the author read a part of the newspaper. Yan Chai happened to step on a land mine while he was fighting as a child soldier in Cambodia. The fact that Yan Chai became a landmine victim when he was fighting surprised the students greatly because they expected he had been playing or helping his family in a farm. In the third class, the students wrote their messages using "no more" and "we need" to express what they wanted to stop or what they needed as they referred to Yan Chai's message "No more land mines. We need peace." The author thought that it might be difficult for the students to answer the question without any input, so she used some picture cards to make them think about what they wanted to stop or needed such as wars, land mines, bullying (a picture of children talking behind back), fighting (a picture of two children quarreling), food, smiles, a meeting (a picture of their school meeting), music, and so on. These inputs might have influenced the students' answers. Examples of their answers include "No more wars, land mines, hunger, bullying, etc." "We need smiles, food, music, meetings, etc." When the author told the students to answer with their own ideas, the following answers came up: "No more suffering." "We need happiness, life, living things, the sun, and the earth." Student T, who seldom speaks out in class and has difficulty writing English, even wrote "No more bullying. We need hap(p)iness." In the fourth lesson, Craig Kielburger, who advocated better conditions for victims of child labor and started Free the Children was introduced (Kielburger and Major, 1998). The reason for discussing what he did for other children was to make the students realize that even a child like them can start something for someone who faces a problem.

In the final lesson the students made a poster including what they think is necessary to attain peace. Picture cards that show the students' answers for the question "What do you think is important for peace?", which was asked before the lessons to understand peace, were used. Their answers include "consideration" "pick up trash" "do not pollute air/water" and so on. Then the question "What is peace?" was asked for their peace poster.

Words that the students wrote in their peace posters include "free (freedom)" "play" "world peace" "smiles" "keep (protect) nature" "friends" "science", and so on. One student wrote sentences in Japanese: "*Minna de sekai wo heiwa ni, minna de minna wo shiawase ni, minna de minna wo taisetsu ni*" ("All should work for world peace. All should make us all happy. All should value us all"). Another student wrote "*minna ga jiyu ni tanoshiku dekimasu you ni*" ("I wish everyone in the world be to free and have fun"). These examples illustrate that their key concept for peace is *"minna ga shiawase nara heiwa"*, which can be translated as "When all people are happy, the world is at peace." This concept was also found in classroom observation.

Results of questionnaires and interviews with children

Questionnaires asking about landmines and peace were given to the students before and after the lessons. Of 24 students, 18 could answer both questionnaires. The questions included these: (1) Can you associate any word with land mines? (2) What do you know about land mines? (3) What do you think is important for peace? (4) Do you want to know how children live in other countries? (5) Do you want to know about problems children face in other countries? (6) Do you want to discuss "peace" in class? (7) Do you think land mines have significance for us living in Japan? (8) Do you want to do something for children suffering from land mines? (9) Do you think you can do something for children suffering from land mines? The students answered according to a scale of 1–4 (from 1, "I totally disagree," to 4, "I totally agree") for questions 4 through 9. In a follow-up informal interview, sessions were conducted after class for two girls and two boys who provided informative and thoughtful answers for the given questions. Needless to say, classroom observation and the students' portfolios were effective resources which helped to understand their perceptions of peace and war.

Results: Changes in the children's perceptions

The results for questions 1 through 3 are shown in Charts 1 through 6. Details of the results for each question are followed by the charts. In the pre-survey of question 1, one-third of the students answered "No, I can't," 28% mentioned feelings such as fear or despair, and 22% described the functions of land mines such as "a land mine is a bomb which explodes when someone steps on it". On the other hand, in the post-survey, the result showed that only one student answered "No, I can't," whereas the ratio of the students who expressed feelings increased to 33% (from five to six students), and the ratio for land mine descriptions increased from four to seven students, or 39%. One student associated land mines with war in the post-survey. This may indicate that the students increased their knowledge about land mines through the lessons.

Charts 1 and 2: Q1. "Can you associate any words with land mines?"

N = 18 (M: 12/F: 6) *the same hereinafter

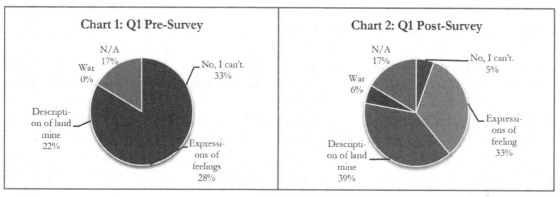

Charts 3 and 4 also show that approximately one-third of the students mentioned that they didn't know anything about land mines, whereas 39% of the students, 7 of 18, mentioned their functions, and a couple of them talked about their negative consequences, such as losing one's leg(s) or arm(s). In the follow-up interview which was conducted after class individually, one student explained several kinds of land mine which disclosed his deep knowledge about land mines. In the post-survey, the ratio of "consequences" increased while the ratio of "nothing" decreased. The picture of Yan Chai having lost his leg by a land mine shown in class might have impressed the students with its consequence. The reason for the increase of "N/A" can be explained by a following comment by a student: "Why should we answer the same question?" This may indicate that some students might think that it would be ridiculous to answer the same question on their knowledge both before and after the lessons.

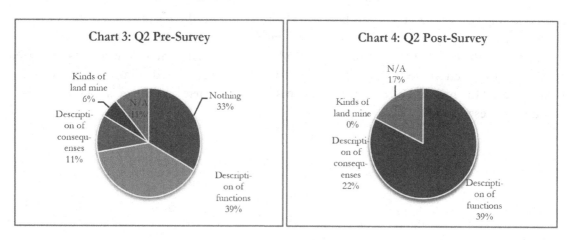

Charts 3 and 4: Q2. "What do you know about land mines?"

Charts 5 and 6: Q3. "What do you think is important for peace?"

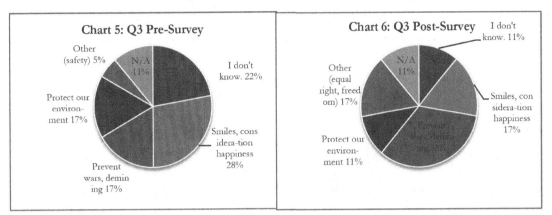

The third question was about peace: "What do you think is important for peace?" In the pre-survey, there were three students who mentioned it would be important to protect our environment for peace. The fact that the students could relate environmental problems to peace was unexpected to this author. This may suggest that children not in war, who cannot have actual images of war, may relate peace or a peaceful society with what they can improve in their life such as environmental problems. Although four students answered "I don't know", about 66% of the students had some ideas regarding means to attain peace: preventing wars or demining, smiles, consideration to others, happiness, and safety. In the post-survey the number of students who could think of means to attain peace slightly increased from 12 to 14, or about 78%. The students who listed prevention of wars or demining and direct counter measures increased and more varieties of answers in the category of "other" were found in the post-survey, such as science, freedom, and equal rights.

The bar graph (Graph 1 below) shows the results of questions 4 through 9. The students answered these questions according to a scale of 1–4 (from 1, "I totally disagree" to 4, "I totally agree"). It should be pointed out that the average scores for questions 4, 5, 7, and 8 increased by more than 0.28, which might indicate changes of the students' perceptions, although the differences are not statistically significant because the sample is small. The students might have increased their interest in children in the world, especially their problems (the average score for question 5 increased by 0.61) as well as their willingness to help children suffering from landmines (increased by 0.31). From classroom observation, some students did not show any interest in this issue at all before the lessons, merely giving irrelevant answers for the questions. To my surprise, however, they all recorded higher scores after the lessons, particularly for questions 6, 7, and 8.

It should be noted however, that the average score for question 9 showed only a slight difference of 0.06 before and after the lessons. This may suggest a difficulty in encouraging primary graders to take action by themselves, although Craig Kielburger was introduced in lesson 4 as a role model at their age who took action to help other children of his age group.

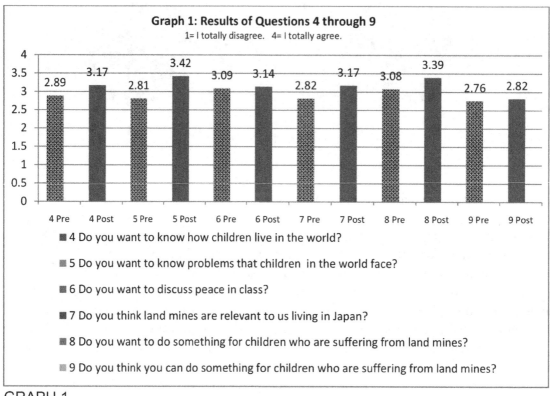

GRAPH 1

Conclusion

Global issues have been found in English textbooks for secondary education in Japan since the 1980s. However, not many empirical studies have been conducted on students' perception of the issues through English language lessons. Previous studies on children's perception of peace and war suggest several factors such as age, gender, and social contexts influence their perception. In terms of age, the target students are 10—11 year olds who may have fully developed concepts of war and peace and understand the social dimensions of war. At this stage, gender differences are also found. Moreover, schools may play an important role for children to understand how a society functions as a social system. From a perspective of peace education, it should be noted that peace education in Japan has less emphasis on practical perspectives of war and peace to raise students' social awareness. Considering these backgrounds, this study aims to investigate changes of fourth and fifth graders' perception of war and peace through the English language lessons of "Land Mines and Peace," which aimed to cultivate their practical perspective of war and willingness to take action for realizing peace.

In the English lessons, the students learned about Yan Chai, who lost his leg by a land mine as he was fighting as a child soldier, wrote messages using "No more/We need" referring to Yan's message "No more land mines. We need peace," and created "My Peace Poster," including what they believe is necessary for peace. The investigation of their perceptions of war and peace is based on results of questionnaires before and after the lessons, semi-structured interviews, classroom observation, and their portfolios. First, by investigating the students' messages in the "No more/We need" worksheets, the following examples were found: "No more wars, landmines, bullying, suffering." "We need smiles, meetings, happiness, life, living things, the sun, and the earth." It should be remarked what "meetings" mean to them. As mentioned in the previous section, the researched school is one of eight children's villages in Japan, in which curriculum is greatly influenced by works of A. S. Neill, who advocated "free education" for children. Adapting Neill's educational philosophy, the school aimed to create a democratic learning community and hold weekly meetings, where all participants including the students, teachers, and staff members have equal rights to make school decisions. The students seem to consider this school meeting as very important because this is a means to manage their school in a democratic way, which should also be an essential tool to attain peace at school.

Second, in "My Peace Poster," the students wrote "free (freedom)" "play" "world peace" "smiles" "keep (protect) nature" "friends" "science" and so on. They mentioned not only direct countermeasures like preventing wars or demining but also peaceful attitudes such as smiles, awareness of human rights such as freedom, and consciousness of environmental problems such as "do not pollute air/water." This may indicate that the students perceive peace from multiple perspectives. It can be said that peace for the students may not merely mean absence of war (negative peace) but a condition in which "everyone can keep smiling," their common definition of peace, which leads to positive peace. The students seemed to reflect what they could do, including smiling, respecting others' rights, and protecting their environment, to think about means for realizing a peaceful world. It's worthy to note that several students mentioned responsibilities of an individual for the society (i.e., "All should work for world peace. All should make us all happy. All should value us all"). Whether this awareness is an influence of the school context should be investigated further.

The results of the questionnaires and the interviews show that the students' knowledge or image of land mines includes not exclusively kinds and consequences of landmines but emotional expressions such as despair and fear. This may indicate that they understand that land mines or war can be very traumatic experiences for the victims. In addition, it was found that their interest in problems that children in other countries face, an emotional connectedness with land mine child victims, and willingness to support the children were increased after the lessons. This may pose a possibility of changing students' perception through English language lessons with global issues, a theme (content)-based approach.

However, this study presents the following challenges for further research and practice. First of all, as the result of question 9 shows, the students' confidence to take action by themselves to support children facing a problem remains low, which means that their practical perspective was not promoted as expected. Further research and practice should be conducted for the promotion. One of the solutions may be a direct encounter with children abroad to talk about their problems. As their motivation to help the children grows, they will gain confidence about how they can help. Second, for improving their English language skills, it is necessary to clarify how content-based English lessons, as in this study, can improve students' English, keeping a good balance of language and content input. It is important to increase students' interest in global issues so that they can think of actions to take for realizing a peaceful world, while increasing motivation for learning English or a foreign language to express their ideas and opinions, which will also be a tool for peace, at the same time. Last but not least, it is worth investigating how a school context can play a role in constructing a student's perception of war and peace, because the students mentioned the importance of their school meeting for peace, which enables them to manage the school in a democratic way. This experience should promote their understanding of how a conflict should be solved in a community to live with others in a peaceful way.

Vriens (1999) claims that peace educators have a responsibility to decide what to do with information they present for their children, knowing that the children have a limited ability to grasp problems of life and death at a global level.[6] Paying attention to this claim, however, I would like to challenge their limitation by English language lessons with global issues because it has become essential for children to develop their identity as global citizens equipped with language tools to communicate in this global society. I believe that teachers should be aware that a core of students' identity could be constructed by experiences to attain peace by democratic means in their local community such as the classroom or school, and every single lesson can provide this experience. I will continue this challenge and share my experience with other teachers in order to raise as many future global citizens as possible.

References

Alvik, T. (1968) The development of views on conflict, war, and peace among school children: A Norwegian case study. *Journal of Peace Research*, 5(2): 171–195.

Asakawa, K. and Matsui, K. (2003, 1st September) Promoting peace in English language classroom-'A culture of peace' as its theoretical background and practical implication for conflict resolution in daily bases. *Conference Proceedings, JACET 42nd Annual Convention*, Sendai: 198–199.

Bronfenbrenner, U. (1979) *The ecology of human development: Experiences of nature and design.* Cambridge, MA: Harvard University Press.

Bronfenbrenner, U. (1988) Interacting systems in human development. Research paradigms: Present and future. In Bolger, N., Caspi, A., Downey, G. and Moorehouse, M. (eds.) *Persons in context: Developmental processes.* Cambridge: Cambridge University Press.

Cooper, P. (1965) The development of the concept of war. *Journal of Peace Research*, 2(1): 1–17.

Deng, L. (2010) *Children's perceptions of war—A comparison study between Taiwanese American children and Non-Taiwanese American children.* Saarbruecken, Germany: LAP (Lambert Academic Publishing).

Globe International Teachers Circle (2005). *New global education in English [Shin eigode manabou kokusairikai kyouiku].* Kanagawa: Bell Works.

Hall, R. (1993) How children think and feel about war and peace: An Australian study. *Journal of Peace Research* 30(22): 181–196.

Iino, A. (1994) Teaching about the United Nations through the hunger issue in an English as a foreign language class. *Social Education* 58(7): 438–439.

Ishimori, H. (2008) The possibilities of introducing global issues through content-based instruction in English language classes [*Global issuewo ishikishita naiyoutyuushinshidouhouniyoru eigonojyugyouno kanousei*]. *The Journal of International Education* 14: 82–103.

Kielburger, C. and Major, K. (1998) *Free the children: A young man's personal crusade against child labor.* New York: HarperCollins.

Löfgren, H. (ed.). (1995) *Peace education and human development*. Malmö, Sweden: University of Lund, School of Education.

Machida, J. and Takiguchi, M. (2010) *Theme-based approach for elementary school English activities. [Te-mademanabu Shogakko Eigokatsudou] Book 2*. Tokyo: Sanshusha.

Maruyama, Y. (1993) History and prospect of peace education at our school 2—Reports on the students' perception of peace [*Honkouni okeru heiwakyouikuno ayumito tennbou (sono2)—Seitono heiwaninnshikini kannshite*], *Bulletin of Nagoya University School of Education Affiliated Upper and Lower Secondary School* 38:43-50.

Murakami, K. (2007) Changes in English education over education for international understanding [*Kokusairikaikyouikuwo meguru eigokyouikuno hensen: Gakusyushidouyouryou oyobi kyoukasyowo tegakarini*]. *Bulletin of Saitama Gakuen University (Faculty of Humanities)* 7:205-220.

Murakami, T. (2013) Evaluation of Hiroshima study: Surveys of the pupils of attached Momoyama elementary school in 2011 [*Hiroshimagakushuwo okonau heiwakyouikuno hyouka—Fuzokumomoyama shogakkouno 2011nenndochosawo jireitoshite*]. *Bulletin of Kyoto University School of Education* 122: 55-71.

Myers-Bowman, K.S., Walker, K. and Myers-Walls, J.A. (2005) Differences between war and peace are big: Children from Yugoslavia and the United States describe peace and war. *Peace and Conflict: Journal of Peace Psychology* 11(2): 177-198.

Neill, A.S. (author) Lamb, A. (ed.) (1992) *Summerhill School—A new view of childhood*. NY: St. Martin's Press. (1st edition, Penguin Books, 1960).

Nishio, O. (2011) *Theory and practice of peace education at schools in Japan [Gakkoniokeru heiwakyouikuno shisou to jissen]*. Tokyo.Gakujyutsu Shuppan Kai.

Raviv, A., Oppenheimer, L. and Bar-Tal, D. (eds.) (1999). *How children understand war and peace: A call for international peace education*. San Francisco, US: Jossey-Bass Publishers.

Valsiner, J. (1988) Ontogeny of co-construction of culture within socially organized environmental settings. In Valsiner, J. (ed.) *Child development within culturally structured environments: Social co-construction and environmental guidance in development*. Norwood, NJ: Ablex.

Vriens, L.J.A. (1987) *Pedagogiek tussen vrees en vrede: Een pedagogische theorie over uredesopvoeding [Pedagogy between fear and peace: A pedagogical theory of peace education]*. Thesis, Utrecht University. Antwerp, Belgium: Internationale Vredesinformatiedienst. Cited in Vriens, 1999.

Vriens, L.J.A. (1999) Children, war, and peace: A review of fifty years of research from the perspective of a balanced concept of peace education. In Raviv, A., Oppenheimer, L. and Bar-Tal, D. (eds.) *How children understand war and peace: A call for international peace education.* San Francisco, US: Jossey-Bass Publishers, 27-58.

Vygotsky, L.S. (1978). *Thought and language.* Cambridge, MA. MIT Press.

Yagi, O. and Hiramatsu, Y. (1991) Perceptions of junior and senior high school students about international understanding [*Kokusairikaini kannsuru chugakusei/koukouseino ishiki*]. *Bulletin of Nagoya University School of Education Affiliated Upper and Lower Secondary School* 36:25-42.

Yoshimura, M. (2005) Promoting awareness of the linguistic and cultural diversity through English language activities in Japanese primary schools [*Tagengo/tabunkawo hagukumu syougakkoueigokatsudouno kokoromi*]. *International Understanding(Bulletin of Institute for International Understanding Tezukayamagakuin University)* 36: 186-196.

CHAPTER 2

The media literacy deficit in Japan: Exploring the link between digital citizenship, cultural diversity and critical thinking

Lisa Friedli

In the name of peace, education and cultural diversity, media literacy is an essential 21st century skill that enables individuals to decipher media messages effectively and responsibly. In the same sense that literacy, or knowing how to read, is the bedrock of any education, knowing how to read visual imagery, and media's powerhouse- advertisement, empowers individuals in the digital world. From personal to social, from local to international, the spheres of media use are growing larger every day and if we cannot navigate their complexities we will fall victim to them. It is therefore in the wake of technology's massive expansion, that we as users bear the responsibility of lucidity and caution in the virtual world. We are in fact interpolated to become digital citizens, and as such must learn to select and process the information we receive from media in a manner that is conducive to our personal health and the health of our global community.

Open access to information and the responsible use and interpretation of it, is necessarily linked to social democratic principles. A digital citizen in principle seeks to "control the interpretation of what they see or hear rather than letting the interpretation control them" (*Media Lit Kit*, 2003, p. 21). The Center for Media Literacy in Los Angeles has in fact promoted informed inquiry in the media world for over 30 years, because "[w] ithout this fundamental ability, an individual cannot have full dignity as a human person or exercise citizenship in a democratic society where to be a citizen is to both *understand* and *contribute* to the debates of the time" (*Media Lit Kit*, 2003, p. 21). The same echo is heard in reference to Japanese democratic principles as media researcher Midori Suzuki proclaims the "critical use of the media is expected to strengthen the democratic structure in society without making the audiences passive and isolated by believing all and any information provided by the media" (Suzuki, 1997, cited by Shibata, 2002, p. 102). Despite the progressive research of Suzuki and other media literacy forerunners, Japan is nonetheless faced with a deficit of media literacy education that spans all levels from tertiary to higher education. First and foremost there has been a considerable lag in the timely dissemination of the concept of media literacy in Japan. Take for example the 2010 article out of Tsukuba University (reputed for its media studies programs) entitled *Media Literacy: A New Type of Communication Skill.* The fact that there is a gap of three decades between the inception of media studies in Western contexts, and the publication of this article on media literacy in Japan as a "new" skill is rather striking.[1]

Moreover, the findings of the article in question reveal that at this late date "media literacy education still has a number of issues to address and is therefore under development" (Sakamoto and Suzuki, 2010, p. 72). As a final word on media literacy in Japan the article's authors reveal that "mass-media related education-including TV programs and newspapers- is not included in the official curriculum" (Sakamoto and Suzuki, 2010, p. 72).

Since the core component of media studies—media literacy—does not appear in the Japanese national curriculum, rather Sakamoto and Suzuki explain the focus has shifted to "the ability to access and effectively use media tools" in public schools (Sakamoto and Suzuki, 2010, p. 70). This ability to use media tools is specified in their article as students learning to retrieve information, to use video cameras and software applications, and to make media by shooting a video. There is only the vaguest mention of how students might be equipped to analyze the information they encounter in online media. The researchers in fact suggest that students through the act of making media would somehow passively acquire these skills: "It has been noted that active use of media tools can improve individuals' understanding of media" (Sakamoto and Suzuki, 2010, p.70). Ultimately the authors explain the shift and focus from media literacy to media use in Japan as a necessary measure, as it seems that "[i]ndependence in learning has been valued in terms of the newer concept of academic performance established by the Ministry of Education, Culture, Sports, Science and Technology (MEXT) and the trend of Japanese media literacy coincides with it" (Sakamoto and Suzuki, 2010, p. 70). The "newer" concept Sakamoto and Suzuki imply is simply a curriculum based on the individual, pragmatic use of media promoted for fear that media literacy, and its correlate critical thinking, encourage "the avoidance of media" (2010, p. 70). One can only speculate as to the logic, or lack thereof, behind an argument that is tantamount to stating that teaching children reading skills would encourage them to avoid books, when quite the opposite is true.

In today's world learning to read media well, to decode, to analyze, is an essential component of digital citizenship, both personal and political. Yet there remains a distinct reticence to incorporate medial literacy and digital citizenship into Japanese media studies courses. Whereas we might point to different cultural values between East and West in creating this gap, the future of Japanese media studies and the protection of cultural diversity demand that the issue be further investigated and debated. As we know, media messages are everywhere from subways to cellphones. We are in fact bombarded with them and they hold a certain power of persuasion that is intensified by the technological possibilities of film, editing, special effects, and sound. Children are growing up online, and the future, it seems will be even more media saturated. All companies and businesses use media to advertise their products, and all other types of media from magazines to social networks are paid for by advertising. The relationship between consumer culture and media is therefore quite strong, and media companies do their best to reach us, touch us and influence us for their financial gain. Companies, and their media, seek to create lifelong consumers of certain products and life styles and often chose children as a target audience in order to do so. Not to mention the fact that children in developing nations may in fact spend more time using media (such as television, movies, video games and the Internet) than they spend with their families or studying.

Media images quite literally hold the power to shape the present and the future of communities and nations, but they also shape who we are as people. Media images perpetuate ideas, but also ideologies and stereotypes for us to internalize. Here lies the threat to peace and cultural diversity on both a macro and a micro level: internalizing messages we receive without discerning their provenance, effect and value, is irresponsible and dangerous. The uncritical acceptation, or internalization, of media messages changes people, society and the world in a way that is not necessarily conducive to human interests. To my mind, human interests are still those brought forth during the enlightenment, namely; free inquiry and debate and the cultivation of justice and ethics. Yet naturally the definition of human interests is to be decided and debated by digital citizens, and that is precisely why one must be media literate: in order to sustain and protect one's personal, and, by extension, communal interests.

The process of media literacy begins by understanding that all media contains messages intended to further the needs and ideas of their creators and sponsors. To recognize the artifice, the mask, the theater, of media communication is not so easily accomplished: we must filter important messages, from the unimportant, and this despite the flashing lights, the special effects, and the attractive yet often misleading images. Moreover, there is another underlying factor that complicates critically interpreting media, and that is our absolute acceptance and trust of photos, films and text as truthful, real and unaltered documents. Children, young adults and the media illiterate are especially vulnerable to being manipulated or duped by what they see or hear in the media. UNESCO researchers in media literacy point to the blind faith that we, the public have for the media, as fast becoming a natural reflex of uncritical acceptance. Information we receive from technology is "deified or naturalized" to the point that we no longer question its veracity or provenance (UNESCO, 2010, p. 20). The goal therefore of media literacy is to break the chains of our acceptance of media messages as natural, and therefore true. In order to promote cultural, political and personal autonomy in a global context,

UNESCO defines media literacy education in the following terms: "Humanity should govern the development of technology instead of technology governing the development of humanity" (UNESCO, 2010, p. 21). Digital citizens understand that media messages are created by people to seem real and convincing. Subsequently they seek to discover who is creating the messages and for what purpose. However, the ultimate, and most crucial task of the digital citizen is to interpret the message received, and to decide whether to accept or reject the message, in whole or in part. For example what may appear to be an entertaining short film or cartoon may in fact be product advertising, or political propaganda that has been disguised as entertainment.

Effectively interpreting media ultimately contributes to peace in the sense that all media are messages, and understanding their political, financial or social spin puts the receiver in the position of responding strategically, in the interest, or according to, the needs of their society and themselves. Technological consumers who become media literate are able to recognize bias, manipulation and propaganda. Furthermore, for these digital citizens, a loaded message has less power to manipulate. Its insidious and hidden intents to persuade, entice or convince are diffused in advance. Being media literate in this sense can be likened to knowing how to recognize, intercept and dismantle time bombs, rather than being broadsided by them with no warning or defense. Furthermore, while this is a rather strong simile to use, the power of media to promote, influence, persuade, manipulate or brainwash our perception of the world, our society and ourselves as individuals is too rampant to deny. In the broader scheme of things, religious fanaticism, war-mongering imperialism, the distribution of potentially dangerous pharmaceutical and agro-chemical products, anorexia, teen pregnancy and crime can all be traced to the use, misuse, and interpretation of media messages. Media literacy is both a form of empowerment and self-defense, that is easy to gain and imperative to master in our global media world.

Although this article strives to represent the cosmopolitan voice of the digital citizen, one cannot deny the overwhelming predominance of North American industries in the media business. From social networks, to search engines to software: America and American points of view are globally disseminated. Thus while critical thinking in media literacy could be considered just another Western model imposed on the rest of the world, I argue that it serves, on the contrary, as a safeguard for free inquiry and debate. A case in point is neatly illustrated by the first formal drafts of media literacy curricula, which were in fact drafted by the Canadian ministry of education in 1989 to protect their nation and culture from the barrage of American media that their citizens were receiving. Canadians sought to preserve their culture by teaching citizens to recognize American cultural imperialism in media messages.

It is from this stance of cultural protectionism, indeed with the intent of preserving cultural differences, that I consider critical thinking as a necessary component of media literacy. In Japan, however, viewing media literacy and critical thinking as Western components of media

21

studies is a common perspective. Toshie Takahashi of Waseda University, for example, calls for the de-Westernization of media studies. Takahashi in fact likens Western viewpoints to an invasive force, referring to them directly as "the interpenetration of Western theories and concepts" in media studies (Takahashi, 2007, p. 334). By today's standards "subjective thinking people" are tantamount to digital citizens, although this early intention of the Ministry has definitely altered course in the new millennium. As concerns Takahashi's interest in de-Westernizing media studies, it is interesting to note that her research does not touch upon media literacy or critical thinking, but rather focuses on "the social practices of audiences" and the "psychological and personal levels of audience engagement with media" (Takahashi, 2007, p. 333). I would like to point out that the social habits of audience engagement are deeply researched in Western media studies as well, albeit in marketing courses. In sum, the power paradigm, and perspective underlying Takahashi's argument reveals a much greater interest in empowering media makers, rather than protecting media consumers. This business-oriented model of media studies is the diametrical opposite of the media-literate digital citizen promoted by international entities like UNESCO. In addition, the tendency towards market-side media studies in Japan is also affirmed by a decade of research published by the Japan Society of Information and Media Studies. Reading through the table of contents for all their issues of the *Journal of Information and Media Studies* published between 2003 and 2013, I did not find a single article addressing the critical interpretation of media. All articles published tended towards the justification and legitimization of consumer culture, and marketing strategies for media makers. Typical article titles included: *The Effects of "user registration" and "reply" functions on online users' behavior*; *The public relations from Tokyo Metropolitan Assembly and information awareness of assemblymen in the internet age* and *Current status and issues of the manuals of mobile phones for elderly viewed from components of the manual.* These titles represent knowledge that holds great value to those creating media for commercial purposes, but holds very little value for the cultural and intellectual autonomy of individuals and society.

These are not isolated cases of market-oriented media studies, but rather a pattern of method in Japan. Demonstrating this evolution, Kuniomi Shibata of Tohoku University traces the adaptation and interpretation of the first media studies frameworks from Canada to Japan. His research specifies which aspects of Canadian curriculum were upheld, and which aspects were discarded in the transfer. Ultimately, Shibata's research reveals the complete oversight, if not the explicit removal of the critical thinking component of media studies in Japan. When media studies were first introduced to Japan, they were divided into two categories: the "critical use" of media and the "subjective use" of media (Shibata, 2002, p. 103). Whereas most media studies courses are currently part of "information education", in Japan they tend to focus on the "subjective use" of media, which despite the deceptive use of the term "subjective" pertains solely to software application, and individual technological use with no reference to the interpretation of media. In addition, despite the work of Japanese proponents of the "critical use" of media, the influence of "subjective" or rather individual, pragmatic use of media largely dominates in an educational system that favors business and marketing over the critical thinking component of the humanities.

Shibata's research demonstrates that the critical regard of media literacy is viewed negatively in Japan because its purpose and use in media studies has been both misunderstood, and I quote, "intentionally ignored" (Shibata, 2002, p. 104). We may of course look to cultural differences to explain the Japanese reinterpretation of media studies, as Shibata is keen to point out there are aspects of Canadian media literacy education that would not work well in Japan. For example, Canadian students are taught that "nationalism" as a concept is largely media created, and that nationalism can have negative aspects. As Shibata further explains: "Critical use" in Canada exhibits a unique character as "it preserve[s] Canadian culture by criticizing American culture … However, it should be noted that the relationship between media literacy and 'nationalism' in Canada is optimistically accepted, and therefore cannot be introduced directly to Japan since this could give rise to complicated issues" (Shibata, 2002, p. 102). Further mapping the shift of focus towards market-side, "subjective use" use of media technology in Japanese national education, Shibata has made it public knowledge that media literacy was officially introduced into Japanese public schools, not by public advocacy groups, teachers' unions or literacy councils, but by media industry representatives such as the Ministry of Public Management, and the Post and Telecommunications Bureau. Shibata predicted in 2002 that this 'wolf watching the lamb' structure would "change the nature and substance, of media literacy in Japan" (Shibata, p. 105). I dare say his prediction paints an accurate picture of media studies in Japan today.

Thanks to Shibata's work on media literacy history in Japan, as an educator I have a better understanding of why my university-level media studies students in the Communications Department had never heard of digital citizenship or media literacy. I was however very surprised to find these same students were enrolled in *another* media studies course in the Business Faculty of our university. At first I was concerned for the students, in that they were receiving redundant lessons. One would think that having the same course twice would lessen student motivation and decrease their opportunities to learn at the university; but when I shared my concerns with the students, they informed me that the Japanese counterpart of our media studies course was completely different. The students explained that they learned "just how to use computers". Lessons about software application and web page building were a far cry from our critical thinking based curriculum of media literacy that focused on: media bias, manipulation in advertising, the notion of target audience, the sexual objectification of women in media, the promotion of unattainable stereotypes of beauty, the Internet users' new role in contributing to long- as opposed to short-tail models of media business, et cetera. Though based on happenstance, this specific discrepancy in course content between the two faculties ultimately offered the students a balanced approach to media studies. It is unfortunate that teaching students critical and "subjective" use of the media remains an anomaly in the educational system at large.

As Shibata has shown, the widespread translation of media literacy into technological media applications in the Japanese educational context has an institutional origin that is culturally specific. While I would hope for a more well-rounded education for Japanese students, I do not advocate the use of Western measurements to understand Japanese society. As Takahashi points out, these comparisons "cannot capture the sense of the Japanese traditional cultural values" (Takahashi, 2007, p. 332). Takahashi indeed grounds her research in social scientific frameworks of linguistic and conceptual differences. For example, she compares media use in terms of *uchi* (private) and *soto* (public); but is quick to clarify that these terms do not simply translate to "private" and "public" in English. While the point is well taken (we can all agree that language is full of nuance) the question however remains: can Japan aptly remain Japanese if the barrage of global media coming at them is not analyzed with a critical eye? To give but one brief example: Japanese students in my media studies course had so deeply internalized a Disneyland advertisement that they mistook Western photo models for Japanese. Clearly, for Japanese students to discern what *is* Japanese from what is Western (let alone for them to de-Westernize culturally) they must first become media literate.

There is no denying that mediatized information does flow from *soto* (outside/public) towards *uchi* (inside/private), and in this sense the rough translation of the terms does serve its purpose. In the interest of self *and* communal preservation of the private or *uchi*, is it not always the case that that one must protect it from outside, *soto* forces? In the end Takahashi and I both agree that we need to work towards a better understanding of the role of media in the context of globalization. It is self-evident that insider and outsider views of a culture necessarily differ, but is Takahashi's call to de-Westernize media studies the best choice for Japan? While teaching critical thinking and media literacy might lead to questioning authority or disrupting tradition, can the Japanese face the global onslaught of media unarmed? Maintaining citizens as functionally illiterate in the media world creates a vulnerability to manipulation and persuasion that could actually be much more disruptive and corrosive to Japanese tradition and society than protectionist policy advocates realize.

The argument underlying this article is that the explosive globalization of media, and its hand maiden, marketing, threatens cultural heritage and diversity not only in Japan, but also in the world at large. My intention, both in the classroom, and in the parameters of this chapter is therefore not to make Westerners of Japanese students, but to guide them in acquiring skills that allow them to make more informed decisions about what they consume, but also about what they accept and reject in their lives. When we are equipped with the understanding of how ideas and ideologies are presented, created and intended, we can make informed decisions that enhance our human experience, rather than diminish it. One might argue that accepting or rejecting information most often results in fairly innocuous consequences, like buying a product we don't need. However, one might argue that even a product we don't need will still *have* a lasting effect on the environment, on the planet's limited resources, and on the workers exploited in its manufacturing and distribution. Lest we forget, there *are* decisions made based on mediatized information that have dire consequences such as voting for a politician that leads a nation to war, or taking medication or ingesting foods that have serious health consequences.

Given the long Western tradition of philosophical debate and inquiry, it is rather clear that the critical thinking component of media literacy is a Western way of processing information. It may very well push Japanese students to think "outside the box" as concerns analyzing the media, and could possibly lead to some form of social unrest; but is ignorance and functional media illiteracy in the face of rampant globalization a more viable option? In Japan, both business and the government are faced with this dilemma as "fresh ideas and innovation provide the impetus for profit, [but] can also pose potential difficulties for organizational stability, as people choose to reject established ways of thinking or behaving" (Rear, 2008). Generally speaking, thinking outside the box denotes creative thinking skills that enable individuals to find imaginative solutions to problems or to invent new ways of doing things. I would like to suggest that these modes of inquiry, both creative and critical thinking, also function well *within* cultural and social parameters. That is to say, critical thinking does not preclude or undermine the understanding, and recognition of the rules and values of any given culture. With this in mind, I would argue, that guiding Japanese students to acquire media literacy skills does not make them less Japanese or incite non-conformity. Thinking critically about the importance of cultural heritage, in light of the current globalization, if not the Americanization of world media, would to the contrary tend to galvanize an individual's adherence to social behaviors and beliefs that maintain their traditions and quality of life. At present, the Japanese national focus on information education's "subjective use" of media and the pragmatic, vocational use of technology could have serious consequences for Japan's future if it is not balanced with media literacy and the "critical use" of media approach in public education. Media does have the power to colonize the mind, and media literacy offers the most effective pre-emptive measure to combat this technological invasion.

References

Dobashi, Y. and Kawashima, S. (2005) The effects of "user registration" and "reply" functions on online users behavior. *Journal of Information and Media Studies* 4(1): 77-93. [Online]. Accessed from <https://www.jstage.jst.go.jp/article/jims/4/1/4_1_77/_article> on 6th November, 2013.

Medialit (2003) *Media Lit Kit*. Accessed from <https://www. medialit.org/sites/default/files/ mlk/01_MLKorientation.pdf> on 3rd September, 2013.

Rear, D. (2008) Critical thinking and modern Japan: Conflict in the discourse of government and business. *Electronic Journal of Contemporary Japanese studies*. [Online]. Accessed from <http://www.japanesestudies.org.uk/articles/2008/Rear.html> on 10th November, 2013.

Sakamoto, A. and Suzuki, K. (2010) Media literacy: A new type of communication skill. *Proceedings: Science of Human Development for Restructuring the Gap Widening Society*, 9. [Online]. Accessed from <http://teapot.lib.ocha.ac.jp/ocha/bitstream/10083/51389/1/ Proceedings09_08Sakamoto&Suzuki.pdf> on 1st November, 2013.

Sannami, I., Iba, S. and Nakayama, S. (2013) Current status and issues of the manuals of mobile phones for elderly viewed from components of the manual. *Journal of Information and Media Studies*, 12(1):14-27. [Online]. Accessed from <https://www.jstage.jst.go.jp/article/ jims/12/1/12_14/_article> on 6th November, 2013.

Shibata, K. (2002) The substance of the "critical" approach in media literacy in Canada. *Keio Communication Review* 24:93-110. [Online]. Accessed from <http://www.mediacom.keio. ac.jp/publication/pdf2002/review24/7.pdf> on 30th October, 2013.

Takahashi, T. (2007) De-Westernizing media studies: a Japanese perspective. *Global Media and Communication* 3:330-335. [Online]. Accessed from https://www.academia.edu/296449/ DeWesternizing_media_studies_a_Japanese_perspective on 3rd November, 2013.

Unesco (2010) *Media Literacy and New Humanism*. Accessed from <http://unesdoc.unesco.org/ images/0019/001921/192134e.pdf>. Accessed on 2nd November, 2013.

Yamamoto, T. (2005) The public relations from Tokyo Metropolitan Assembly and information awareness of assemblymen in the internet age. *Journal of Information and Media Studies* 1(1): 43-57. [Online]. Accessed from <https://www.jstage.jst.go.jp/article/ jims/4/1/4_1_77/_article> on 6th November, 2013.

CHAPTER 3

Toward a utopian peace education

Nick Kasparek

Introduction

This chapter attempts to connect peace education (hereinafter PE) theory to broader theory concerned with transformation, theory that is open to the future and the chasm that separates us from it. It attempts to follow an edifying type of philosophy of education and offer a new idealization of the field, highlighting certain components of peace education theory as the most promising for its coherence and relevance (Rorty, 1996). The author argues that a *utopian turn* for this theory would be an important way for it to open itself to wider social theory, the world, and the future. This utopianism would not aim at perfection, but like novelist Kobo Abe (1971), it would attempt to make us "confront the cruelty of the future, produce within [us] anguish and strain, and bring about a dialogue with [ourselves]" (p. 221).

This chapter attempts an immanent intervention into the theoretical discourse within the field of peace education. There is a concern that the field is both under-defined and under-theorized. This fundamental uncertainty is related to trends in the broader intellectual world grouped under the name of *postmodernity*. Some peace education scholars have attempted to respond to the challenges and opportunities they see in postmodernity, but there has remained a sense that PE is a modernist project; many scholars have simply added a few concerns about diversity and the contingency of social structures and have given up on grand programs for the reconstruction of society.

In this way, there has been a trend within the field of turning away from big goals and instead focusing on small-scale change. While there is much to commend in it, this postmodern peace education is in danger of imagining the future as an endless continuation of the present, reifying "harsh realities" of violence and inequality in the name of pragmatism and achievable goals. Like the rest of society, it rejects utopianism when this could be its greatest strength. This chapter therefore identifies implicit utopian hopes and desires in peace education and argues for a peace education that embraces the utopianism of the "culture of peace" discourse. It suggests a disruptive utopian peace education, one that encourages both teachers and students to confront the future, thus inspiring dialogue within them.

The contemporary context: postmodernity

As Lyotard famously tried to express with the controversial term "postmodern," there is now a strong sense of suspicion toward "grand narratives" and that "progress" itself is an uncertain concept, as it seems to imply a specific end point, a deterministic outcome in which we can no longer fully believe (Lyotard and Brugger, 2001). Rather than any sense of totality, now we seem to have an infinite fragmentation of presence, or an "eternal present" (Eagleton, 2000, p. 86). The name "postmodernity" is one useful attempt to "name the system" as connected totality (Jameson, 1998, p. 49). Žižek (2010) describes this system as a paradoxically anti-utopian utopia: The desire to impose a positive good is taken as the root of all evil, yet "its modest rejection of utopias ends with the imposition of its own market-liberal utopia" (p. 38). This hegemonic ideology is utopian in another sense as well: it entails the "belief that the existing global system can reproduce itself indefinitely" despite widely acknowledged impending catastrophes *(Ibid.*, p. 363).

This extends to educational thought. As the philosopher of education Paul Smeyers (2006) notes, "What is labelled postmodern educational theory focuses on a particular aspect of the present *Zeitgeist*. Indeed, the obsession with efficiency and effectiveness has finally parted company altogether from controversial, political questions of what we should be trying to achieve" (p. 2). Against this trend in educational theory, however, peace education and its political goal of a "culture of peace" returns attention to these bigger questions.

Peace education as anachronism?

Reardon (2000) defines *peace education* as the "transmission of knowledge about requirements of, the obstacles to, and possibilities for achieving and maintaining peace; training in skills for interpreting the knowledge; and the development of reflective and participatory capacities for applying the knowledge to overcome problems and achieve possibilities" (p. 399). Modifying Salomon's (2002) classification of the types of peace education based on sociopolitical context, this paper focuses more narrowly on peace education in relatively wealthy contexts. In this, the author follows Kent's (1977) conception of peace education as most effectively a "pedagogy of the middle class," in that it can lead to reconceptualizations of peace, social justice, and the good society for those who consider themselves already fairly satisfied with and invested in the status quo.

Reardon (2000) describes another key term of the field, *culture of peace*, as having become a "kind of short-hand description of what peace educators see as the goal of global transformation" (413); for peace educators this becomes the ethos of all education and school culture. She further conceives of the possibility of determining what is "humanly destructive" and "humanly enhancing" and identifies the *culture of peace* concept as a "culture of human enhancement," which seems to presume a metaphysical human essence that can be made better, a distinctly modernist ambition.

Many internal and external criticisms of the field stem from a similarly modernist concern that *peace education* is under-theorized, where theory is taken as the unifying foundation for action (Dolby and Rahman, 2008). For some scholars, this simply leads to the field's lack of recognition within academia (Wintersteiner, 2010) or overly modest goals for practice (Cook, 2008), suggesting, for example, that the "multiplicity" of definitions and normative statements of the purpose for "peace education" is possibly "the most severely undermining factor of peace education as a scholarly and pedagogic field" (Ben-Porath, 2003). Page (2008) further argues that peace education philosophy is "fideistic" and needs more substantial justifying foundations, while Cox and Levine (2005) likewise suggest that peace education in practice only succeeds in preaching to the choir.

Yet these criticisms place unreasonable demands on theory in the contemporary world. The philosopher Richard Rorty (1989) points out that "liberals have come to expect philosophy to do a certain job—namely, answering questions like 'Why not be cruel?' and 'Why be kind?'—and they feel that any philosophy that refuses to do this must be heartless" (p. 94). However, these questions remain unanswerable, since they operate as our contingent final vocabularies - the level at which we can dig no deeper. Asking for definitive philosophical rationales for peace reveals a continuing modernist metaphysical faith in an "ur-language" that all would understand if we could just find it. This doomed search for an ur-language undermines, from the outset, Page's (2008) and Snauwaert's (2011) respective philosophical foundations. Peace education critics and proponents want philosophy to do foundational understudy work of establishing the field's truth, which has proved impossible and unproductive.

Peace education, with its focus on a comprehensive system of contingent goods, thus seems to sit uneasily within the tension between our desire to give meaning to our practice and our suspicion about broader narratives. This tension is at once the source of its potential creative energy and of its potential failure. The umbrella concept of peace education (and its related names) could be a pragmatically useful package for transformative ideology in this seemingly post-ideological age. But this is also a potential threat to its own goals of transformation, as well as to revolutionary change by attempting to enforce a superficial consensus and declare an end to the search for clarity. Peace education could therefore either exemplify or challenge what philosopher of education Thomas Popkewitz (2008) sees as endemic in contemporary education: a premature foreclosure of possibilities enforcing "unspoken norms about what is possible and desirable" (p. 154). As Ruitenberg (2009) notes, this danger exists even in self-described "emancipatory" pedagogy and progressive pedagogy, such as peace education, by emphasizing certain outcomes whereby teachers risk stultifying students rather than engaging their intelligence.

One of the most prolific philosophers dealing directly with peace education today, Ilan Gur-Ze'ev (2010), highlights a related danger, namely, that peace education "is praised and paid tribute to by most theoretical orientations, political establishments, and the so-called radical movements," and then asks, "Who today dares courageously to challenge this idol or offer a systematic negation of the very *principle of peace*?" (p. 171) Following Karl Schmitt's reflections on international law, he presents the challenge that "peace education, actually, is one of the most advanced manifestations of [violence] and is a serious threat to human edification" (*Ibid.*, pp. 174–175). He contends that peace education is at best a distraction from the worst violence, and at worst, a sophisticated tool to maintain the violence inherent in the status quo. Unfortunately, this provocative criticism has thus far not inspired meaningful engagement, only mischaracterization (Ben-Porath, 2006) and very limited acceptance (Kruger, 2012). Real engagement would demand contending also with time's own out-of-jointness (Derrida, 1994; Jameson, 1999). As Gur-Ze'ev's (2001; 2010) series of "post-" titles indicates, PE's grand modern project of achieving a culture of peace programmatically is challenged by the widespread contemporary suspicion precisely toward such ambitions, schemes, and narratives.

It remains true that PE is in dire need of better internal *and external* critics who contend with this fundamental challenge, since it is they who can offer the impetus to improve it (White, 1988). Peace education scholars Haavelsrud and Stenberg (2012) thus challenge us to forge links with social theory but warn that this may be "the greatest challenge in the field" (p. 78). The connecting pieces are available, but the theories remain separated by a chasm. This chasm is not simply temporal - a need to bring modernist peace education up to date with postmodern theory - as Foucault (1984), Lyotard and Brugger (2001), and countless others have argued, these are not simply eras but attitudes or tendencies across time. Nonetheless, we would do well to open the field to temporal issues in another way, namely, to engage with the future to escape the eternal present.

Utopianism in peace education

Like peace education, utopianism is a broad and complex concept, and one that inspires mixed reactions. *Utopia* is Thomas More's (2012) playful invented term that combines the Greek *topos*, or place, with an ambiguous "u" from either the negative prefix "ou" or the good prefix "eu." Sargeant (2010) explains that this complex pairing produces our contemporary understanding of utopia as a nonexistent good place. These imaginary lands were first identified in works of fiction, but utopia also came to be used for practical experiments in better living and as a tool for social theory. In political theory and elsewhere, however, it is easy anti-utopians, who see utopia as a dangerously attractive idea that inspires only failure and violence, a common view that Levitas (2000) summarizes as "where there is vision, the people perish" (p. 31). Peace education scholar Lynn Davies (2008) exemplifies this broader sentiment: "The desire for some sort of Utopia is in the end highly dangerous" (p. 18).

In this ideological climate, it might seem foolhardy for peace education to turn to the field of utopian studies for new ways of rethinking its postmodern problems. Utopianism has its own definitional crises and faces fierce wholesale denunciations; peace education scholars can be forgiven for denying utopianism. Indeed, in the peace education literature, "utopian" is almost exclusively used in its common, derogatory meaning: unrealistic, impossible dreaming. It is the straw man opposed to serious attempts to develop realistic theory and practice. Scholars such as Ben-Porath (2003) argue against "burden[ing] the field of peace education with too many hopes and dreams, which albeit admirable, cannot be satisfied all at once" (p. 532). These realist critics ask bluntly with Davies (2008), "Should we not aim for comfort with the inevitable messiness of life?" (p. 19).

Despite this anti-utopianism, though, utopian desire remains an animating force within the field. Utopianism is what leaves scholars and teachers unsatisfied with contemporary ideas and practices and drives them to find better ones. We must therefore resist realist peace education scholarship not because it is wrong now, but because it denies the *real* future; as Fritzman (2001) summarizes Hegel's thought:

> The advocates of history's end are correct in claiming that the resources for radical change are not present now, but they fail to see that those resources will have been present as a result of radical change. The future is not possible now, for Hegel, although it *will have been* after it becomes real. (p. 298)

Thus, to counter the foreclosure of new realities, it is important to add serious theorizing of utopian desire and the importance of utopia to the field of peace education.

More broadly, anti-utopianism has inspired a rich theorization of utopia from those who find in it positive social hope, and it is precisely this response that could be edifying for peace education theory. Because explicitly *anti-peace education* is hard to find,[1] the field would do well to borrow intelligent ideas from *anti-utopian* critics. From Ernst Bloch's (1995) work on hope and utopia[2] in modernity to contemporary *anti-anti-utopian*[3] scholarship, utopia has found new life as more than the scapegoat for political failures, a straw man to argue against, or a derogatory label for others' ideas. It is in this spirit, then, that the author proposes that we view peace education and its scholarship as already utopian, and in need of more explicit utopianism.

31

Webb's (2008) typology of five modes of hope - patient, resolute, estimative, critical and transformative - helps distinguish peace education as utopian. Patient hope is anti-utopian in that it rejects human intervention. Estimative and resolute hope can be utopian, while critical and transformative hope have great utopian potential. The modes of hope common in peace education reveal the field's nascent utopianism and suggest the most promising strands of peace education theory for a utopian turn.

The anti-utopian *patient hope* is equally antithetical to peace education. *Resolute hope* in PE emphasizes the well-being of students and student achievement. This is utopian in terms of changing the coordinates of what is hoped for, such as relational happiness in the work of Noddings (2003) or peace of mind in Hicks' (2004) writings. *Estimative hope* in the field promotes a science of peace-building and conflict prevention. While transmitting this knowledge to students could proscribe the limits of what is possible, it still supports a deep utopianism. Indeed, we can find this estimative hope paired with utopianism in Reardon and Snauwaert's (2011) recent writing:

> In all peace education, we need to make clear that all the knowledge necessary for the making and building of peace is *not yet* available to us; that our task as peace learners and peace makers is to contribute to the building of the fundamental peace knowledge base, involving all existing fields of human knowledge and perhaps inventing new ones. (p. 11)

There is still a faith in the progress of knowledge here, but we also find a key utopian "not yet" (Levitas, 2009).

Even more promising is *critical hope*, "a passionate suffering and restless longing for that which is missing" (Webb, 2008, p. 204). In this mode of hoping, negative elements are identified and attacked in a continual process toward improvement. The end result is left completely open, but the idea of something better and radically new is vital. Critical peace education is especially strong in finding *violence* to then imagine away. But the most powerfully utopian hope is *transformative hope*. This hope trusts the human "capacity to construct, both imaginatively and materially, new ways of organizing life" (Webb, 2008, p. 204). Some degree of content is risked in envisioning the end result of such construction. This utopian image then mobilizes human effort toward this goal.

As Lewis (2009) points out, though, education theory should recognize that utopianism derives as much from anxiety as it does from hope. Thus, Levitas' (2000) analysis of the *function* of utopia, and its three forms - *compensation*, emphasizing that even anti-utopian hopes carry utopian dreams; *critique*; and *change* - is also important to finding utopianism in PE. Peace education adopts all three of these forms of utopianism, even when it is explicitly anti-utopian.

For instance, as a recent meta-study of peace pedagogies in the *Journal of Peace Education* (Haavelsrud and Stenberg, 2012) points out, some peace education scholarship focuses on molding pro-social individuals in an isolated classroom, removed from broader contexts. These "pockets of peace" within the curriculum and classroom offer participants *compensatory* utopias, but Levitas' (2009) framework suggests that these disconnected spaces must be linked to a social totality for them to be effective beyond temporary compensation.

Peace education as critique has a long history, as the critical analyses of our "war cultures" in peace studies is a cornerstone of much peace pedagogy. This critical project is implicitly linked to a vision of a society without violence, and this vision forms the criteria for determining and judging forms of violence. Here, *peace* is the "something missing" fueling a utopian desire, and *violence* in all its forms is "the negative" that must be negated (Webb, 2008). Some vague conception of an ideal works as the ground from which to judge - and always find lacking - contemporary society.

Finally, the transformative potential of peace pedagogy is the one most often called for within theory-conscious peace education scholarship, and this transformative hope is often what sets it apart from conflict studies. The *culture of peace* becomes both the tool through which one can judge the present and the goal for which one must aim. This vision need not be fully formed or laden with detailed content, but some idea of what would characterize the ideal society animates the recurring call for social change aided by education. This vision often includes a listing of contemporary liberal and social democratic keywords such as "ecology" and "human rights," which are themselves given significant room for overflowing meaning. For instance, Davies' (2008) "informed and critical idealism" and "positive extremism" represent the provisional outlines of one such peace educational utopia, borrowing positive visions from liberal humanism and universal human rights.

Embracing peace education's transformative utopianism

Leaders in the fields of both utopian studies and peace education thus typically reserve their greatest praise for transformative potential. Nonetheless, there has been little interaction between these fields. The work of Hicks (2004) takes important steps in this direction by reviving more utopian-friendly themes in the scholarship of various peace scholars. He proposed greater integration of "future studies" into peace pedagogy, including eliciting students' "preferred futures," which comes very close to utopianism. However, his one mention of utopianism was in quotation marks, and conforms to the common pejorative meaning, referring negatively to students' dreams for the future as typically overly idealized and unrealistic (Hicks, p. 171).

For greater engagement with utopia in its own name, we must turn to the broader field of educational theory. Webb (2009) notes that "utopian" has been losing some of its pejorative meaning in this theory, particularly in radical pedagogy. However, he finds that in an attempt to avoid the tragic possibilities of utopia, many calls for utopian education and the examples of utopianism in education are often emptied of their transformative power. By eschewing actual visions of the future as too constraining and prescriptive, these theorists essentially take the utopia out of utopianism, leaving only implicit goals and piecemeal reformism behind.

Giroux and McLaren (1995), two influential radical pedagogy theorists, explicitly advocate utopianism for education in a way that could inform a utopian peace education in postmodernity. As self-described "postmodern dreamers," they reject grandiose blueprints for change as limiting possibilities, and follow postmodern thought in de-authorizing and challenging "the master narratives of liberal, postindustrial democracy and the humanist, individual, and patriarchal discourses that underwrite it" (Giroux & McLaren, p. 55). However, rather than totality itself, they abandon only the reductive use of totality. There is still a place for imagining the whole, and for critiquing and transforming it.

The philosopher Paul Ricoeur (1986) shows the postmodern potential of understanding utopia in this way. He argues that, against previous oppositions of *utopia and ideology* versus *science and reality*, utopia is better seen as the *counterpart* of ideology: ideology provides the legitimation of authority and the status quo, while utopia functions as its radical undermining. With the postmodern acknowledgement of the impossibility of the value-free intellectual and an "objective" god's-eye view, utopia as "nowhere puts the cultural system at a distance; we see our cultural system from the outside precisely thanks to this nowhere" (Ricoeur, p. 17). In other words, utopia provides the functional ground that a Hegelian absolute *Geist* promises (*Ibid.*, p. 312), namely, an exterior glance on our reality that opens the "field of the possible... beyond that of the actual" (*Ibid.*, p. 16).

This represents one vital route open to postmodern utopian education theory, which can inform a similar critical peace education theory. Levitas (2000) further develops the possibilities for contemporary *transformative* utopists, one that involves but goes beyond critique. She contends that we must risk some form of representational or *architectural* utopia, about which Jameson (2010) reminds us:

> these seemingly peaceful images are also, in and of themselves, violent ruptures with what is, breaks that destabilize our stereotypes of a future that is the same as our own present, interventions that interrupt the reproduction of the system in habit and in ideological consent and institute that fissure, however minimal and initially little more than a hairline fracture, through which another picture of the future and another system of temporality altogether might emerge. (p. 415)

More than a "nowhere" ground from which to critique contemporary ideology or the means for disrupting it, then, utopia itself constitutes a disruption.

Levitas (2010) also sides with Bloch (1995) in seeing utopian imagining as a key tool for identifying and representing desire and attempting to fulfill it, while recognizing that there will always be an element of misrecognition involved. In other words, utopia in the postmodern sense involves a necessary but impossible *salto mortale*, or leap of faith, into some positive representation, but with the awareness that it can never be fully formed or taken as perfect. As she asserts elsewhere (2009), utopias are necessarily multiple and provisional. Utopia cannot retreat to a modest status as a heuristic tool in postmodernity, but must involve some element of risk for representation to engender hope. It must involve the architectural mode of utopia, what Levitas (2009) calls the imaginary reconstruction of society (IROS) method, and present at least "a possibility for consideration, if not necessarily a possibility" (p. 66). Moylan (2009) similarly argues that the utopian method requires both moments of the critical dialectic: "the negative, denunciatory moment and the positive, annunciatory moment," which challenge each other productively (p. 208).

Utopianism is then disruptive and transgressive in challenging our current socially conditioned and condoned desires and teaches us "to desire in a different way" (Levitas, 2000, p. 39). It estranges and defamiliarizes our perceived worlds and challenges its appearance of closure. Utopian representational failure is inevitable, but as Jameson (1982, cited by Levitas, 2000) argues, the attempt is all the more valuable for this, for it helps us see what we are "unable or unwilling to imagine" about the future (p. 39). Thus, we can find a postmodern ethics that demands that utopians "recognise the contingency of their hopes and desires," yet remain committed to them (Levitas, 2000, p. 40); we must risk taking *responsibility* despite the impossibility of any assurances. And it is precisely this radical responsibility and indeterminacy that peace education also must take seriously if it is to engage with postmodern thought.

Implications for theory and practice

Peace educationists would therefore do well to follow Reardon and Snauwaert's (2011) recent recommendations for the field. They explicitly reject set definitions for *peace*, presenting this instead as a perpetual challenge for all those engaged in peace education - namely theorists, teachers, and students. In their place, she recommends - in utopian fashion - provisional *visions*. On the topic, they write:

> Peace is—or will be—what we think it is…. We will know it when we see it.
> If we are committed to seeing it, we need to be able to envision it. *Visions of*
> *the unprecedented* lend themselves more to description than to definition, i.e. 'It
> would look like or be like this… (p. 11, emphasis added).

With this, the definition is left open to radical change and to the intelligence of students. By doing so, they stand against the narrowing of the definition to focus only on "the absence of violent conflict," and against the perpetual crisis for the field; yet crucially, they also leave it open to the effort to imaginatively fill it with content. They implicitly invite the transformative imagination of everyone involved in the practice of peace education, and indeed suggest that this could be its defining feature.

In this, they point to a way of avoiding a common problem: intellectual reification that mistakes names of problems for solutions. Adapting Jameson's (2010) argument, *peace education* needs to become our animating dilemma, with *peace* its central *aporia*, rather than a solution or program to be implemented. Rather than peace education's usual mission of bringing the contemporary world more in line with one in which the ideal of peace is presumed, we could follow Derrida's (1994) alternate option of going "beyond the 'facts,' beyond the supposed 'empirical evidence,'" and continually putting into question "the very concept of the said ideal" (p. 108). This would answer the demands of contemporary peace education scholars and critics with a more fundamental demand. As such, the lack of consensus on definitions and foundations would then become the field's source of energy.

This re-conception of *peace* as an eternal problematic will require a rethinking of teaching as well. No longer can educators and theorists operate from the assumption of greater knowledge; their goal cannot be the explication of the *facts* of what peace is and how to achieve it. Rather, we need to recognize our own ignorance and its accompanying emancipation. Rancière's (1991) ignorant but emancipated schoolmaster Jacotot suggests:

> To teach what one doesn't know is simply to ask questions about what one doesn't know. Science isn't needed to ask such questions. The ignorant one can ask anything, and for the voyager in the land of signs, his questions alone will be true questions compelling the autonomous exercise of his intelligence. (p. 30)

In other words, peace educators do not need to *know* all about peace to ask students about what they see, what they say, and what they think about different visions of peace. Rather than as verifiers of findings, then, teachers must focus on being verifiers of searches. Asking students about what they desire and why, and demanding the application of their intelligence to these searches for utopian peace, is the fundamental element of a transformative utopian peace education.

Conclusion

In this paper, it has been argued that peace education scholarship has engaged too little with the disturbance of postmodernity. The field has instead lowered expectations and adopted the rhetoric of anti-utopianism in misguided attempts at legitimization and differentiation. Meanwhile, there remains a reluctance to give up on essentialism in its most metaphysical forms, in the search for solid theoretical foundations, or on the positivist dream of accumulating enough data and knowledge to rationalize social relations.

Against these anti-utopian dreams, a turn to utopian studies would open up new possibilities for engagement and a deeper interrogation of the field's premises, something Gur-Ze'ev (2010) rightly identifies as necessary. Peace educators should heed Reardon's (2011) warning about reifying Galtung's (1975) classic concepts of negative and positive peace in order to repeat his original act, that is, to fundamentally question what constitutes *violence* and *peace* today. Peace education could then emerge as a laboratory for provisional counter-utopias to the contemporary liberal (anti-)utopia. As Jameson (2005) illustrates, the "moment of truth" of any utopia is its "critical negativity as a conceptual instrument…to discredit and demystify the claims to full representation of its opposite number" (p. 175). Utopian peace education's responsibility would then be "to radically negate" the violence of the status quo and its educational reproduction: it must become *anti-anti-peace education.*

Peace education theory could then contend with Gur-Ze'ev's (2001, 2010) attacks and Žižek's (2008) warnings against categorically condemning all violence, namely, that "to chastise violence outright, to condemn it as 'bad,' is an ideological operation par excellence, a mystification which collaborates in rendering invisible the fundamental forms of social violence" (p. 174). Indeed, if we engage with Žižek's (2008) definition of violence as "a radical upheaval of the basic social relations," (p. 217) and follow his (2004) conception of the utopian gesture as being "the gesture which changes the co-ordinates of the possible" (p. 123), utopian peace education will have to take seriously the implication that it is potentially violent—the challenge then becomes how the field can embrace this symbolic violence without abandoning *peace*. In other words, it will have to risk becoming unrecognizable to itself.

Peace education theory should not be concerned with finding consensus or authentication. Rather, peace education theory, after a utopian turn, would dare to disturb the "peace" of the systemically violent status quo in our societies; it would avoid becoming just an ineffective extension of the progressive education that George Counts (1932) criticized nearly a century ago: a project of a "liberal-minded upper middle class…who are full of good will and humane sentiment, who have vague aspirations for world peace and human brotherhood..." (p. 5). It would instead recognize and refine these aspirations as potential ruptures of the present totality of infinite presence. Like Abe Kobo's (1971) novel, this utopianism would foster the "image of a future that intrudes on the present, a future that sits in judgment" (p. 220).

The time has come for peace education to step into this future and fulfill its utopian promise.

References

Abe, K. (1971) *Inter Ice Age 4 [Dai Yon Kanpyo-ki]*. Translated from the Japanese by E.D. Saunders. New York: Berkley Publishing Corporation.

Ben-Porath, S. (2003) War and peace education. *Journal of Philosophy of Education* 37(3): 525–533.

Ben-Porath, S. (2006) *Citizenship under fire: Democratic education in times of conflict*. Princeton University Press.

Bloch, E. (1995) *The principle of hope [Das Prinzip Hoffnung]*. Translated from the German by Plaice, N. Plaice, S. and Knight, P. MIT Press.

Cook, S.A. (2008) Give peace a chance: The diminution of peace in global education in the United States, United Kingdom, and Canada. *Canadian Journal of Education* 31(4): 889–914.

Counts, G.S. (1932) *Dare the schools build a new social order?* New York: The John Day Company.

Cox, D. and Levine, M. (2005) War and violence: The problem of teaching the like-minded. *Peace Review: A Journal of Social Justice* 17(2–3): 247–259.

Davies, L. (2008) *Educating against extremism*. Sterling, USA: Trentham Books Limited.

Derrida, J. (1994) *Specters of Marx: The state of debt, the work of mourning, and the new International [Spectres de Marx: l'état de la dette, le travail du deuil et la nouvelle Internationale]*. Translated from the French by P. Kamuf. New York: Routledge.

Dolby, N., and Rahman, A. (2008) Research in international education. *Review of Educational Research* 78(3): 676–726.

Eagleton, T. (2000) *The idea of culture*. Malden, MA: Blackwell.

Foucault, M. (1984) What is Enlightenment? [Qu'est-ce que les Lumières?] In: Rabinow, P. (ed.) *The Foucault reader*. New York: Pantheon Books, 32-50. Also available at <http://foucault.info//documents/whatisenlightenment/foucault.whatisenlightenment.en.htht>. Accessed 19 June, 2015.

Fritzman, J.M. (2001) Return to Hegel. *Continental Philosophy Review* 34(3): 287–320.

Galtung, J. (1975) Violence, peace, and peace research. In: *Peace: research, education, action*. Oslo: Prio Monographs, 167–191.

Giroux, H.A., and McLaren, P. (1995) Radical pedagogy as cultural politics: Beyond the discourse of critique and anti-utopianism. In: McLaren, P. (ed.) *Critical pedagogy and predatory culture: Oppositional politics in a postmodern era*. New York: Routledge, 29–57.

Gur-Ze'ev, I. (2001) Philosophy of peace education in a postmodern era. *Educational Theory* 51(3): 315–336.

Gur-Ze'ev, I. (2010) Philosophy of peace education in a postmetaphysical era. In: Salomon, G., and Cairns, E. (eds.) *Handbook on peace education*. New York: Psychology Press, 171–183.

Haavelsrud, M. and Stenberg, O. (2012) Analyzing peace pedagogies. *Journal of Peace Education* 9(1): 65–80.

Hicks, D. (2004) Teaching for tomorrow: How can futures studies contribute to peace education? *Journal of Peace Education* 1(2): 165–178.

Jameson, F. (1982) Progress versus utopia; or, can we imagine the future? *Science Fiction Studies* 9(2): 147–158.

Jameson, F. (1998)*The cultural turn: Selected writings on the postmodern, 1983–1998*. New York: Verso.

Jameson, F. (1999) Marx's purloined letter. In Sprinker, M. (ed.) *Ghostly demarcations: A symposium on Jacques Derrida's Specters of Marx*. New York: Verso, 26–67.

Jameson, F. (2005)*Archaeologies of the future*. New York: Verso.

Jameson, F. (2010) *Valences of the dialectic*. New York: Verso.

Kent, G. (1977) Peace education: Pedagogy of the middle class. *Peace & Change* 4(3): 37–42.

Kruger, F. (2012) The role of TESOL in educating for peace. *Journal of Peace Education* 9(1): 17–30.

Levitas, R. (2000) For utopia: The (limits of the) utopian function in late capitalist society. *Critical Review of International Social and Political Philosophy* 3(2–3): 25–43.

Levitas, R. (2009) The imaginary reconstitution of society: Utopia as method. In: Moylan, B., and Baccolini, R. (eds.) *Utopia method vision: The use value of social dreaming.* Oxford: Peter Lang, 47–68.

Levitas, R. (2010) Back to the future: Wells, sociology, utopia and method. *The Sociological Review* 58(4): 530–547.

Lewis, T. (2009) Too little, too late: Reflections on Fredric Jameson's pedagogy of form. *Rethinking Marxism* 21(3): 438–452.

Lyotard, J. F. and Brugger, N. (2001) What about the postmodern? The concept of the postmodern in the work of Lyotard. *Yale French Studies* 99(1): 77–92.

More, T. (2012) *Utopia [Libellus vere aureus, nec minus salutaris quam festivus, de optimo rei publicae statu deque nova insula Utopia].* Translated from the Latin by D. Baker-Smith. London: Penguin Classics.

Noddings, N. (2003) *Happiness and education.* Cambridge: Cambridge University Press.

Page, J. (2008) *Peace education: Exploring ethical and philosophical foundations.* Charlotte, NC: Information Age Publishing.

Popkewitz, T. (2008) *Cosmpolitanism and the age of school reform.* Routledge.

Rancière, J. (1991) *The ignorant schoolmaster: Five lessons in intellectual emancipation.* [*Le Maître ignorant: Cinq leçons sur l'émancipation intellectuelle*]. Translated from the French by K. Ross. Stanford University Press.

Reardon, B. (2000) Peace education: A review and a projection. In: Moon, B., Brown, S. and Ben-Peretz, M. (eds.) *Routledge international companion to education.* New York: Routledge, 397–425.

Reardon, B and Snauwaert, D. (2011) Reflective pedagogy, cosmopolitanism, and critical peace education for political efficacy. *In Factis Pax* 5(1): 1–14.

Ricoeur, P. (1986) *Lectures on ideology and utopia.* New York: Columbia University Press.

Rorty, R. (1989) *Contingency, irony, and solidarity.* Cambridge: Cambridge University Press.

Rorty, R. (1996) Idealizations, foundations, and social practices. In: Benhabib, S. (ed.) *Democracy and difference: Contesting the boundaries of the political.* Princeton, NJ: Princeton University Press, 333–335.

Ruitenberg, C. (2009) Giving Place to unforeseeable learning: The inhospitality of outcomes-based education. *Philosophy of Education*: 266–274.

Salomon, G. (2002) The nature of peace education: Not all programs are created equal. In: Nevo, B. and Salomon, G. (eds.) *Peace education: The concept, principles, and practices around the world.* New Jersey: Lawrence Erlbaum Associates, 3–13.

Sargeant, L.T. (2010) *Utopianism: A very short introduction.* Oxford: Oxford University Press.

Smeyers, P. (March 2006) What philosophy can and cannot do for education. *Studies in Philosophy and Education* 25(1–2): 1–18.

Snauwaert, D. (2011) Social justice and the philosophical foundations of critical peace education. *Journal of Peace Education* 8(3): 315–331.

Webb, D. (2008) Exploring the relationship between hope and utopia: Towards a conceptual framework. *Politics* 28(3): 197–206.

Webb, D. (2009) Where's the vision? The concept of utopia in contemporary educational theory. *Oxford Review of Education* 35(6): 743–760.

White, P. (1988) Countering the critics. In: Hicks, D. (ed.) *Education for peace: Issues, principles, and practice in the classroom.* New York: Routledge, 36–50.

Wintersteiner, W. (2010) Educational sciences and peace education: Mainstreaming peace education into (western) academia? In: Salomon, G. and Cairns, E. (eds.) *Handbook on peace education.* New York: Psychology Press, 45–59.

Žižek, S. (2008) *Violence: Six sideways reflections.* New York: Picador.

Žižek, S. (2010) *Living in the end times.* New York: Verso.

CHAPTER 4

Education and spaces of, for, and by Ainu: Lessons from the 2013 New Zealand Ainumosir Exchange Program

Akemi Shimada, Jennifer Louise Teeter, Takayuki Okazaki

The word Ainu means "human" and the Ainu homeland is called *Ainu Mosir*,[1] meaning the land where humans live. Although the Ainu are indigenous to the northern Japanese island of Hokkaido, today they live throughout Japan; however, their culture and language has witnessed a transformation through a long history of practices and policies aiming for assimilation.

The contemporary lives of Ainu are multifaceted and varied, including those who are open about their Ainu heritage, those who have only just embarked on a journey to reconnect with their Ainu identities, and those who keep their Ainu ancestries hidden. Even today, Ainu still experience prejudice and discrimination, the results of which keep some trapped in a cycle of poverty. And to avoid social stigmas, many hide their Ainu roots. Since Ainu only make up 0.1% of the Japanese population, Ainu are indeed a small, but important, minority group whose voice often remains unheard.

The misunderstood position in which Ainu find themselves is exemplified by the comments posted on Twitter on August 11, 2014 by Sapporo Assemblyman Yasuyuki Kaneko, who asserts that the Ainu do not exist: "But, here are no such people as the Ainu anymore, are there? But they constantly demand rights they don't deserve. How can this be reasonable?"["*Ainu minzoku, mō i nai' kaneko*"] (Yamayoshi, 2014). The continued prevalence of these kinds of discriminatory statements by politicians demonstrates the level of misunderstanding and ignorance Ainu face by not just the general public, but by governmental representatives, even in areas where the Ainu population is comparatively high.

Out of this precarious situation, the Aotearoa Ainumosir Exchange Program (AAEP) was formed to inspire a new generation of Ainu youth to take action on behalf of their society and to learn from the native Māori of New Zealand about their endeavors for cultural survival. As a part of the program, five Ainu youths, two elders and a support group from Tokyo and Hokkaido took part in a five-week cultural exchange to New Zealand with the Māori in January and February 2013.

This chapter will provide a brief introduction of the current Ainu situation, before discussing the origins and activities of AAEP and two initiatives that have grown out of the experiences of the Ainu youth who took part on the program; the first one revolves around adapting the Te Ataarangi[2] method of language revitalization to the Ainu situation and intertwines the Silent Way with Māori cultural protocols creating a technique that is effective for teaching people of all ages their heritage language. The second initiative is the *cas ankar* (our fortress that we build on our own) movement to build a Tokyo-based community center for, by, and of Ainu people. At present there are no centers for Ainu in Tokyo, and those that are present in Hokkaido are governmental-run, meaning there are restrictions on how Ainu can make use of the facilities. This movement came about as a result of the AAEP participants experiences on a Māori *marae*.[3]

Historical background

Colonization and assimilation policies

The Ainu are indigenous to Hokkaido, the northern part of Honshu, the southern part of Sakhalin, and the Kurile Islands. Historically, they have a dynamic trade relationship with the people of mainland Asia, as well as different parts of Japan. However, during Japan's Edo period (from 1603 and 1867), trade with mainland Japan was restricted to the Matsumae Domain, which in part caused trade relations to deteriorate to a point where Ainu were placed at an unfair disadvantage. For example, whereas Ainu received 28 kilograms of rice in exchange for their hundred dried salmon in 1641, they only received 11 in 1669 (Shōchūgakusei Muke Fukudokuhon Henshū Iinkai, 2008, p. 17). In the 18th century, when the Matsumae Domain allowed merchants to control the trade, most Ainu men were no longer treated as traders, but rather as slave-like workers who were forcibly separated from their communities to fish herring and salmon exclusively. Furthermore, towards the end of the Edo period, the livelihood of Ainu communities was weakened drastically by starvation, unfamiliar diseases including smallpox and syphilis, and the rape of Ainu women by Japanese men. The population around this time had reportedly diminished by 50% (Ogawa, 1993).

In 1870, in the second year of the Meiji period, the Meiji government unilaterally incorporated all of *Ainu Mosir* (what was referred to as Ezochi by Japan) into its territory and subsequently banned Ainu customs including deer hunting, salmon fishing, tattooing, and other ceremonies, while subjugating the Ainu to assimilation policies. The *Kaitakushi* (Colonization Commission), under the assumption that Hokkaido was a terra nullius, denied Ainu access to territorial hunting and gathering grounds and imposed a system of private land ownership. Colonization agents forcibly relocated Ainu families, redistributing fertile lands to *Wajin* (ethnic Japanese) owners (Katō, 1980; Ogawa, 1993).

The view of Ainu by the Japanese government at the time is exemplified by this excerpt from parliamentary debate:

The natives are not knowledgeable enough to appreciate assimilation into the Empire, nor to be able to revere the Emperor, nor to understand the system. Their resources and ways of life have been gradually taken from them. They are at the brink of starvation so a law to protect them must be passed (cited in Keira, 1995, p. 11).

These comments, while acknowledging Meiji usurpation of Ainu resources, demonstrate the derogatory lens that framed colonization.

As one of its policies of total assimilation, the Meiji government enacted the Former Aborigines Protection Act by which the Ainu were forced into agriculture, and established Former Aborigines' Schools, which provided assimilatory education only to Ainu children. The first school specifically for the Ainu was established in 1877. While school attendance was less than 10% in 1886, it rose to 30% by 1898 as colonization gradually chipped away at Ainu ways of life (Ogawa, 1991). An additional 25 *Dojin Gakko* (Former Native Schools) were established in 1901 throughout Hokkaido (Abe, 2008).

In these schools, belittling and scolding by teachers served to reinforce the discouragement of using the Ainu language (Abe, 2008; Yamamoto, 1995). A disproportionate amount of classroom time was dedicated to teaching the Japanese language, even outside of Japanese language classes. Physical education classes were largely dedicated to the recitation of songs in Japanese and Japanese language classes were conducted for half of the week (Teeter & Okazaki, 2011). Judicial courts and the United Nations now recognize that these types of restrictions on native language "often curtail the development of children's capabilities and perpetuates poverty" (Skuttnab-Kangas, 2008, p. 1).

Another arm of colonization policy included attempts to force Ainu into farming. The Kaitakushi refused to acknowledge Ainu ownership of *iwor* (shared traditional hunting grounds/life spaces) and distributed scraps of land to the Ainu (Yamamoto, 1995). In comparison with Japanese companies and landholders, Ainu were allocated much smaller portions of land, which were often barren. They could only keep the land if they managed to cultivate it (Keira, 1995).

Ainu identity in contemporary Japan

In a 2006 Hokkaido governmental poll of people who claimed Ainu heritage, 23,782 people identified themselves as Ainu, and among these, only 304 professed to understand the language. Discrimination still exists on the island, and many hide their heritage. Nevertheless, as founder and President of the AAEP Akemi Shimada elaborated:

> Some estimates of the total Ainu population are between 100,000 to 500,000, if Ainu outside of Hokkaido are included. It is estimated that 5,000 to 10,000 Ainu live in the Tokyo metropolitan area. (Shimada, 2013)

The Ainu language is not used as an everyday language in the same way it once was. Indeed, UNESCO has declared Ainu a critically endangered language (United Nations Educational, 2009).For many Ainu over 50 years old, their parents spoke the language to them when they were growing up, but they were not under the ideal circumstances to teach their children, as Shimada explains:

> My parents spoke Ainu, but did not teach us when we were kids. So I can't speak Ainu. UNESCO has declared the Ainu language as an endangered language. Most Ainu language teachers are *wajin* (non-Ainu Japanese). (Shimada, 2013)

Shimada also went on to describe how discrimination still permeates within society today:

> Teachers at school discriminated against Ainu kids. I tried hard not to let discrimination get me down, but sometimes I just couldn't take it. Although discrimination isn't as harsh as before, it still definitely exists. That's why Ainu can't identify as Ainu. People look at Ainu at the supermarket, for instance, with caution, worrying that they will steal something. Also, people have refused to marry Ainu because they are Ainu, so they have moved outside of Hokkaido to get married. There is no discrimination against Ainu outside of Hokkaido, but I think that is just because *Wajin* don't know anything about Ainu. In big cities like Tokyo, there is another form of discrimination where Ainu are mistaken for illegal immigrants and get stopped and questioned by the police. (Shimada, 2013)

Shimada's comments are illustrative of the difficult situation that many Ainu currently find themselves in, as she asserts:

> No matter what we try to express to the country, or to society, our voices remain unheard. Given these circumstances, Ainu have lost the strength to

rise up against those who would rather silence them. We can't speak of our ancestors with pride. (Shimada, 2013)

It was only 10 years ago that Shimada herself felt comfortable disclosing her Ainu identity publically "Since then," she explained, "I have strived to lift myself up and voice my opinions. I do this not only for myself, but with the intention of engendering Ainu youth to be able to do the same." (Shimada, 2013)

Japanese government Ainu policy

There remains no internationally recognized definition of what constitutes an Ainu, and as such the Japanese government has always denied their existence as an indigenous people. In August 2007, however, the United Nations enacted the Declaration on the Rights of Indigenous People, and Japan ratified the declaration, with the exception that it would not recognize the collective rights of Ainu people (Tsunemoto, 2012). While as a declaration, it is not legally binding, it is, nonetheless, considered an epoch-making UN human rights document that clearly states the rights of indigenous groups.

Finally, on June 6, 2008, the Japanese Diet enacted a declaration recognizing Ainu as indigenous people of Japan. It is explained, however, that the reason for this decision was politically motivated: Japanese politicians felt pressured to recognize Ainu as indigenous before the Group of Eight Summit in Toyako, Hokkaido, in the same month, in order to avoid being accused of violating human rights. While the declaration was passed unanimously, few politicians and bureaucrats knew what an indigenous person was in a legal sense, let alone the rights to which indigenous people as a collective were entitled.

At present, the Council for Ainu Policy Promotion, a governmental body that deliberates on Ainu policy, has come up with two proposals. The first it to construct an enormous facility, the "Symbolic Space for Ethnic Harmony," which is considered by many Ainu to be the equivalent of an Ainu theme park, which will include a museum and traditional Ainu *cise*, or house, inside. The second proposal is to conduct a survey of Ainu living outside of Hokkaido. Notably, this council includes only five Ainu members out of 15 (Ainu seisaku suishin kaigi, 2014).

The priorities of the panel are questioned by members of the Ainu community in a variety of ways, ranging from a focus on issues related to repatriation of looted human remains to more general concerns regarding the scope of these policies. While it is planned for the human remains of Ainu that are currently stored at Hokkaido University and other institutions to be gathered and relocated in the newly proposed facility, many contend that deliberation on the unjust process that led to the remains to be stored in these universities today has not been sufficient. Accordingly, a lawsuit seeking to rectify the looting of Ainu graves by collectors and researchers has been initiated against Hokkaido University for the proper return of these remains ('Ikotsu irei shisetsu', 2014).

Another problem with the way Ainu policy is decided revolves around how those residing outside of Hokkaido are not sufficiently taken into consideration. Welfare policies enacted in 1947 only applied to Hokkaido-resident Ainu. Granted, the Council is considering a nationwide survey of Ainu, yet current deliberations suggest that any implemented policies will only represent a small fraction of the Hokkaido welfare measures. The vast majority of Ainu people are dissatisfied with governmental policy and have expressed a desire for more comprehensive initiatives that make more efficient use of allocated funds and incorporate aspects of the United Nations Declaration on the Rights of Indigenous Peoples.

Regarding the construction of the Symbolic Space for Ethnic Harmony, Ainu people across the country have voiced several criticisms, particularly regarding the funding, management, and the purpose of the facility. Most believe that expenditure numbering anywhere from four to 10 billion US dollars for a gargantuan symbolic space cannot be justified. Rather than concentrating all of the funds into what is basically another Ainu museum in only one Ainu community, Shiraoi, many have suggested that these funds would be better spent to revitalize the spirit of every Ainu community. In regards to management of the facility, uncertainty remains as to what extent Ainu will be involved in the management and running of the facility. Many expect that job opportunities that will be provided for Ainu will be minimal. Being able to spread knowledge of the Ainu world through a new museum would certainly benefit the status of Ainu in Japanese society to some extent; however, the majority of Ainu do not believe that building another museum should be made a priority, especially when there are still many of their people living lives of poverty.

The Aotearoa Ainumosir Exchange Program

Amidst the situation with the Japanese government failing to adequately address Ainu concerns in terms of policy, the grassroots-based, non-government affiliated Aotearoa Ainumosir Exchange Program was conceived. The inspiration for creating the AAEP stems back to 2009 when Shimada had the chance to visit New Zealand for an indigenous leadership program organized by the Advancement of Māori Opportunity (AMO):

> I was uneasy at first about collaborating with indigenous peoples from other countries, but for two weeks Bentham Ohia, the principal of a Māori-run university, stayed by my side and encouraged me. "You are Ainu, Akemi." He constantly told me this. I had never experienced this kind of encouragement in Japan. This liberated me. The person I am today is thanks to the Māori people I met. (Shimada, 2013)

Following this, in January 2012, Māori Party representative Te Ururoa Flavell was invited to come to Japan as a guest for the inauguration of a Ainu political party. Te Ururoa met with Ainu leaders in Tokyo and Hokkaido, and learned about the Ainu situation. Te Ururoa later returned to Tokyo and consulted with Shimada about her goals and aspirations and she expressed that she wanted young Ainu to experience what she had witnessed in New Zealand. This conversation, in part, led to the establishment of the AAEP.

The AAEP organizing committee was formed in Japan, with Shimada as president, with the guiding mission of contributing to the development of future generations of Ainu leaders. The Māori situation differs significantly from the situation in Japan in which Ainu find themselves. The program aims to provide Ainu youth with chances to gain insight from a variety of Māori initiatives. Through this program, it is hoped that Ainu will gain inspiration for their own community-based initiatives in all fields, whether they are economic, social, cultural, or political. The program strives to reach out to all Ainu, in their diverse situations, and provide opportunities for participants to discover for themselves their Ainu identity in a modern context, become independent as Ainu, and make important strides for a new future for their people. This information was publicized through the program website, pamphlets, and a variety of events.

The program host organization on the New Zealand side, AMO, is an indigenous leadership program that was formed in 2003. It focuses on leadership for community capacity-building and emphasizes five core universal cultural values: Relationships, Responsibility, Reciprocity, Redistribution, and Respect. AMO is also as sister organization of Americans for Indian Opportunity (AIO), which was established by Ladonna Harris from the Comanche Nation in the United States and other Native Americans supporters (Harris and Wasilewski, 2004).

For the initial pioneer exchange program, applicants underwent a screening process to ensure they met certain eligibility requirements and were committed to the objectives of the program. Applicants were also required to be of Ainu descent and over 18 years of age, unless accompanied by a parent. Two rounds of screenings were used to select participants. The first round involved submission of an essay on motivations for joining the program, and the second round was based on interviews. As a result of the thorough screening process, two Ainu from the Tokyo metropolitan area and five from Hokkaido were selected to participate. The youngest was 13, and the oldest 45 years old. Three of the participants were members of the same family (mother, father, and daughter). Interpreters and other people who were delegated the responsibility of documentation also accompanied the group, so that the participants could participate as fully as possible.

In collaboration with the organizing committee, a team began fundraising independently for the five-week program. Besides fundraising at Ainu events and through personal contacts, an additional $11,870 was also collected through the generous contributions of supporters from the Indiegogo campaign from December 3, 2012 to January 20, 2013 just prior to departure. Donors received Ainu-designed postcards, *mukkuri* (an Ainu jaw harp), and special edition t-shirts and woodblock prints designed by Ainu artist Yuki Koji in exchange for their contributions.

Pre-departure preparation included an orientation, a pre-departure study packet, and a list of items to bring for the exchange prepared by the host organization in New Zealand. A Māori educator, Mr. Matarahi, was invited to Nibutani to take part in the orientation from September 21 to September 23, 2013, focusing on lecturing about Māori work to regain their language, culture and pride. He also taught the participants about culturally-appropriate behavior on a Māori *marae*. The study packet prepared by the organizing committee included papers on Māori history, the Treaty of Waitangi, T. W. Ratana, the Ratana Movement, Juji Nakata, Māori Electorates, the Māori Party, the returning of land and resources, as well as compensation agreements based on the Treaty of Waitangi, Māori language revitalization, the recent situation of Ainu, and chronological tables of Māori and Ainu history.

The comprehensive five-week program covered a series of entwined themes related to identity, culture and language, self-determination, education, and performing arts. Throughout the trip, the participants stayed in *wharenui* (meeting houses) on *marae* grounds and immersed themselves in Māori culture. These two aspects had a strong impact on the participants and led to the development of two Ainu-led initiatives upon the groups' return to Japan, namely employing the Māori Te Ataarangi language teaching methodology to Ainu language education, and a movement modeled on Māori *marae* life that Ainu developed independently.

aynu itak Language Society

The Māori revitalization movement began in the 1970s as a grassroots, community-based movement. Similar to the Ainu language situation, a significant driver of the loss of language use is attributed to the policies of the colonial government, especially the native school system where instruction was restricted to the English language and European culture (Hond & Brewerton, 2014a; Simon *et al.*, 2001). In the 1970s, Ainu also sought to revitalize the language, which led to Shigeru Kayano's attempt to create a primary school in 1980 with Ainu as the main language of instruction. Nonetheless, the Ministry of Welfare denied his petition for funding, as the language of instruction was not Japanese, and he resorted to establishing a private language school instead (Teeter & Okazaki, 2011). Similarly, private Ainu language schools and cultural revitalization groups were established throughout Hokkaido and in Tokyo and after the passage of the Ainu Cultural Promotion Act, governmentally-funded classes were provided as well (Ōta, 2009).

One approach of this Māori revitalization movement was the Te Ataarangi teaching method developed by Katerina Te Heikoko Mataira and Ngoingoi Te Kumeroa Pewhairangi who adapted the mathematician Caleb Gattegno's Silent Way approach, which applies Cuisenaire rods to Māori cultural contexts (Brewerton, 2013). Gattegno called this method "the Silent Way" in order to emphasize the silencing of the teacher for the benefit of the learner (*ibid*). Adaptations of Mataira and Pewhairangi incorporated other teaching approaches and an emphasis on engendering "immersion environments to support the full participation of all members of a community, respecting their distinct identity and encouraging internal leadership" (Hond, 2013, p. 227).

The cultural values that guide the method are: collectivity, acknowledging that all people have knowledge, families as an essential resource, humility, mutual respect, the sacred nature of every person and dialect, ensuring that barriers are never placed on a person, and the speaking of Māori at all times (Hond & Brewerton, 2014b). Learners are encouraged to follow several learning principles when engaging in Te Ataarangi:

- Maintain a Māori immersion environment by only speaking Māori
  Respect the customs, beliefs of others
- Respect the learning paces of others—do not rush other people to respond or add information not presented in class
- Allow everyone the chance to speak and do not interrupt so that everyone has a voice in the classroom
- Empathize with the learning processes and emotions of others (Hond & Brewerton, 2014a)

In the second week of the program, Dr. Ruakere Hond led the participants through workshops in the method over four days in Parihaka. They first learned basic Māori constructs through Te Ataarangi and then learned how to teach Ainu using the method. Rather than focus on vocabulary development, the beginning stage of Te Ataarangi is dedicated to introducing learners to as many grammatical constructs as possible in the beginning. According to Hond and Brewerton (2014a), by the time learners reach the intermediate stage, they are eager to absorb more vocabulary on their own. In this approach, rather than expecting students to memorize vocabulary words, students naturally learn words as they suit their needs and are fluently able to use them in sentences.

Many of the participants, including those with little interest in learning Ainu before, became motivated to learn Ainu as a result of the warm, accepting, and enjoyable approach that Te Ataarangi brings to facilitating language learning. Another attractive aspect of this approach is the ability to involve members of all generations regardless of educational training. Additionally, since this approach is different from those that participants had experienced while learning

Ainu in Japan where the focus is largely on reading and writing, they found that they were quickly able to speak both Māori and Ainu with fluency. The type of fluency referred to here is not fluency in the entire language, but rather fluency in the types of phrases that they had learned (Hond, 2014). Another core strength that the participants recognized was how the Te Ataarangi approach recognizes the tenet that language vitality and revitalization are intrinsically linked to cultural strength (Hond, 2013).

Upon their return to Japan in February, the *aynu itak* Revitalization Society was established, focusing on the adaptation of the Te Ataarangi to the Ainu language situation. Program participants residing in Kyoto, Tokyo, and Hokkaido take part in Ainu language Skype lessons weekly led by Kenji Sekine. Video teleconferencing interfaces have also been used to utilize the Te Ataarangi methodology.

In order to deepen their knowledge of the Te Ataarangi approach, a prominent Te Ataarangi educator from Ngati Porou, Erana Brewerton, was invited to lead demonstration workshops in Tokyo and Hokkaido Ainu communities in August 2013. Erana provided a presentation in Tokyo on the method in the Yaesu Tokyo Ainu Culture Center. Members of the audience also had the opportunity to experience learning Māori at the end of the presentation. Four days were also spent in Nibutani, Hokkaido, engaging in intensive experiential learning workshops with 20 participants from various regions of Hokkaido and Tokyo. Prominent Ainu educators, both Ainu and Japanese, also came to contribute their knowledge to discussions on curriculum development. The Nibutani workshops focused on developing teaching techniques for basic commands, colors, numbers, and telling the time. A visit was also made to Ainu language classes tailored to children.

Later, in August and September 2014, Hond and Brewerton were invited to Japan again to lead more workshops focusing more intensely on curriculum development and teacher training. Since there was limited time in Tokyo the previous year, events were scheduled for three days in Tokyo at the Ainu Culture Center. The first event was an introduction to the methodology. The second focused on assessing the needs of the Tokyo metropolitan Ainu community. The third event focused on the actual practice of the Te Ataarangi method, with a special emphasis on teaching children. After Erana's departure, workshop participants immediately scheduled an event for the following week with an emphasis on introducing the method to Ainu learners.

The Nibutani workshops again took place over four days from August 24th to August 27th, 2014. Significant progress was made in curriculum development and training teachers in using the method. With the collaboration of 25 workshop participants and two Ainu language educators, 12 introductory lessons were developed and 50 ideas for future lessons were brought to the table. Participants were separated into two groups—one focusing on curriculum development, and the other on teaching methods. Each group then shared their approaches with one another, creating a cohesive learning environment. Three workshops were then held in Akan. This time, the number of participants tripled from the previous year, with 15 attendees. Since many of the participants were interested in participating after work until 9:30 p.m., two of the workshops were scheduled for 10:00 p.m. over two days. A children's focused workshop was also scheduled on the second day, where Ruakere and Erana provided advice for maintaining an immersion environment using the Cuisenaire rods, and games which utilize language were introduced using the rods.

Future activities of the *aynu itak* Revitalization Society will include monthly curriculum development and learning meetings. There is also discussion about sending Ainu educators to learn more Te Ataarangi over the span of a month.

casi ankar Movement

This section will focus on and describe the development of a grassroots movement to create an independent Ainu-run space in the Tokyo metropolitan community. Throughout the participants' voyage, they were welcomed to a *marae*, which serves as a community meeting place founded on Māori cultural values. The fostering of Māori identity through the maintenance of connections to land, ancestors, and future generations was evident not only in the first week, but throughout the visit, especially on the *marae*. When approaching the *marae* of the *wharenui* where the participants were hosted, the presence of ancestors, including those of the participants, was constantly made evident. In the ceremonies to welcome the participants onto the *marae*, ancestors were summoned through *karanga* (a ceremonial call to let the ancestors know of the arrival of the guests). Additionally, a *marae* is in fact designed to represent the body of an ancestor. By entering the *marae* in a physical sense, the participants were entering the world of the ancestors. Inside the *wharenui*, photos of ancestors adorned the walls.

Shimada was inspired by the warm welcome she received on the *marae* and the function it provided as a place for people to come together to discuss, eat, and sleep together in an Ainu environment. Thus the movement for Ainu to have their "own place of activity, their own fortress," *casi ankar*, was conceived. Since Ainu outside of Hokkaido are not counted in welfare policies, those in Tokyo do not have a place in Tokyo that they can use as they wish despite there being 143 Ainu community centers in 27 different municipalities throughout Hokkaido (Ainu Seisaku Suishin Kaigi, 2011). Modeling initiatives after grassroots Māori strategies, the approach to creating this type of community center was changed from one where members petitioned the government, to one where Ainu worked completely independently of the government with youth as the focal point. Out of the nearly 100 Ainu actively working on Ainu issues, 50 or 60 are involved in this project.

Through the exchange program, the participants learned of many Māori-led initiatives completely independent of the government. Shimada describes this as follows:

> I received so much stimulation and learned so much about the Māori initiatives from my visits to *marae*. I learned that the reason Māori have been able to accomplish so much is not only due to the rights that were recognized through the Waitangi Treaty and their population, composing 15% of the New Zealand population, but because Māori paid for things at their own expense and made sacrifices. (Shimada, 2013)

The *casi ankar* organization was opened to public on October 5th, 2013, at the annual Ainu Thanksgiving Festival in Shin-Yokohama. Shimada described the organization as a place for Ainu to reconnect with their ancestors and Ainu essence:

> The *casi ankar* will breathe life into the Ainu in Tokyo. Tokyo will become something much different from what it is today, a city where a new type of civilization will take root. Purely and simply, Tokyo will become an Ainu city. The first person to say that Tokyo is an Ainu City was a researcher named Mark Watson. This means that Tokyo will not just be a place where Ainu live, but rather in the true sense of the word, Tokyo will become a multicultural city. *casi ankar* will mark one step forward to a type of peace where different cultures are accepted. Gaining the strength of young Ainu and the support of Māori, we are working to take this first step forward. (Shimada, 2013)

At present, *casi ankar* is working on fundraising and awareness-raising through a variety of events throughout the Tokyo metropolitan era.

Conclusion

Based on the knowledge gained through first hand experiences immersed in the Māori world through the Ainumosir Exchange Programs, a fresh group of Ainu individuals has found the impetus to rise up to create on their own the kinds of changes they would like to see in their society. While acknowledging that every Ainu person has their own unique experience in defining their identity, the general public's lack of knowledge about Ainu, and continued discrimination, adds an additional hurdle for many seeking to embrace their identity and heritage. The relics of governmental colonization, imperial education, and welfare policies still cast a shadow on Ainu education in the public sphere, causing many to question whether current governmental policies are truly bringing benefits to Ainu people.

Witnessing how Māori maintain their genealogical connections to land, ancestors, and identity through museums founded on Māori values; successfully becoming able to speak Māori and give voice to Māori cultural traditions in the Māori language through Te Ataarangi; participating in celebrations of successful and ongoing struggles to maintain rights as indigenous peoples; taking part and learning about the founding of inclusivity, Māori-led elementary through university education adapted to the various needs of youth, both Māori and non-Māori; collaborating in the traditional and modern Māori arts; sharing Ainu culture, learning, and experiences with Māori through the entire journey—all of these experiences empowered the participants to reconfirm their commitment to developing innovative approaches to sharing their Ainu culture and heritage in their communities.

Finally, the *aynu itak* Revitalization Society and *casi ankar* are developing the competency to remain independent from the government, which continues to insufficiently address Ainu needs. They are working to create spaces and educational strategies of, for, and by Ainu with Ainu culture forming the backbone. While these initiatives are already emboldening Ainu communities for positive change, it is certain, as AMO chair Bentham Ohia at the end of the AAEP exchange, stated over and over again: "What's good for Ainu, is good for Japan, is good for the world."

References

Abe, Y. (2008). Ainu minzoku ni totte no kyōiku (Education for Ainu people). *Kaihō Kyōiku, 491*, 7-14.

'Ainu minzoku, mō i nai' kaneko sapporo shigi tsuittā hasshin 'yūgū okashii' to setsumei ("Ainu people don't exist anymore", Sapporo parliament member tweets, describing Ainu's favourable treatment to be strange.). (2014). *Hokkaido Shimbun*, 17 August, Retrieved from: http://www.hokkaido-np.co.jp/news/donai/557277.html [August 20, 2014].

Ainu seisaku suishin kaigi (Council for Ainu Policy Promotion). (2011). Dai san kai 'seisaku suishin sagyō bukai' giji gaiyō (Summary of proceedings of the lifestyle policy group 3rd meeting). Retrieved from: http://www.kantei.go.jp/jp/singi/ainusuishin/seisakusuishin/dai3/gijigaiyou.pdf [August 10, 1014].

Ainu seisaku suishin kaigi (Council for Ainu Policy Promotion). (2014). Ainu seisaku suishin kaigi meibo (Council for Ainu policy promotion members), *Ainu seisaku no gaiyō (Outline of Ainu Policy)*. Retrieved from: http://www.kantei.go.jp/jp/singi/ainusuishin/meibo.pdf [August 1, 2014].

Brewerton, E. (2013). Māori language revitalisation and Te Ataarangi method. Presentation. Tokyo: Tokyo Ainu Culture Center.

Harris, L. and Wasilewski, J. (2004). Indigeneity, an Alternative Worldview: Four R's (Relationship, Responsibility, Reciprocity, Redistribution) vs. Two P's (Power and Profit). Sharing the Journey Towards Conscious, *Systems Research and Behavioral Science*, 21 (1): 1-15. Retrieved from: http://www.humiliationstudies.org/documents/WasilewskiIndigeneity.pdf [August, 15, 2013].

Hond, R. (2013). Matua te reo, matua te tangata Speaker community: visions, approaches, outcomes. Doctoral thesis presented at Massey University, Palmerston North, New Zealand.

Hond, R., & Brewerton, E. (2014a). Lecture: How Māori revitalized their language. Presentation. Sapporo: Hokkaido University Center for Ainu and Indigenous Studies.

Hond, R., & Brewerton, E. (2014b). *Māori ga dō yatte kotoba o torimodoshi ta no ka Te Ataarangi to Māori go fukkō (*How Māori brought back their language—Te Ataarangi and Māori language revitalization). Presentation. Tokyo: Tokyo Ainu Culture Center.

Ikotsu irei shisetsu ni 'hantai'= ainu ra, kenkyū mokuteki o kenen—henkan motome soshō mo. Hokkaido. (2014). *Jiji*, 23 August, Retrieved from: http://www.jiji.com/jc/zc?k=201408/2014082300186 [August 26, 2014].

Katō, N. (1980). Hokkaido sanken ikkyoku jidai no tai Ainu seisaku to sono jitsujō (Policy towards Ainu during the sanken-ikkyoku era when Hokkaido was divided into three prefectures of Hakodate Prefecture, Sapporo Prefecture and Nemuro Prefecture from 1882 - 1886 and the actual state of affairs). *Hokudai Shigaku, 20*, 14-26.

Keira, M. (1995). The Ainu people. In E. Yamamoto & T. Keira (Eds.), *Ainu women, aboriginal people of Japan : keeping the hearts of our eldresses alive today.* Hokkaido, Japan: Yay Yukar no Mori.

Ogawa, M. (1991). 'Ainu gakkō' no setchi to 'Hokkaido kyūdojin hogohō,"kyūdojin jidō kyōiku kitei' no seiritsu (A historical study on "Aine School" (an elementary school in Ainu Comunnity) in Hokkaido(1):The Forming process of the educational system for Ainu children in the 1870's~1900). *Hokkaido daigaku kyōikugakubu kiyō, 55*, 257-325. Retrieved from: http://eprints.lib.hokudai.ac.jp/dspace/bitstream/2115/29364/1/55_P257-325.pdf [June 5, 2010].

Ogawa, M. (1993). The Hokkaido former aborigines protection act and assimilatory education. In N. Loos & T. Osanai (Eds.), *Indigenous minorities and education : Australian and Japanese perspectives of their indigenous peoples, the Ainu, Aborigines and Torres Strait Islanders* (pp. 237-249). Tokyo: Sanyusha.

Ōta, M. (2009). Asahikawa Ainugo Kyōiku no genjō to kadao (The current situation and challenges in Asahikawa Ainu Language Education). *Rekishi Chiri Kyōiku*, 742(1), 36-47.

Shimada, A. (2013) "Fostering Ainu Youth." Plenary address given by Akemi Shimada, founder and president of the AAEP, at Peace as a Global Language conference, Rikkyo University, Japan.

Shōchūgakusei Muke Fukudokuhon Henshū Iinkai. (2008). *Ainu Minzoku: Rekishi to Genza (The Ainu People: History and the Present Day)*. Sapporo: Zaidanhōjin Ainu Bunka Fukkō: Kenkyū Suishin Kikan.

Simon, J. A., Smith, L. T., Cram, F., Hohepa, M. K., McNaughton, T., & Stephenson, M. (2001). *A civilising mission?: Perceptions and representations of the native schools system.* Auckland, NZ: Auckland University Press.

Skuttnab-Kangus, T. (2009). Linguistic Genocide: Tribal education in India, *National Folklore Support Center Newsletter*, 32 (1), pp. 4-6. Retrieved from www.tove-skutnabb-kangas.org/pdf/ Tove_Skutnabb_Kangas_India_tribal_education_and_participating_in_crimes_against _humanity.pdf [July 1, 2010].

Tsunemoto, T. (2012). Towards Ainu- and Japan-specific indigenous policies, *The Ainu: Indigenous People of Japan*. Sapporo: Hokkaido University Center for Ainu and Indigenous Studies.

United Nations Educational, Scientific, and Cultural Organization. (2009). UNESCO Interactive Atlas of the World's Languages in Danger. Retrieved from <http://www. unesco.org/culture/ich/ index.php?pg=00206> [June 6, 2010].

Yamamoto, E. (1995). My life in the Ainu community of Akan: teaching our children to sing with pride and dance with joy. In E. Yamamoto & T. Keira (Eds.), *Ainu women, aboriginal people of Japan : keeping the hearts of our eldresses alive today*. Hokkaido, Japan: Yay Yukar no Mori.

Yamayoshi, K. (2014). Sapporo assemblyman criticized for denying the existence of Ainu – AJW. *The Asahi Shimbun*, 19 August, Retrieved from: http://ajw.asahi.com/article/behind_news/ social_affairs/ AJ201408190034 [August 20, 2014].

CHAPTER 5

Towards the creation of a dynamic learning environment to promote learning for peace

James D. Short

2014—Only connect?

The majority of educators who are currently in the early to mid-stages of their careers came of age during or shortly after the period of momentous change that took place around the world at the end of the Cold War. Following the collapse of the Soviet bloc at the beginning of the 1990s, the likelihood of nuclear war breaking out between the superpowers diminished drastically and a new, optimistic era seemed to stand before humanity. However, subsequent tragic events such as the civil war in the Balkans and the genocide in Rwanda cast a dark veil over much of that optimism. The next significant temporal milestone, that of the new millennium, seemed to offer another opportunity for humanity to embark upon a more understanding and peaceful path. Yet events such as 9/11, the Second Gulf War, the 2008 economic crisis, and the unravelling of many of the advances of the Arab Spring, have served to dispel much of that second groundswell of optimism. Our world in 2014, despite its continued technological advances and hyper-connectivity through social media and the broad range of 24-hour news sources, remains to a large degree unstable, insecure, and riven with economic disparity between the haves and the have-nots (Oxfam, 2014). This is the international society in which our students, born in the late 90s and the 2000s, are growing up and coming of age. On a broad level, the international picture frequently appears far from promising, and the challenge facing our students of trying to make sense of this situation and then locating their own place within it is clearly a daunting one.

In attempting to tackle this challenge, a key factor relates to the collection and analysis of information. Whereas prior to the advent of the internet, one could say that to generate a relatively sound understanding of a topic, one could pursue fairly clearly demarcated investigative strategies, the growing reality in our contemporary world, increasingly influenced by data-source giants such as Google, multilingual Wikipedia and the blogosphere, is that students can find themselves at a loss when looking for reliable information that can be used to deepen their understanding. Regarding news about current world events, formerly relatively reliable information could be drawn from major news outlets such as NHK, the BBC and CNN, supplemented to some extent by newspapers and magazines with differing political sympathies. However, now the almost ubiquitous nature of smartphones and tablets means that anyone with internet access can become an on-the-spot journalist with the ability to colour eyewitness accounts of unfolding events in any manner they choose. Whilst on the one side this phenomenon represents something of a revolution in terms of the free dissemination of information, arguably it also has the potential to create confusion, distrust and information-overload, which can leave viewers and listeners at the mercy of a constant influx of 'info-noise'. As a consequence, for educators of the social sciences and languages, it is held that as part and parcel of imparting knowledge and facilitating understanding amongst our students, providing guidance about navigating the constant influx of information about our 21st century world represents a significant educational responsibility.

A pertinent issue related to this task, which is clearly linked to the never ending merry-go-round of news headlines, commentary, and analysis (much of it focused on dark and depressing topics), can be summed up in the following question: in reality, is the world that we live in such a chaotic and uncaring place? If someone were unable to draw him or herself away from the news cycle focusing on the latest terrorist atrocity, natural or environmental disaster or suffering in a war-torn society, it would be hard to answer 'no' to such a question. It is widely acknowledged that an unwritten rule exists within the news media that 'good news doesn't sell', which commonly leads to headlines being dominated by the shocking details of the latest disaster. Adams (2013) draws attention to CNN as being particularly culpable in this regard due its policy of placing 'embedded reporters' in moving or actually fighting military units, who then send back news reports from conflict hotspots in different parts of the world. This practice led Adams to describe CNN not as the 'Cable News Network', but as the war-focused and to some extent conflict-aggrandizing CWNN – 'the *culture of war* news network' (Adams, 2013, pp. 234-235).[1]

At times when the majority of incoming news appears discouraging, having the wherewithal to step back and recognise that the violent and tragic events on the television, computer, or tablet screen by no means represent the majority of all human interactions, and to recall and appreciate the myriad of acts of kindness and consideration which permeate and sustain societies throughout the world, serve to give balance to internal or external debates about the overall state of the world. Jeannie Lum of the University of Hawaii addresses this issue in the following way: while recognising that peace educators and researchers strive to identify and draw attention to conditions of violence, oppression, and suffering around the world and then propose practicable policies for their improvement, these negative conditions do not and should not represent the entirety of their pedagogical or research focus. Conversely, Lum (2013) describes the positive aspects as follows:

> The other side of the coin represents the positive face: that of drawing attention to people taking everyday actions from the kindness of their hearts that support conditions for peace—compassion, respectful relations, equality, freedom, health, and well-being of humanity and the world as a whole … Inspiring creativity, reflective thinking, diversity, holistic problem-solving, social intelligence, cooperation, communicative dialogue, and an orientation to seek knowledge and understanding. This includes activities such as raising funds and taking action for those who are in need of food, clothing, shelter, medical care and emotional support … bringing disaster relief to areas experiencing flooding, starvation and disease … Notable examples such as that of Darnell Barton, the bus driver who stopped his bus on the middle of a bridge and reached out to a woman on the other side of the railing who was about to jump to her death while others walked, rode or drove by. (pp. 218-219)

Hence with regard to the hyper-connected world of 2014, recognising the many competing pressures which are incumbent upon our students, the author holds that it is important to consider whether they have or are given sufficient time to actually consider the great variety of good deeds done by people every day during the course of their normal studies. Without such a balancing perspective, it is possible that they could come to feel disoriented and demoralised, potentially leading to emotional or psychological distress. A case in point can be seen in the concerns raised by a third grade student at Toyo University, Mr. N. [name withheld], who after watching the movie *13 Days* about the Cuban missile crisis, asked the author in June 2014 why human beings were always fighting and making war.[2]

It is precisely for the purpose of addressing concerns such as those voiced by Mr. N. that the author is teaching the subject of Peace Studies. It is held that within this underlying psycho-educational context, the clear importance of specifically targeted learning about and for peace becomes readily discernible.

Contributing towards the growth of peace-related learning

Since the end of the Cold War there has been significant growth in peace-related learning in many countries around the world. In an essay published in August 2013, Werner Wintersteiner traces the development of the Global Campaign for Peace Education (GCPE), a movement which grew out of the wide-ranging activities of UNESCO and the Hague Appeal for Peace during the 1990s. In its key declaration published in 1999, in clear, forthright language, the Hague Appeal for Peace (as cited in Wentersteiner, 2013) called for the following:

> In order to combat the culture of violence that pervades our society, the coming generation deserves a radically different education—one that does not glorify war but educates for peace, non-violence and international cooperation. The Hague Appeal for Peace has launched a world-wide campaign to empower people at all levels with the peacemaking skills of mediation, conflict transformation, consensus-building and non-violent social change.
>
> The campaign insists that peace education be made compulsory at all levels of the education system. It demands that education ministries systematically implement peace education initiatives at a local and national level. It calls on development assistance agencies to promote peace education as a component of their teacher training and materials production. (p. 140)

On the basis of these premises, since 1999 the GCPE has sought to promote the teaching of peace education courses in educational institutions around the world, and also to support the continued expansion of peace-related learning and research. Regarding the success achieved by this initiative in the last decade and a half, the peace scholar, educator and women's rights advocate Barbara Wien (2010) described how peace education is now spreading rapidly and scaling-up throughout the world:

> From Pakistan to South Central Los Angeles, from Iraq to the Philippines, from Afghanistan to Kenya, we are finding more and more peace education programs in after-school programs, summer camps, schools, refugee settings, community centers, houses of worship, college campuses and thousands of other venues. A rich storehouse of knowledge is building, infusing and integrating peace scholarship into public spaces, communications, curricula, and research. Particularly powerful are the peace education programs being developed by soldiers and former combatants, some of them as young as 15.

One example of the developments contributing towards the success of this initiative was the opening in 2012 of the Fundamental Concepts of Peace Studies course within the Law Faculty of Toyo University, Tokyo. This course was created as part of the university-wide curriculum restructuring which took place within Toyo to coincide with the 125th anniversary of its founding in 2012. The course represents the first opportunity for all Toyo undergraduates, both Japanese and non-Japanese, to undertake specifically targeted peace learning in English. As the result of something of an ad-hoc creation process which began in November 2011, the course opened in April 2012 and is now in its third year.[3]

The following sections of this chapter discuss lessons learned from the process of creation and subsequent delivery of this course, and a number of additional issues which have come to light during its first five semesters.

Course creation

Following the decision to open a course of Peace Studies within the Law Faculty of Toyo University taken in November 2011, the author had slightly less than five months to design and create it before the beginning of the next academic year, at which time a thoroughly revised curriculum would be implemented across the university as a whole. With hindsight it has become clear that this period of time was inadequate to prepare sufficiently for the opening of the course in April 2012. As hitherto no blueprint existed within the faculty for what a new Peace Studies course might look like—much less one which would be delivered in English—to a large extent the author found himself in the position of constant creation.

In order to address this challenge, the first priority was to articulate an overall structure for the course, and this in turn necessitated the selection of an appropriate textbook. On the advice of Japanese and American colleagues, the decision was taken to select *Peace and Conflict Studies* (second edition) by David P. Barash and Charles P. Webel.[4] This textbook provided the structure for the course, which followed its division into four distinct parts: Part 1—The Promise of Peace, The Problems of War; Part 2—The Reasons for Wars; Part 3—Building 'Negative Peace'; Part 4—Building 'Positive Peace'. The next priority was to ascertain what specific content from the textbook would be delivered within each of the four parts, and then to devise and create the actual teaching materials which would be utilized to deliver the content in the classroom. At this point, over and above the lack of a general course blueprint, the author came up against a significant difficulty.

As a number of academic analyses have demonstrated, Peace Studies represents a very broad educational discipline which incorporates concepts and issues from a number of different fields, including those of politics, economics, psychology and ecology.[5] As a consequence, it became clear that attempting to cover the full range of topics contained in Barash and Webel's textbook during the course of two 15-week semesters would not represent a viable strategy. Foremost in the author's mind at this point were the likely recipients of the course: Japanese undergraduate students in their second or third year of study with moderate to good English ability, who were in all probability coming to the subject for the first time. It is here that the crux of the issue comes to light: considering the broad range of content that constitutes Peace Studies, the significant cognitive demands that a large amount of this content would likely place upon learners, coupled with the linguistic medium through which it would be delivered —English not being the learners' native tongue—in such circumstances what could be seen as the most appropriate teaching strategy for the new course? Following extensive consultation with colleagues from within Toyo University and externally, the author came to the conclusion that the nature of the likely audience necessitated a teaching strategy which would elucidate the fundamental themes and subject matter of Peace Studies, but which would eschew an excessive focus on specific detail and the overuse of complicated vocabulary which could inhibit students' overall understanding. This was the principle which guided the creation of the course from late 2011 until April 2012, and which continues to underlie the ongoing process of revision and refinement up to the present date. In practice, finding an effective means of tackling the central pedagogical challenge of making the specific content both digestible and understandable *in English* represents the most significant difficulty that has arisen in relation to the development of the course.

In 2013 this challenge was further exacerbated by the addition to the class of several highly motivated exchange students from the United States who registered for the course in the spring and autumn semesters. These students were naturally able to digest the English subject matter of each class lecture far more rapidly than their Japanese counterparts, and were also more accustomed to expressing their opinions in relation to it in a discussion format. More will be said about this issue below.

The result of the five-month creation process which began in November 2011 was that by the beginning of the new academic year, the author had succeeded in creating an overall topic framework for the two semesters and specific guidelines for the teaching method and course evaluation; this information was then uploaded to the university's online syllabus. However, in terms of specific lecture preparation, this was far from complete and the author had managed to flesh out only two-thirds of the content earmarked for the first semester. As a consequence, from the very first class of academic year 2012-2013, he was in the position of delivering some pre-prepared content, while adjusting the teaching method for pace and difficulty as he went along, at the same time as trying to keep ahead of the curve by preparing the remaining lectures of the semester before the students caught up. This was clearly a far from ideal situation.

First year of classroom delivery: April 2012 – January 2013

Prior to April 2012, neither the author nor the department for educational administration of the Law Faculty (the *Kyoumuka*) had an idea of how many students would choose to register for the new Peace Studies course. Coupled with the fact that the preparation was far from complete, this situation added to a sense of unease about whether it would prove to be a success or not. At this stage, "success" was taken to mean whether or not justification would be found within the faculty to keep the course open for longer than the initial planned period of two years. In March 2012 the director of the administrative department had informed the author unofficially that should less than five students register for the course in each of the first two years, difficulties might subsequently arise in convincing senior law professors of the merits of keeping it open. As it transpired, during the first year a total of 23 students registered, of whom 15 attended regularly.

With regard to the teaching method, in keeping with the author's central aim of creating an engaging learning environment by means of delivering the range of content in an engaging and digestible manner, the individual 90 minute classes were largely structured according to the following pattern:

1. Explanation of the class theme by means of a PowerPoint presentation incorporating many images, with Japanese vocabulary explanations included where appropriate (30-35 minutes).
2. Distribution of presentation handout, confirmation of understanding of main points of the presentation in groups (10-15 minutes).
3. Group discussion on specific questions related to the theme posed by the instructor; the instructor circulating to provide additional explanations and assistance where required (15-20 minutes).
4. Reporting back session—one or two students from each group report the results of their discussions to the whole class (10-15 minutes).
5. Follow up: after class the PowerPoint presentation file is sent to all students by e-mail in order for them to review the material.

Two example slides taken from the first semester lecture focusing on the role of leaders in war, entitled 'The decision-making level' are included in the appendix at the end of the chapter; the second of these slides contains a number of Japanese vocabulary explanations.

In addition to the standard class structure described above, twice per semester students were required to make short presentations about topics related to the previous lecture that they had researched, such as the lives of terrorists who later became political leaders, the activities of international NGOs, and the human rights records of particular countries.

With regard to formal evaluation, students were assessed according to three criteria: i) attendance, ii) classroom performance, and iii) performance in written tests. For the latter, considering the quantity and relative difficulty of much of the content, students were required to take a review test following each of the four parts of the course, meaning that there were two written tests per semester. During the first year of delivery the author also periodically gave the students short quizzes in order to check their understanding of particular concepts. However, these were steadily phased out during the second and third years for reasons which will be explained below.

Results of the first year

As may be already apparent, prior to and during the first year of delivery, the author had a number of serious concerns about the content and efficacy of the course. The first of these related to the prosaic logistical fact that the cycle of 15 lectures for the first semester had yet to be completed by the time the students first took their seats in the classroom.

Further concerns focused on the following issues:

- In general, was the lecture content appropriate, too detailed or not detailed enough?
- Considering the language barrier, how much of the content was being well understood?
- Were the discussion and evaluation questions posed during class and in the review tests appropriate, too easy or too difficult?
- Were the students making effective use of the textbook?

In accordance with university policy, classes of all Toyo teaching staff require that formal objective evaluations be carried out once a semester by means of student completion of anonymous questionnaires. Prior to the 2012-2013 academic year these evaluations were habitually carried out in classes that contained the largest number of students. However, with the introduction of the new curriculum, in cases where courses were being taught for the first time, these also became the subject of formal evaluation; consequently in July and December 2012 the students of Peace Studies had the opportunity to express their opinions about it. For good or for ill, the author was grateful for this since his impressions up to that point of how well the classes had been progressing had been based solely on subjective analysis. This analysis, which had focused on student attendance, the quality of class work (particularly discussion responses and group presentations), and performance in quizzes and review tests, had revealed a good level of student interest in the content and sound comprehension of the main concepts. However, it was clear that these personal impressions required objective corroboration which could be provided by statistical data.

In general, the spring and autumn questionnaire evaluations revealed that the students were largely satisfied with the content and delivery of the course, especially with regard to the explanation of the content using PowerPoint presentations and the frequent opportunities they had to discuss the concepts and related issues with other students. Specific weaknesses were identified in relation to the difficulty of the textbook, which had not proved useful in supporting students' pre and post-class study, and the author's use of the blackboard to provide additional explanations.[6] On the strength of these results, it appeared that the first three of the above concerns about the course were not too serious, and that therefore a complete rethink and/or restructuring might not be required prior to the start of the second year of delivery in

April 2013. However, the fourth concern in relation to the textbook had proven accurate, and so it was clear that this issue would require attention.

In order to enhance student understanding of the content, during the course of the winter vacation (February—March 2013) the author undertook a large scale revision of the majority of the PowerPoint presentations for the first semester, adding several more images and Japanese vocabulary explanations. Furthermore, new slides were created for the group discussion questions for each topic which were more intellectually demanding than those that had been posed during the previous year. Henceforth, generating answers to these questions would require a higher degree of critical thinking since they were no longer to be found in the text of the presentation handouts. With regard to the textbook issue, considering the fact that replacing Barash and Webel with a different textbook would almost certainly require a significant revision of both the overall topic framework and many of its associated lectures, due to the fact that the two rounds of class evaluations had revealed a good level of student satisfaction with the existing method of content and delivery, the decision was taken to continue with the same text for another year in an effort to identify more effective means of maximising its utility to the students.

Second year of classroom delivery: April 2013—January 2014

On the strength of one year of experience, two completed (and revised) cycles of lectures, some high-quality student responses in the end of semester review tests from the previous July and January, coupled with two rounds of generally encouraging class evaluations, the author entered the classroom at the beginning of April 2013 with rather more confidence than a year earlier. However, he was almost immediately thrown off his stride by the presence in the classroom of six exchange students from the United States. This presented an immediate conundrum since the developments and incremental improvements that had brought the course to its seemingly acceptable condition at this point would now be put seriously to the test by the additional educational needs and intellectual faculties of six native speakers.

Henceforth, were any problems to arise in relation to planning, content or delivery, no longer would the author have the potential luxury of a language barrier or different educational and cultural norms to mask any discernible deficiencies.

Over and above a genuine fear of being found incompetent in the eyes of these American undergraduates – the first native speakers the author had ever taught at university level—the most pressing question which was to dominate much of the first six weeks of the Spring 2013 semester was: would the course as it currently stood be appropriate for what had now become a multicultural classroom? A year earlier it is highly likely that Toyo University's 100 or more foreign exchange students had been made aware of the existence of a course of Peace Studies taught in English for which they might register. However, perhaps due to scheduling difficulties, particularly relating to required classes of Japanese language or to other undetermined factors (a lack of interest in the subject?), none had chosen to do so. Nevertheless, amongst the total of 30 students who attended the first class in April 2013 (a number which was to fall to around 24 during the following weeks), the author's teaching method in particular was quickly brought under sharp scrutiny.

The presence of the American students had immediate ramifications for the pacing and evaluation of the course. In fact, it soon became clear that delivering a slightly revised version of the previous year's curriculum would in all likelihood fail to meet the educational needs of both sets of students. The reasons for this were as follows: if the classes were to proceed at a similar pace to that of the first cycle, the American students would likely find this rather pedestrian and unstimulating, and could well then decide to quit the course. Were this to happen, it would likely have a detrimental effect on their Japanese counterparts since the latter would then lose the opportunity to engage with the content and related issues in what could potentially develop into a lively international classroom. Conversely, were the pace to be quickened significantly in order to capture and maintain the interest of the American students, then it was possible that a number of the Japanese students would experience difficulty in comprehending the material in English, and would almost certainly struggle to express their opinions about it in classroom discussions. Hence a balance or effective compromise needed to be struck between the needs of the two groups of students in order to identify an appropriate teaching method; and to achieve this, once again the author found himself largely improvising as he went along.

The first step in this process involved the author requesting the understanding and cooperation of the American students for what would likely develop into a rather unorthodox class which would progress at a slower pace than they might prefer.[7] It was made clear that in terms of evaluation, they would be assessed in accordance with the online syllabus but with two additional criteria: the first of these would be their ability to coordinate discussions with their Japanese counterparts in order to facilitate greater overall understanding of the material in English; the second would be their ability to produce written work and review test responses of an equivalent standard to that required for a regular university course in the United States.

Two further adjustments which came about during the course of the classes of the spring semester related to the use of short quizzes and the language used during class discussions.[8] Regarding the first of these, during the previous year the quizzes had been used to confirm students' understanding of key concepts such as 'structural violence' or the difference between terms such as 'ethnic group', 'nation' and 'state'. However, it quickly became clear that these quizzes would be rather redundant for the American students, and would therefore represent a loss of class time. As a result, they were phased out during the first few weeks of the semester and a greater emphasis placed upon explaining important terminology during the course of the lecture presentations. Regarding the language used in class discussions, in order to maintain the thread of a discussion and to maximise students' opportunities to explain their opinions about a particular topic in detail, a flexible attitude was adopted whereby the use of both languages became acceptable, with the author providing translation into the other language where necessary. It is conceivable that this approach provided an opportunity for both groups of students to improve their comprehension of technical discussions taking place in the other language, but no specific measures were taken to examine this. A final change made to the review tests for the four parts of the course saw a reduction in the number of specific 'knowledge-type' questions, such as *"Name the three delivery systems used to send nuclear missiles to their targets"*, and a concomitant increase in questions which required more intellectual and/or analytical input, such as *"Should governments negotiate with terrorist groups?"*

Results of the second year

With revised and enhanced lectures, more focused and exacting discussion questions, coupled with a clearer idea of appropriate overall pacing for Japanese second and third year students, in April 2013 the author had a degree of confidence that the second year of delivery would progress in a generally similar manner to that of the previous year. However, the unexpected addition to the class of the American students to a large extent invalidated this prediction and necessitated a significant revision to the teaching method. Over and above the aforementioned subjective criteria the author utilized to evaluate the progress of the course during the spring semester of the 2013-14 academic year, the formal evaluation of July 2013 provided the first opportunity to assess the Japanese students' opinions about it in detail. As a result of the changes brought in to accommodate the American students, comparable concerns relating to the difficulty of the content, pacing of the classes and level of understanding in English arose as had been the case a year earlier. Within what had become an international learning environment, the author hoped that the evaluation data would shed light on whether the Japanese students found themselves able to: i) comprehend the content of the lectures progressing at a faster pace; ii) participate meaningfully in class discussions taking place in English or Japanese; iii) feel generally comfortable studying in a learning environment in cooperation with their American peers.

Considering the marked differences in tenor and overall atmosphere of the classes in comparison to those of the previous year, the author was somewhat surprised to find that the results of both the spring and autumn evaluations bore a number of similarities to those collected twelve months earlier. To a large extent the students expressed a favourable opinion of the delivery of the content through PowerPoint presentations and had enjoyed the opportunities to discuss various content-related issues with both their Japanese and American colleagues. It was clear once again that they had found the textbook very difficult and as a result had barely referred to it when preparing for in-class presentations and the review tests.[9] In the 'free comment" section at the end of the evaluation questionnaire several students remarked that the content of some of the lectures had been difficult to grasp, and that expressing their opinions about it—especially in English, had proved very challenging. However, several also said that they had found this experience rewarding[10] and had formed opinions about issues which they had not considered before.

With regard to studying in cooperation with the American students, none of the Japanese students remarked that they had disliked this or had felt that they were being left behind due to the pace of the discussion in English proceeding too quickly. On the other hand, it was clear that on some occasions group discussions with the American students had proved to be a struggle.

On the strength of the two sets of evaluations, the author surmised that the recommendable elements identified from the first year of delivery were continuing to stimulate the interest of the Japanese students, and that the addition of their American counterparts coupled with the changes made to accommodate them, had introduced some additional challenges, but had ultimately represented a positive development.

With regard to the opinions of the American students themselves, due to the fact that they were unfortunately not the subjects of the formal evaluations,[11] the author had to rely on subjective analysis in order to evaluate this. The first source of data utilized for this analysis was records of classroom attendance. Considering his fears of being found wanting in the role of university lecturer by native speaker undergraduates, the author was relieved that during the 2013-14 academic year none of the American students decided to vote with their feet and quit the course. Over and above this condition, with the exception of a small number of absences which were likely due to illness, most of the six students attended nearly all of the classes. The second source of data was the quality of the students' classwork, and in general this was found to be highly creditable. In addition to the quality of individual presentations and responses during whole class discussions, in line with the additional evaluation criterion of coordinating group discussions in order to facilitate greater understanding in English, almost without fail this task was addressed with commitment and maturity.[12] The final source of data was the students' performance in the review tests, and in this regard four out of the group of six produced test answers which displayed creditable analytical insight.

In the absence of any objective data which could corroborate personal impressions, the author refrains from making any categorical statements in relation to the American students' overall opinions of the course. However, on the basis of their classroom attendance, the quality of their class work and the performance of four of the six students in the review tests, the author proposes that it is likely that they found attending the Peace Studies course to be a worthwhile educational experience.

Conclusion: lessons learned, future prospects, and looking back in order to look ahead

In April 2014 the Peace Studies course entered its third year at Toyo University. According to one measure, that of the risk of insufficient students choosing to attend the course bringing about its swift closure after two years, it can be said to represent a success. However, on the basis of the process of creation and its delivery so far, what lessons have been learned, and on the strength of this what possible predictions can be made for the future? Furthermore, with regard to the wider context within Japanese university education, in what ways can the experience from November 2011 until the present inform the promotion of learning for peace in other educational contexts?

Before addressing these key questions, the author will describe the current condition of the course as its fifth semester draws to a close in July 2014. Two major differences can be discerned between the current academic year and the previous ones described above. The first of these is that there are currently no foreign exchange students taking the course. As a result of changes made to the timetable within the Law Faculty, Peace Studies is now being taught at the same time as the obligatory classes of Japanese language that all foreign exchange students must attend; this naturally means that it has become impossible for them to register for it. Therefore the changes made to the content and delivery of the course in 2013-2014 to accommodate the American students have become largely superfluous and the author has had to revert to the previous teaching method utilized in 2012-2013.[13] A second difference is that the English abilities of the current class of students are significantly weaker than those of their predecessors in the previous two years, which has necessitated the simplification of some of the lecture content, the discussion questions and the review tests. At the time of writing, the results of the spring 2014 formal evaluation have yet to be received.

The section on course creation above describes the process of creation of the course which began in November 2011, and in many ways describes a method of course creation that should probably best be avoided. After initially being permitted the opportunity to create a Peace Studies course within the Law Faculty where none had existed before, the author quickly discovered that being presented with a blank slate means, unsurprisingly, that one has to create almost everything from scratch: hitherto no blueprint existed, therefore something pedagogically sound had to be created within a short period of time and then delivered as effectively as possible in the classroom – somehow or other. It is clear that a more structured and methodical process of creation would certainly be advisable. Subsequently, beginning the delivery of a cycle of lectures for a new course before that cycle had been actually completed on not one, but *two* occasions evidently represents quite a professional challenge. In addition, selecting an expensive imported textbook for the course, which has unfortunately proved to be all but impenetrable to the majority of the students, suggests that another approach to text selection must be sought in future.

With that said, the experience of the five semesters of delivering the course has at the same time identified some successful strategies which could offer valuable guidance for the promotion of learning for peace in other educational contexts in Japan. In this regard, three specific strengths have been identified:

Firstly, notwithstanding the significant difficulties that the students have faced in tackling the detailed content contained in Barash and Webel, the author holds that the textbook's framework of topic themes represents an appropriate structure for an undergraduate course in Peace Studies at a Japanese university. Therefore he proposes following this thematic structure, but not placing undue emphasis on having students attempt to decipher large quantities of complicated text. An alternative approach could be adopted whereby Barash and Webel remains a key reference text for the course, but a stipulation is made that not all students need to purchase it, and instead groups of two or three students purchase one copy jointly and then tackle specific classroom and/or homework tasks set by the instructor which relate to particular important sections within it. The textbook could also be supplemented by additional reference material drawn from other sources including, if appropriate, some material in Japanese.

A second recommendable feature of the course has been the utilization of PowerPoint presentations to introduce new topics. During the first year of delivery the author was concerned that these presentations contained an inordinate number of images and were lacking sufficient textual explanations. However, he now holds that on the contrary the insertion of additional images plus further Japanese vocabulary explanations which were made during each cycle of revision and improvement since 2012 has served to enhance students' overall levels of understanding of the key concepts and specific content. The distribution of handouts of the PowerPoint slides printed in fairly large size (four slides per page, arranged horizontally), plus the uploading of all the presentations to a common-access reference website is also to be recommended.[14]

A third feature which has proved successful has been the time devoted in each class to group and whole class discussions. Considering the not insignificant specific difficulties of the course relating to the novelty and complexity of the content coupled with the language of delivery, from the inception as much as possible the author sought to allocate generous amounts of class time to this activity in order for students to gain a solid understanding of the topic in question and thereby the ability to express their own opinions about it with confidence. Aside from the language difficulties experienced by some Japanese students when interacting with their colleagues from America during the second year of delivery, the two cycles of completed classroom evaluations both revealed that the students regarded these activities to be beneficial since they aided their overall understanding and therefore their enjoyment of the course. This regular peer-to-peer interaction also had a positive effect on the quality of the students' group presentations which were made twice per semester.

With regard to lessons learned from the teaching of Peace Studies in a multicultural classroom, on a general level where opportunities for such a scenario exist within other educational contexts, the author is strongly in favour of teaching the subject to students of more than one nationality. Considering the potential benefits which can be gained from drawing out diverse perspectives about specific issues, developing understanding of different cultural frames of reference, and attempting to come to terms with global problems through a mutually-respectful multicultural discourse, the author holds that the advantages of such an educational environment are self-evident.[15] At the same time as stating this, it is also undeniable that the challenges to instructors of managing such an environment, that is to say delivering complex educational content to two very different audiences simultaneously, are quite significant, especially in situations where serious language difficulties exist between the two groups of students. The author is aware that the relative degree of success achieved during the 2013-2014 academic year is due to a significant degree to the cooperation and positivity displayed by both the American and Japanese students who studied the course during that period. As a result, it would be unwise to make generalisations to the effect that this approach could be easily applied in other institutions. The two additional criteria for class evaluation given to the American students evinced a generally positive response and so are included in this discussion as possible assessment approaches for other instructors to consider when teaching native English speakers together with Japanese students.

Regarding the future development of the course, it is clear that many areas of improvement remain, not least relating to the fact that it could be argued that facilitating sound understanding of some of the concepts central to Peace Studies would represent an appropriate challenge for a graduate-level seminar. However, thanks to student interest and institutional backing at Toyo University, the author remains optimistic about the opportunities for continued improvement, is hopeful that the multicultural classroom of 2013-2014 can become a permanent feature of the course, and that these observations can be of benefit to other educational practitioners who are working towards the promotion of learning for peace in Japan.

References

Adams, D. (2013) Education for a culture of peace: the culture of peace news network as a case study. *Journal of Peace Education,* 10(3): 230-242.

Alger, C. (2009) Peace studies as a trans-disciplinary project. In Webel, C. and Galtung, J. (Eds.) *Handbook of Peace and Conflict Studies.* Abingdon, Oxon and New York: Routledge, 299-318.

Barash, D. and Webel, C. (2008) *Peace and Conflict Studies,* 2nd edition. Thousand Oaks, Ca.: SAGE Publications.

Berger, Mark T. and Weber, H. (2011) *War, Peace and Progress in the 21st Century,* Abingdon, Oxon and New York: Routledge.

Lum, J. (2013) Peace Education: Past, Present and Future. *Journal of Peace Education,* 10(3): 215-229.

Matsuo, M. (1995)Peace Studies in Japan: The Current State. *Journal of International Development and Cooperation,* 1(1).

Matsuo, M. (2001)Whither Peace Studies? Fragmentation to a New Integration? *Journal of International Development and Cooperation* 7(2).

Mushakoji, K. (2009) Peace studies and peace politics: multicultural common security in North-South conflict situations. In Webel, C. and Galtung, J. (Eds.) *Handbook of Peace and Conflict Studies.* Abingdon, Oxon and New York: Routledge, 86-93.

Oxfam (2014) *Working for the Few,* Briefing Paper for the World Economic Forum. [Online] Accessible from <https://www.oxfam.org/sites/www.oxfam.org/files/file_attachments/bp-working-for-few-political-capture-economic-inequality-200114-en_3.pdf>

Short, J. (2011) Educating for a Culture of Peace—a synthesis of contemporary developments in Peace Education theory and the drive for its application across the educational sphere. *Toyo University Law Faculty Journal,* 54 (3): 21-54.

Short, J. (2013) Curriculum development in peace-related learning within the Japanese higher education sector: The structure and content of a new one year undergraduate course in Peace Studies. *Toyo University Law Faculty Journal* 57(2): 1-32.

Wien, B. (2010), Peace Education reaching critical mass. [Online] Accessible at <http://www.peace-ed-campaign.org/newsletter/archives/77.html>

Wintersteiner, W. (2013) Building a global community for a culture of peace: the Hague appeal for peace global campaign for peace education (1999-2006). *Journal of Peace Education* 10(2): 138-157.

CHAPTER 6

The world through music: using the Putumayo World Music site to enhance cultural awareness and linguistic use in an EMI classroom

Susan Laura Sullivan

Introduction

In a world where 'accidental' drone victims are officially regarded as 'bugsplats' (Robinson, 2011, p. 5; Schwartz, 2013, pp. 15-16), and where many global policies cultivate the existence of 'unpeople', that is, people who are 'dispensable' amongst the world's population (Chomsky, 2012; Curtis, 2004 in Chomsky and Polk, 2013, p. 33; Orwell, 1949 in Chomsky, 2012), activities designed to overcome personal and cultural defences towards others are sorely needed. Bennett's *DMIS* (1986/2011) has often been referred to and used as a guide in all types of literature, ranging from child development, to 'developing cross-cultural competency' in military leaders (Abbe *et al.*, 2008). It graduates from three ethnocentric to three ethnorelative stages pertaining to cultural awareness and sensitivity (Bennett, 1986/2011; Bennett, 2004). All stages have sub-divisions and, though presented in a linear framework, progress through the stages is not necessarily consistently sequential or permanent (Bennett, 1993 as cited in Bourjolly *et al.*, 2005, p.44; Bourjolly *et al.*, 2005). The three main categories within the ethnocentric grouping are: 'I. Denial of Difference, II. Defense Against Difference, and III. Minimization of Difference'. Ethnorelative stages are defined as: 'IV. Acceptance of Difference, V. Adaptation to Difference, and VI. Integration of Difference' (1986/2011, pp.1-11; 2004). Elements of these stages will be discussed throughout the chapter.

According to the model, within the ethnocentric stages, there are many defences that students can display towards developing an awareness of their own and other cultures. People who are in a state of denial (the first stage of the model and a form of defence) about the validity or even existence of a variety of cultures probably do not yet have an 'experience of difference' (Bennett, 2004, p.74). This can be due to a hegemonic outlook, particularly in societies which 'have received largely mono-culturalsocialization' (2004, p.74). In this case, there is no real knowledge of even one's own culture, and this can lead to 'dehumanizing' those perceived as being different (1986/2011, p.1). In the worst-case scenario, these ethnocentric defences can lead to the overt or insidious justification of abuse of others as a form of political and cultural expediency (Bennett, 2004).

Connection (a form of empathy) rather than disconnection, both for Japanese students, and other nationalities, can be encouraged in lessons through the aforementioned 'experience of difference' (Bennett, 2011, p. 1; Bennett, 2004, p. 74). Easing students into this state can be accomplished through exercises which incorporate pre-existing interests and knowledge. This can connect students to other cultures in an accessible, meaningful and non-threatening way, which can lead to a broader and more nuanced view of both themselves and the wider world (Bennett, 1986/2011, pp. 2-3). Music, particularly for university students, is one such interest (discussed further in section two).

In sympathy with this notion of using pre-existing interest and knowledge is the idea, well known in TESOL circles, of tapping into and opening student schemata, and transferring pre-existing information within into new fields (Widdowson, 1984, p.223; see also Carrel & Eisterhold, 1987; Hadley, 2001, p. 161). This transference usually involves top-down processing skills which, along with encouraging students to use pre-existing knowledge, help ease the burden of comprehension when lessons are conducted in second or other languages (Carrel & Eisterhold, 1987; Grabe, 2004; Hadley, 2001). In language acquisition literature, this is said to heighten the chances of gaining said acquisition (Hadley, 2001). Further to this, music is a strong candidate for encouraging student curiosity. Curiosity is a major component of intrinsic motivation, and students who are thus driven can display a higher level of learner autonomy, which can lead to a greater sense of achievement and success, both for the completion of the task at hand and for course and linguistic goals (Vallerand, 1997, as cited in Dörnyei, 1998, p. 121; Dörnyei, 1998). Some level of familiarity is conducive to new ideas being more readily absorbed and accepted. Taking into account the favourable effects of studying content that is music-related, this chapter will detail how using the Putumayo World Music website in a general comparative culture course, conducted in English in Japan, can broaden both university students' cultural knowledge and attitudes, and linguistic knowledge and use.

Music within Japan

Within Japan, students have a compulsory nine years of music study (Sonoda, 2014, p. 118). Many continue to play in various types of music clubs (circles) throughout school and into university, and are conversant in the jargon, and definitely have knowledge, of the musical form, both in a trained and popular sense (Sonoda, 2014).

Along with those who have continued their formal studies, most university students and young adults connect to and love some form of music. In Japan, the popular music tends to be Japanese, Korean and English-lyric pop (de la Torre, 1996-2014). The majority of the foreign music popular among the below 25s (excepting K-Pop) consists of songs sung in English from English-dominated countries, particularly the inner circle countries of the U.S., the U.K. and to a lesser degree, Canada (de la Torre, 1996-2014; Billboard, 2014; Kachru, 1985). Students often give these countries as the following choices, after Korea and China, when asked to name foreign countries (this writer's own experience), and a form of 'neo-colonialism' and 'gatekeeping' might be a by-product or cause of commercially promoting this music (Pennycook, 1994, as cited in Kachru, 2005, p. 160; Foucault, 1981, as cited in Savignon, 2005, p. 639; see also Kachru, 2005, McKay, 2011).

At variance with this is the U.S. Putumayo recording label, established in 1993 with the aim of highlighting music and styles of music from certain areas of the world. Not all musicians on the label are well known worldwide, or even in their own countries. Some music is recent; some goes as far back as the 1930s (Nieset, 2013). It is a gateway to music styles and sounds from different regions for many listeners (2013). Even though studying music from certain regions might focus on limited fields of culture, they are still new areas for many students. Once their curiosity is piqued, deeper interaction can be sought (Bennett, 2011, p. 4; Dörnyei, 1998; Taylor, 1976, p. 317). Accordingly, using the Putumayo world music site for classroom purposes can be employed with students of all countries, including my own, to engage them with knowledge of other nations in a way that is immediate to them (through music), and has relevance to them (through music).

Naturally, as an outsider with restricted understanding of the wider Japanese community, my knowledge of student awareness of world music is mostly entrenched in my own experience, research, observances and culture. According to the Japan Music Marketing website, once past 25 years of age, the music taste of many Japanese is well known for its diversity. However, it seems less so in the under 25s (de la Torre, 1996-2014), and this is the age group with which this chapter concerns itself. Nonetheless, a foreign teacher in an foreign language academy situation, teaching world music to the students of a culture different from her own, is definitely playing the role of cultural 'gatekeeper' as outlined in the second paragraph of this section, no matter how much autonomy the class has. All teachers of any subject play this role to a degree.

Even so, using the Putumayo site and music does expose students to more than the popular culture endorsed and filtered by the mainstream music industry. The dominant music available often promotes and supports a 'sameness' of local and world culture, as suggested in the paragraphs above. At the same time, because the content of this comparative culture class is music-based, and as part of the course students need to locate videos (content and media they are receptive towards), learners are potentially more open to appreciating, rather than devaluing, the difference that also exists between music cultures (as implied by Bennett, 1986/2011, p. 2, p. 4). This can encourage moving away from a homogenous outlook, both in terms of perception of local and global music, which can be a form of lowering defences to other cultures, even if only in changing perception. This not only ties into the early stages of Bennett's model, but also into 'adaptation', the fifth stage, and will be discussed further in the chapter (Bennett, 2004, p. 70). More detailed methodology (process) of the classes will be discussed below and within the section on linguistic advantages.

Process

Over five to seven weeks, first-year comparative culture classes at Aichi University are allocated/choose a broad area of the world, such as Europe, the Middle East, Africa, Asia, or Latin America (Putumayo uses these categories). Each album promoted by the website contains samples of its music, and students choose a track from their allocated/chosen area. They then research the artist, and from there, learn more about the history of the performer(s), the style of music, the instruments used, and the countries of origin, amongst other things.

Students, in pairs, use Prezi (presentation software) to introduce their findings. Classes are 90 minutes long and meet once a week. There are usually two separate presentations per class. The students go through the same information twice for maximum potential audience retention, to share presenting and technical workloads, and to develop their fluency and automacy skills. Their work is later used as a scaffold to discuss musical preferences (written on Edmodo, a social learning platform similar to Moodle), to provide feedback and to develop macro skills. It is also a lead-in to their second assignment.

Rationalization: Cultural aspects

On March 19, 2014, a Tokyo court ruled that a Ghanaian man suffocated to death due to unlawful measures of restraint employed by Narita airport security guards (Johnson, 2014, p. 1). One key word attached to Johnson's article was 'xenophobia' (2014). Australia, my homeland, also has a history of xenophobia, elements which are still perpetuated in its asylum seeker policies, and in its recent attempt to repeal parts of the racial discrimination act 'which [currently] makes it unlawful to "offend, insult, humiliate or intimidate" people based upon their race' (Deen, 2014; see also Clark, 2014, p. 2; Laughland & Davison, 2014). Only a short while ago did the current Abbott government change its stance and decide not to pursue rescinding the act (Griffiths, 2014).

Discrimination can be normalized in policies and actions such as the now defunct *White Australia Policy* (Deen, 2014; Shirrefs, 2014, p. 4), and as seen in the behaviour of the Japanese officials at Narita. Within the DMIS, Bennett outlines some of the features students display in stage two, 'Defense against Difference', as being: polarized in terms of viewing cultures, which often includes casting their own culture as the apogee of evolution, and often having an unfavourable stereotypical view of others. Defence can include '[a] tendency towards social/cultural proselytizing of "underdeveloped" cultures' (Bennett, 1986/2011, p. 3). Reflected societally, within my experience as an instructor, Japanese student ideas about areas unfamiliar to them are well-meaning, but often contain elements of the above. It should be noted though that students are communicating in English, and their expression might be more nuanced in their native language. In any event, a quick read of the comments section of any story about asylum or immigration in Australia, and across much of the world, illustrates that these kinds of opinions are not unique to Japan.

The power of music

The world's music can make cultures more accessible to those leading fairly insular lives. Whether Japan is a monocultural, fairly homogenous society, or multicultural and heterogeneous, or a mixture of the two, is a popular area of discussion. Burgess (2007, 2010) and Jones (2014) contend that, in attitude and law, its outlook remains fairly monocultural. Linguistically and culturally, Cunningham and Hanford in Kosaka (2014) imply the same. For the purposes of this paper, I agree with the positions of the above authors, especially keeping in mind the age group of the students participating in this lesson. Subsequently, as outlined in the introduction, those whose upbringing is imbued with a homogenous outlook tend to have a more limited outlook, as they only have their own cultural reference points to inform them (Bennett, 2004, p. 74). The situation can arise where 'they are unable to experience the difference between their own perception and that of people who are culturally different' (p.74). To counter this, connection as opposed to difference, or difference which elicits connection, can be explored through music. In fact, this is one of the governing principles of the NGO, Musicians Without Borders (2014).

The founder of Putumayo, Dan Storper, hopes to encourage people to explore more work by the artists featured on the site. Reportedly, U.S. fans have traveled afar to the places of origin of much of the music due to its impact on their lives (Nieset, 2013). Similarly, students using the Putumayo site to complete this project have mentioned researching musicians, or aspects of music or regions, beyond assigned requirements, and valuing learning about areas of the world they had not previously considered (M. Iwasaki, personal communication, Edmodo comment, January 7, 2014). Their 'experience of difference' can change their outlook. Culturally, this can tie in with stage IV of Bennett's model, 'Acceptance of Difference' (1986/2011, pp. 6-7) which will be explored in the following paragraphs.

Student reflection

Earlier in Bennett's model (1986/2011) is the suggestion that to develop students' comfort with understanding that their culture can coexist with others, it is important to initially '[p]rovide reassurance and information about similarities' (p. 4), and to concentrate initially on 'objective culture' such as music (p. 3). Using music to broaden students' cultural understanding of the world also helps them to understand their own personal and local culture better as well as they reflect on their own experience, likes and dislikes. This raises self-awareness. For example, a student in a 2013 class observed that she rarely listened to female vocalists, but she enjoyed the voice of a singer (Dobet Gnahore) featured in another group's presentation so much that she sought out additional tracks. Further comments on other videos showed that she continued to enjoy female vocalists from the Putumayo website (M. Nishikawa, personal communication, Edmodo comment, November 5, 2013). These reactions were garnered from the Edmodo interface, where the week's presenters posted videos featured in their presentations and students were required to comment.

From this writer's point of view, Nishikawa's words show that her individual world broadened as she reassessed her personal identity (could she still define herself as someone who did not listen to female vocalists?), and she also widened her scope of interaction with both gender and music as a direct result of exposure to new information and cultures. She related to this piece of music from the perspective of an 'insider' rather than an 'outsider'. The music was not produced by her culture, and the lyrics were neither Japanese nor English, but she assessed it from the point of view of her personal opinion and reaction to the music. Therefore she adapted so that this representation of a culture separate from her own (Gnahore is from the Ivory Coast) can be included within her current perception of self and her own culture, particularly the music she enjoys within that culture.

This somewhat ties in with the ethnorelative fourth and fifth stages of Bennett's six-stage model, 'Acceptance of Difference' and 'Adaption to Difference'. Both stages involve recognising the diversity not only in another culture, but in one's own culture, and also cover, particularly in the fifth stage, 'self-reflexive consciousness' which, among other things, can see a learner changing behaviour in order to problem-solve (Bennett, 2011, pp. 8-9). Nishikawa listened to a song by a female vocalist (Dobet Gnahore) and consciously realised she was doing so. This was a form of conflict, because she did not view herself as someone who listened to female vocalists, so she needed to reassess (problem solve) the situation, and adapt. Additionally, she did not hold her own culture as the 'acme' of 'civilization', and nor its opposite. This 'slice' of material culture was valued for its difference, and therefore any defences that might have been held against cultural awareness were lessened. Obviously, these presentation classes did not delve into the deeper aspects of developing cultural awareness that Bennett's model explores, and from a 10- minute presentation, it is highly unlikely that Nishikawa's limited exposure to and experience of Gnahore's culture has resulted in much of a worldview perception shift, but enough 'experience of difference' was encountered in this case that the student's self-knowledge and broader knowledge of other cultures was positively considered. This 'experience of difference' led to a societal shift (female singers are worth listening to / not all female singers sound the same / have to be the same) and self-perception shift (I now listen to some female singers).

Building upon students' knowledge, deepening curiosity and connection can encourage both increased FLA (this concept is expanded upon in the next section), and a more aware stance towards cultures separate from the majority culture (Hadley, 2001; Bennett, 2004, 1986/2011). Another example is when students learned that world famous *oud* player, the late Hamza El Din, studied the *biwa* in Japan in the 80s, and lectured in Nubian music at Tokyo University. He met his wife in Japan (Lusk, 2006). The *biwa* is a unique Japanese stringed instrument, but it is also related to the other stringed instruments of the world, such as the *oud*, the lute, and the *pipa*, and understanding this shared musical element can foster cultural awareness and connection. Through research, students find 'reassurance and information about similarities', whilst exploring the diversity that exists between cultures (Bennett, 2011, p. 4). To extrapolate: the uniqueness of the *biwa* is still valued by the students, and indeed, by other cultures (as seen by El Din's wish to study it), but students are also able to see the uniqueness and value of instruments supposedly peculiar to other cultures, such as the *oud*. Despite their uniqueness, these stringed instruments also contain obvious similarities. The similarities, the connection between the *oud* and the *biwa*, encourage a musical conversation which highlights the knowledge and propinquity that exists between the instruments, players and appreciators of the music, without devaluing distinctive aspects of the same. Similarly, El Din and his wife obviously connected despite their different backgrounds. In this way appreciation, exploration, and acceptance of differences *and* similarities can be undertaken: not only through the songs and music explored, but by further studying aspects related to them (for example, the study of El Din's life, the country he came from, *et cetera*).

Another group was thrilled when a Brazilian artist included snippets of Japanese in his song (Jorge, 2012; Pre-seminar 1, period 3, multiple private correspondence, Edmodo comments, November 12-19, 2013). This somewhat links to ;[c]ultural category boundaries becom[ing] more flexible and permeable; (Bennett, 2011, p. 9, 'Adaptation to Difference'). In addition to studying certain aspects of non-Japanese cultures, the students were excited to find that Japan also has a cultural influence on the wider world (A. Sugiura, personal communication, Edmodo comment, November 19, 2013). Returning to the introduction, knowledge and discovery that cultural boundaries are not always rigid certainly works towards mitigating defensiveness against developing cultural awareness, and can work towards developing a value of difference, including awareness of difference that lies within the dominant culture, as the students take note of connections (Bennett, 1986/2011, 2004).

Linguistic and pedagogic advantages

Music, because it appeals to students, encourages a weak affective filter, as defined by Krashen (Schoepp, 1991). That is, it has a better chance of opening them up to the language of instruction—English—which can spiral into further interest in the topic (Taylor, 1976, p. 317). That interest can expand beyond music as seen by the examples outlined above. Furthermore, a strong grasp of English is not needed to enjoy music, as it has a commonality of existence amongst most cultures. This can mean that the classes also have relevance to students with a lower aptitude for English, and by using content they are interested in, it is conceivable that their aptitude might increase. Both practical and cultural language skills can increase for all as students need to find the necessary language to express themselves, need to learn paraphrasing skills so that their classmates can follow their content, need to develop interactive quizzes (a requirement of the course) to accompany their presentations, and later need to watch and listen to the videos other groups have chosen in order to write their opinion about the music or song. Some exercises call for the development of creative skills as students imagine and write scenarios influenced by their reactions to the music.

S. Toyama reported, also in reaction to Dobet Gnahore's work, 'when I listened to her song, I was fascinated by her voice … because she was singing bass and had a sense of stability. I became composed then. Of course, her soprano is very beautiful too …' (personal communication, Edmodo comment, November 5, 2013). The student went on to write that the tenderness of the voice seemed to indicate that the song's protagonist was thinking about a loved one. As stated in the Music in Japan section of this paper, the student was able to connect with the song technically through her pre-existing knowledge of musical composition (her mention of the facets of voice seems to indicate this), and was able to expand upon that knowledge in a technical review, and was able to further extend that initial connection into a form of analysis and creativity about the intent behind the song's feeling and possible universal application. The lyrics were not in Japanese or English, but "[t]he ability to recognize patterns and generalize from experience, to predict what's likely to happen in the future — in short, the ability to imagine . . ." (Lemonick, 2013, p. 9), a very human characteristic, was being undertaken, and she was doing it in English, or expressing her ideas in English. In linguistic terms, she was able to broaden her knowledge base (and use), which could then be adopted by her schemata, which, as stated in the introduction, could then be transferred from 'one individual world to another' (Widdowson, 1984, p. 223, see also Carrel & Eisterhold, 1987; Hadley, 2001, p. 161) and expatiated upon. This transfer can be seen in the production of these quite high and sophisticated language and writing skills and ideas. As the discourse of instruction and production was English, this reflection shows that the activity allows the students to negotiate, practice and hone both technical skills, skills of analysis and extrapolation in and through the target language.

Student interest is also sustained in that the course requires them to learn how to make Prezis, and navigate the Edmodo website for classroom communication, computer technologies that most have not yet encountered. This is also carried out in English. Though difficult at first, this interaction of research, pre-existing interest (music), learning new skills, and ongoing production can augment 'flow'. 'Flow' is where students become 'immersed' in their tasks (Nakamura & Csikszentmihalyi, 2005; Csikszentmihalyi, cited in Davies, 2013), and are therefore intrinsically motivated to complete the task. As argued in the introduction, this adds to potential language and general knowledge acquisition.

Through using music and technology, the representation of another society does not become a desiccated recitation of facts, figures and set ideas, or merely a language activity, but evolves into an interactive experience, all of which can lead to further sociological and global awareness. Because study, presentation, research and reflection is mostly conducted in English, and the basic content matter is familiar and appealing, and students communicate with the class on the Edmodo website in the target language, linguistic capabilities are also used and developed, and some form of technological competency is gained.

Level playing field, English as a lingua franca and expansion

Another way in which student defences to cultural differences are dissolved, to a degree, is that they gain a modicum of insider status to the culture through their research and the medium (music). Apart from the appeal of music, particularly to the young as discussed above, another element is that much of the Putumayo music is in a third language, and this means before research is undertaken, everyone including the teacher has outsider status to a point. Therefore, all class members are experts *and* novices in terms of knowledge of content, until they research and communicate their findings (Duff, 2005, p. 56). In theory students start on a 'level playing field', which can motivate them to communicate in the target language, as all information is new, and classroom dynamics of students uncritically fitting allotted roles (teachers and students can routinely encourage this) can potentially be subverted (2005). This can lessen resentment that students might have towards studying in another language, which might lessen any defences they have against learning about other cultures in English. Having a strong technical knowledge of music, as many of the students do, can also help facilitate a sense of insider status. Therefore, the subject matter becomes of value, and wishing to communicate the worth of this, its universal language, can conversely lead to acceptance, awareness and value of difference through the shared experience of the enjoyment of song, and might also override student hesitation of using English.

Related to this, as stated, the music is often neither in the target language nor Japanese, so, while researching, the students can encounter information only available in the featured country's language or English. Often the first 'hit' they get is linguistically incomprehensible to them, but further research can return information in English. This provides them with some relief and confidence, as they have knowledge of English, and they can see that it frequently operates as a *lingua franca*. Along with the musicians of the world, they can use it for communication and research without losing their own identities. It can be a tool of sharing and communication (Kosaka, 2014; Sung, 2013), though, as implied in the section on music in Japan, it can also be used as a tool of exclusion. Hopefully the benefit of finding information and learning about new music outweighs the negative aspects of the permeation of a dominant language.

Furthermore, those students who study a third language are often elevated to 'experts' when a song featuring a language they may be studying is highlighted. This also boosts their confidence as they see that the languages of the world do have a place outside of the confinement of study. On the other hand, some of the lesser-known artists may only have information in the language of their own or adopted countries. When neither English nor Japanese sources are available, the students then need to select a new subject, which is a disadvantage in terms of time constraints. However, culturally, students can see that the music that they enjoy (they choose the songs) is still very much under the domain of its own culture, which means that the hegemony which often accompanies globalisation is not always a given, and that they can enjoy and connect with various cultures of the world, to varying degrees, despite and because of differences (language) and similarities (music).

In conjunction with the above, many of the artists have lived in multiple countries, the fact of which also raises student awareness of global possibility as well as peril (Gnahore fled the Ivory Coast for Marseille, France in 1999, due to civil war) (Lusk, 2007). The bands often consist of people of many different nationalities (2007). This exposes students, particularly from a society mostly viewed as monocultural, to nationalities working together to produce songs which both the creators and consumers enjoy. It is another example of the possible permeability of 'cultural category boundaries' (Bennett, 1986/2011, p. 9). A 2013 group chose Billie Holiday's 'Strange Fruit' as their featured song. The students did not explore the meanings of the lyrics deeply. In fact, they were more impressed by Holiday's voice. However, it provided the class with a perfect springboard to talk about the song's lyrics and the history of lynching in the U.S. which was a welcome challenge in terms of students exploring aspects of culture in a 'non-threatening context' (Bennett, 1986/2011, p. 2). 'Each change in worldview structure generates new and more sophisticated issues to be resolved in intercultural encounters' (Bennett, 2004, p. 74). Student reflection showed that understanding the deeper meaning of the song had an effect on them (D. Hiramatsu, December 25, 2013, personal communication, email). That exposure might have led towards developing their 'intuitive' and 'cognitive empathy' (Bennett, 1996/2011, p.5), or at least drawn their attention to the existence and quality of life of different cultures within a dominant culture. This observation could influence their general outlook towards differing experiences of majority and minority cultures, including within their own. As a follow up, the Putumayo website links to various non-profit organizations and the students investigate global issues associated with them. Having established a connection through their music and research, it is hoped that they also feel something of a connection with these broader issues, rather than viewing them through the eyes of a dispassionate outsider.

Conclusion (the importance of empathy)

Empathy, and particularly cultural empathy, has become a subject of study and instruction in many educational situations, whether under the banner of teaching 'character and resilience', or part of understanding how to better connect with a wider global community (Morris as cited in BBC News, 2014; see also Hacker, 2013; Tomalin, 2008). To feel empathy towards others we need to feel a connection with them (Grossman, 1996, p. 160). We need to view others as *not* so very different from us at a fundamental level, and need to oppose desensitization which can potentially lead us to view others as 'bugsplats' or 'unpeople'. Bennett (2004, pp. 70-71) defines empathy as 'the ability to take perspective or shift frame of reference vis-à-vis other cultures. This shift is not merely cognitive; it is a change in the organization of lived experience, which necessarily includes affect and behavior'. He supplies this as one of the elements of the ethnorelative stage of 'Adaptation' and states '[i]f the process of frame shifting is deepened and habitualized, it becomes the basis of biculturality or multiculturality' (Bennett, 2004, pp. 70-71). Within the plurality of experience is a commonality of difference *and* similarity. Understanding this is a form of empathy, and strengthening empathy helps build healthy societies (Hacker, 2013). Strengthening connection helps build empathy. A recent article stated that '[l]anguage is the key to unlocking culture and in a shrinking, swirling, multicultural world, multilingualism is a crucial tool' (Shirrefs, 2014, introduction). Studying music in English, especially the world's music in English, addresses and appeals to both a multicultural and multilingual understanding of the world. Of course it can be, and is studied, in other languages but this paper concerns itself with English. Both Bennett (2011, p. 8; 2004) and many linguists argue that intercultural sensitivity and multilingualism can promote empathy (Dewaele & Wei, 2012, Hanford in Kosaka, 2014).

An exercise such as bringing world music into the EFL/EMI classroom promotes connection in an attainable manner, and encourages students to develop a view of global interdependency. At best, this can hopefully act as a form of antidote to militarily and societally condoned disassociation and disconnection, and at the least, raise student awareness that a diversity of cultures can mutually exist and contribute to one another. This ties into the 2013 Peace as a Global Language aims of 'bring[ing] us closer together to realise our potential to interconnect, respect and promote recognition for all'. That at the same time linguistic aptitude also improves, or at the least linguistic use and automaticity progresses, is regarded as a welcome side benefit.

Acknowledgement:

Alternate versions of portions of this paper were previously published in the 2014 Spring *Global Issues in Language Education Newsletter* (GILE)91, and as a working paper for the 2014 North East Asian Regional (NEAR) Language Education Conference. The expanded findings, argument and analysis presented here are original to this paper.

References

Abbe, A., Gulick, M.L. V., and J. L. Herman (2007, October). Cross-cultural competence in army leaders: A conceptual and empirical foundation. *United States Army Research Institute for the Behavioral and Social Sciences.* Accessed from <https://www.deomi.org/culturalreadiness/documents/cccompetencearmy.pdf>on 4 August, 2014]

Bennett, M.J. (1986-2011) A developmental model of intercultural sensitivity. *The Intercultural Development Research Institute.* Accessed from <http://www.idrinstitute.org/allegati/IDRI_t_Pubblicazioni/47/FILE_Documento_Bennett_DMIS_12pp_quotes_rev_2011.pdf> on 2 March, 2014.

Bennett, M.J. (2004) Becoming interculturally competent. In Wurzel, J. (ed.) *Toward Multiculturalism: A Reader in Multicultural Education*, 2nd edition. Newton, MA: Intercultural Resource Corporation: 62-77.

Bourjolly, J.N., Sands, R.G., Solomon, P., Stanhope, V., Pernell-Arnold, A., and Finley, L. (2005) The Journey Toward Intercultural Sensitivity. *Journal of Ethnic And Cultural Diversity in Social Work*, 14(3-4): 41-62.

Burgess, C. (2007, 27 March) Multi-cultural Japan remains a 'pipe dream". *Japan Times.* Accessed from <http://www.japantimes.co.jp/community/2007/03/27/issues/multicultural-japan-remains-a-pipe-dream/>on 11 August, 2014.

Burgess, C. (2010, March 1) The 'illusion' of homogeneous Japan and national character: Discourse as a tool to transcend the 'myth' vs. 'reality' binary. *The Asia-Pacific Journal,* 9-1-10. Accessed from <http://www.japanfocus.org/-Chris-Burgess/3310> on 11 August, 2014.

Carrell, P.L., and Eisterhold, J.C. (1987) Schema theory and ESL reading pedagogy. In Long, M.H. and Richards, J.C. (eds.) *Methodology in TESOL; A Book of Readings.* New York: Newbury: 218-232.

BBC News (2014, 12 February) Character can and should be taught in schools, says Hunt. Accessed from<http://www.bbc.com/news/uk-england-london-26140607>on 15 February, 2014.

Chomsky, N. (2012, 9 January) Recognizing the 'unpeople'. *In These Times and the Institute for Public Affairs.* Accessed from<http://inthesetimes.com/article/12501/recognizing_the_unpeople>on 8 April 2014.

Chomsky, N. and Polk, L. (2013) *Nuclear War and Environmental Catastrophe*. New York: Seven Stories Press.

Clark, H. (2014, 8 April) Australia debates repeal of parts of racial discrimination act. *Index: The Voice of Free Expression*. Accessed from<http://www.indexoncensorship.org/2014/04/australia-debates-repeal-parts-racial-discrimination-act/>on 8 April, 2014.

Davies, R. (2013) Web design and second language acquisition; the flow. [Online]. Accessed from<https://www.youtube.com/watch?v=iP5ByQC7O2o&list=UUft-9xIYwARdoqTHEFq2jEQ>on 12 August, 2014].

de la Torre, N. (1996-2013). The music business in Japan, indie music culture and promoting your music in Japan. *Japan Music Marketing, 1996-2013*. [Online] Accessed from <http://japanmusicmarketing.com/article2.htm>on14 November, 2013.

Deen, H. (2014, April 8) Humour isn't a total response against bigotry. [Online] *newmatilda.com* Accessed from <https://newmatilda.com/2014/04/08/humour-isnt-total-defence-against-bigotry>on 8 April, 2014.

Dewaele, J. & Wei. L. (2012) Multilingualism, empathy and competence. *International Journal of Multilingualism; Social and Affective Factors in Multilingualism Research*, 9(4): 352-366. Accessed from <http://www.bbk.ac.uk/linguistics/our-staff/li-weifolder/copy_of_DewaeleLiWei2012.pdf>on July 13, 2014].

Dörnyei, Z. (1998) Motivation in second and foreign language learning. *Language Teaching*, 31(3): 117-135.

Duff, P.A. (2005) ESL in secondary schools: Programs, problematics and possibilities. In Hinkel, E. (ed.) *Handbook of Research in Second Language Teaching and Learning*. Mahwah, N.J: Lawrence Erlbaum Associates: 45-65.

Grabe, W. (2004) Research on teaching reading. *Annual Review of Applied Linguistics*, 24: 44-69.

Griffiths, E. (2014, August 6) Government backtracks on Racial Discrimination Act 18C changes; pushes ahead with tough security laws. *ABC News*. [Online] Accessed from <http://www.abc.net.au/news/2014-08-05/government-backtracks-on-racial-discrimination-act-changes/5650030> on 5 August, 2014.

Grossman, D. (1996) *On Killing: The Psychological Cost of Learning to Kill in War and Society.* London, Ontario: Little, Brown & Company. Accessed from <http://archive.org/stream/ On_Killing/On_Killing_djvu.txt>on 20 April, 2014.

Hacker, T. (2013, January 28) Building empathy builds society. *Seattle Times.*[Online] Accessed from http://seattle times.com/html/health/2020198902_healthhacker xml.html on April 21, 2014.

Hadley, A.O. (2001) *Teaching Language in Context* (3rd ed.). Boston: Heinle & Heinle.

Japan Hot 100 (2014). *Billboard Charts.* [Online] Accessed from<http://www.billboard.com/ charts/japan-hot-100?page=1>on20 April, 2014.

Johnson, C. (2014, 28 March) Court rules Japan officials killed deportee at Narita. *Deutsche Welle.* [Online] Accessed from http://www.dw.de/court-rules-japan-officials-killed-deportee-at-narita/a-17527619 on 2 April, 2014.

Jones, C. (2014, 6 August). Think you've got rights as a foreigner in Japan? Well, it's complicated. *Japan Times.* [Online] Accessed from http://www.japantimes.co.jp/community/2014/08/06/ issues/think-youve-got-rights-foreigner-japan-well-complicated/ on 11 August, 2014.

Jorge, S. (2011) *Japonesa.* [Sound recording]. Accessed from http://www.youtube.com/ watch?v=QelwvRzoxPs&gl=US on 5 July, 2014.

Kachru, Y. (2005) Teaching and learning of world Englishes. In Hinkel, E. (ed.) *Handbook of Research in Second Language Teaching and Learning.* Mahwah, N.J.: Lawrence Erlbaum Associates: 155-173.

Kosaka, K. (2014, 17 August) Could the lingua franca approach to learning break Japan's English curse? *Japan Times.* Accessed from http://www.japantimes.co.jp/community/2014/08/17/ issues/could-the-lingua-franca-approach-to-learning-break-japans-english-curse/ on 19 August, 2014.

Laughland, O. and Davidson, H. (2014, 20 March) Manus Island human rights inquiry to be assisted by Amnesty International. *The Guardian.* [Online] Accessed from http:// www.theguardian.com/world/2014/mar/20/manus-island-human-rights-inquiry-to-be-assisted-by-amnesty-international on 8 April, 2014.

Lemonick, M.D. (2013, 15 April) Why your brain craves music. *Time.* [Online] Accessed from <http://science.time.com/2013/04/15/music/> on 7 December, 2013.

Lusk, J. (2006, 30 May) Hamza El Din. Egyptian musician who fused Nubian and Middle Eastern influences. *The Guardian.* [Online] Accessed from <http://www.theguardian.com/news/2006/may/30/guardianobituaries.egypt/print> on 1 December, 2013]

Lusk, J. (2007) Awards for world music 2006 - Dobet Gnahore. *BBC Radio 3.* [Online] Accessed from http://www.bbc.co.uk/radio3/worldmusic/a4wm2006/a4wm_dobet.shtml> on 16 August, 2014.

Meeropol, A. (1937). *Strange Fruit.* Performed by Billie Holiday (1939) [Single]. New York: Commodore.

Musicians without Borders (2014) [Online] Accessed from <http://www.musicianswithoutborders.org/>

McKay, S.L. (2011) English as an international Lingua Franca pedagogy. In Hinkel, E. (ed.) *Handbook of Research in Second Language Teaching and Learning, Volume II.* New York: Routledge: 122-139.

Nakamura, J. and Csikszentmihalyi, M. (2005) The concept of flow. In Snyder, C. R. and Lopez, S.J.(eds.) *Handbook of Positive Psychology.* New York: Oxford University Press: 89-105.

Nieset, L. (2013, 20 June). Putumayo returns to its roots with acoustic America and American playground releases. *New Times Broward-Palm Beach.* [Online] Accessed from <http://blogs.browardpalmbeach.com/countygrind/2013/06/putumayo_acoustic_america_playground_20_years.php/> on 13 November, 2014.

Peace as a Global Language (2013) Peace and Welfare in the Global Community: November 16-17 Rikkyo University (Niiza Campus). [Online] Accessed from <http://pgljapan.org/> on 10 November, 2013.

Putumayo (1996-2014). [Online] Available from http://www.putumayo.com/

Robinson, J. (2011, November 29)'Bugsplat': The ugly US drone war in Pakistan – Opinion. *Al Jazeera English.* [Online] Accessed from http://www.aljazeera.com/indepth/opinion/2011/11/201111278839153400.html> on 8 April, 2014.

Savignon, S.J. (2005). Communicative language teaching; Strategies and goals. In Hinkel, E. (ed.) *Handbook of Research in Second Language Teaching and Learning.* Mahwah, N.J.: Lawrence Erlbaum Associates: 635-651.

Schoepp, K. (2001). Reasons for using song in the ESL/EFL classroom. *The Internet TESL Journal,* VIII(2), February [Online] Accessed from http://iteslj.org/Articles/Schoepp-Songs.html> on 21 August, 2014.

Schwartz, D. (2013, 8 February) Drone-speak lexicon: from 'Bugsplat' to 'Targeted killing'. *CBC News.* [Online] Accessed from http://www.cbc.ca/news/world/drone-speak-lexicon-from-bugsplat-to-targeted-killing-1.1342966> on 8 April, 2014.

Shirrefs, M. (2014, 30 April) Australia's failure to embrace multilingualism—360 documentaries. *ABC Radio National (Australian Broadcasting Corporation).* Accessed from <http://www.abc.net.au/radionational/programs/360/australias-lack-of-multilingualism-due-to-education-failures/5535654> on June, 2014.

Sonoda, M. (2014) The teaching of music history in Japanese music education. *MusicaDocta: RivistaDigitale de Pedagogia e DidactticadellaMusica: Transmission of Musical Knowledge: Constructing a European Citizenship* (Special edition): 111-119. Accessed from <http://musicadocta.unibo.it/article/view/4314> on 15 June, 2014.

Sung, C.C. M. (2013) English as a lingua franca and its implications for English language teaching. *JALT Journal* 35(2), November: 173-190.

Taylor, B.P. (1976) Teaching composition to low-level ESL students. *TESOL Quarterly* 10(3): 309-319

Tomalin, B. (2008, 29 September) Culture—the fifth language skill. *British Council / BBC.* Accessed from <http://www.teachingenglish.org.uk/article/culture-fifth-language-skill>on April 20, 2014.

Widdowson, H.G. (1984). Reading and Communication. In Alderson, J.C. & Urquhart, A.H. (eds.) *Reading in a Foreign Language.* New York: Longman: 213-230.

PART 2

Peace and conflicts

CHAPTER 7

Natural resources and topography: Rethinking the cause of conflict in Mindanao

Travis Ryan J. Delos-Reyes

Introduction

After the fall of the dictator, the former President Ferdinand Marcos, many changes were seen with the formal restoration of the democratic system in the Philippines. Those who steered the leadership took turns in restoring the peace negotiations to achieve *hudna*, an Arabic term meaning a truce or calmness, which can also be translated as "cease-fire". Despite this, the Southern Philippines continued to face armed struggles with Muslim separatists. Using greed and viability approaches, this chapter will look at the relationship of natural resources and integration of resources to finance an armed conflict. Further, combinations of geographical locations, e.g. rough terrain, which provide secure sanctuary and an ineffective state, shall also be considered. A combination of qualitative and content analysis shall be used. This chapter ends with lessons learned and concluding thoughts.

Basis of the Study

The Mindanao conflict can be considered to have commenced during the Marcos regime after the local uprisings turned into a full-scale war in the 1970s. Akihiro Chiba (2006) maintains that even though most people are aware of the many skirmishes and bloodsheds through the media, still it is not easy to understand the conflict in Mindanao. He further commented that people even dissuade their friends to visit the island because of its precarious security problems. Mindanao is viewed like a terrorist's haven, feared by its own countrymen and looked down upon by the people of the north; hence, it seemed like a separate nation. To better understand the Mindanao conflict, its details are discussed below.

The past: colonization and its effects

Mindanao, once dubbed a land of promise, a land rich in natural resources, has been clothed with conflict to the extent that it is now known as a "War Zone" (Chiba, 2006). The conflict in today's Mindanao has existed since the 17th century. It is a continuous struggle of minority peoples to fight for survival. The perception of destroying the religious, cultural and political tradition of Mindanao's tribes was a cry for protection and justice. Such conflicts arose not only because of a struggle between Muslims and Christians, but also due to poverty, oppression and marginalization. Colonization and development pushed the minorities and the poor into the background (Turner, May, & Turner, 1992).

When a military expedition by the Spaniards during the late 16th century was dispatched to Mindanao, the main purpose was to stem the expansion of Islamic rule. The sultanates of Sulu, Maguindanao, and Buayan resisted the Spanish military's political and religious intrusions (Milligan, 2010). Local leadership at that time was confused owing to the bloody internal struggles for power (Turner, May & Turner, 1992). The reorganization and centralization policy carried out by the Spanish government in Manila was partly in response to need, as well as redefinition of their colonial frontiers, as other foreign powers continued to dominate the Philippines.

By the 20th century, American colonizers suppressed Moro resistance towards the central government in Manila. A campaign of pacification took place, coupled with strong military force and concrete programs that led to the creation of a civilian government in Mindanao under the control of the central government. Eventually, Mindanao was placed under the jurisdiction of the Commonwealth in 1935 and became an integral part of the independent state in 1946. After the end of the Second World War, the Philippines government encouraged people to migrate to the then Muslim-dominated Mindanao by Christians from the north (May, 2002). Milligan (2010) stated that the process of integrating Mindanao as part of the state was forced, thereby creating more tension between and among the Christians and Muslims in a centuries-old conflict. As an addition to the wound created, migration of the peasant farmers from the North and Central Philippines to Mindanao shifted the balance and created still more conflict. The settlers were mainly Catholic migrants from Luzon and Visayas and their descendants now numbered 12 million, or 75% of the population, forming a majority in 18 out of 23 provinces (Santos, 2000).

The influx of these settlers made Mindanao a place of diversity whose ethnicity, culture, traditions, and beliefs never became a source of misunderstanding, apprehensions and even fears among the early Mindanaons. The situation changed when land grabbing and social injustices were committed by certain groups[1] against the region's peace-loving people (Autonomous

Region in Muslim Mindanao, n.d., p.1). The Mindanaons consequently became doubtful of the motives of the government regarding their land due to these acts.

Under U.S. colonial rule, which set unequal limits on private land ownership for Christians and non-Christians, Muslims, who were formerly a majority, became the minority (Amnesty International, 2008). This was the start of an endless battle for land rights in Mindanao.

Although the Moroland was subjugated, the Moros nonetheless continued to long for their own land. The horrors of the past led them to contest the legitimacy of the central government's occupancy in Mindanao. Again in the 1960s, the Muslim Independent Movement (MIM) eloquently expressed the Moro dream of independence from the state in order to establish an Islamic State. These secessionist movements were grounded in the following claims, as Turner, May & Turner (1992) enumerate:

- That the Moro people constitute a distinct Bangsa (Nation);
- That the Moro people have their own particular culture and history;
- That the geographical territory consisting of Mindanao, Sulu and Palawan constitutes the Moro homeland;
- That the Moro people are a majority of the population of this homeland;
- That the central government in Manila has continued the colonial policy of isolation and dispersal of the Muslim communities, which is detrimental both to the Muslim population and Islam;
- That the Muslim inhabitants have the duty and the obligation to wage jihad (holy war) physically and spiritually to change the Moro homeland to Dar al-Islam (House of Islam);
- That Islam is both religion and the ideology of the Bangsa Moro. (pp. 160-161)

An intense rebellion broke out in the early 1970s when martial law was in effect. The rebellion was further escalated by the Philippine government military campaign against the Moro National Liberation Front (MNLF). The insurgents' demands were clear and straightforward—a Bangsamoro—a separate nation for the true owners of the land. This lasted for almost five years, displacing thousands of residents, with an estimate of 50,000 casualties (Hedman, 2009). After the declaration of martial law, President Marcos began to realize that there was a need to bridge the gap between the Filipinos and the Muslims. He further stated that in order to bridge this gap, Muslim aspirations and expectations must be accommodated, so that they would feel as if they were citizens of the country (Majul, 1985). He later ordered and signed Presidential Decree No. 410, dated March 11, 1974, declaring that the Moro ancestral lands were inalienable and not disposable. A village was also created in Manila, called Maharlika Village, for the Muslims, and a mosque constructed for worship. However, hostilities between the military and the insurgents continued. Attempts at negotiations between the government and the MNLF, despite the creation on April 22, 1975 of the Southern Philippines Development Authority (SPDA), did nothing to control the situation (May, 2002).

The situation escalated internationally and was brought to the attention of the Organization of the Islamic Cooperation (OIC) who intervened to find ways to help out (Autonomous Region in Muslim Mindanao [ARMM], n.d., p. 1). This intervention led to the signing of the Tripoli Agreement in 1976, establishing a ceasefire and autonomy in the southern Philippines. The shift from the demand for a separate nation to an acceptance of political autonomy by the MNLF was due to the intervention of Libyan President Gaddafi (May, 2002). However, in 1978, the Moro Islamic Liberation Front (MILF) split from the MNLF, and up to the present day continues to fight for its claim of the land (Amnesty International, 2008).

Theoretical concepts

The literatures on the persistency of the civil wars or armed conflict[2] offer an array of theoretical concepts. Following the terms used by Collier, Hoeffler and Rohner (2009), there are three theoretical factors for the persistence of an armed conflict: greed (later called opportunity), grievance and viability. Conflicts can have crucial causes that take precedence over lesser causes, but because of the complexities of politics, economics and societies, a single factor cannot spark any conflict. According to Collier and Hoeffler (2004a), the first theory involves the aspiration of the rebel group to be victorious, so they invest in rebellion. The rebellion-as-investment approach, the political and/or material payoff to the rebellion, is dependent with its victory. An argument pointed out by Collier and Hoeffler (2000) is that this same aspiration is motivated by greed[3]. Greed, as a definition, is a desire to gain political and/or material payoff. The authors argued that an existence of "lootable" resources that can be a source of financial payoff for the rebellion is a good motive and a facilitating factor (Elbadawi and Sambanis, 2002). The main key for the persistence to sustain an armed conflict is financing. Without good financing to buy guns and assailants, any attempt at rebellion is pointless. Natural resources and external sources of financing are a necessity for an effective armed conflict. In the accrued benefits model, fashioned from Grossman's discount rate analysis, Collier and Hoeffler (1998) argued that the longer the period of the persistence of a war, the higher the cost, and the benefits are reduced. Further, Collier, Hoeffler and Söderbom (2004b) argued that the main prognostic for this is that the higher the payoff from conquest, the longer would be the armed conflict.

The grievance approach, on the other hand, focuses on dissatisfaction and unjust deprivation as the primary motivation for civil war. This approach emphasizes the psychological processes and factors that create discontentment amongst peoples. Taydas *et al.* (2011) explain that the origin of civil strife and violence are collective experiences of peoples, ranging from frustrations, inequalities and antipathies due to political, economic and other factors, which creates a "justice-seeking behavior". Another theory that supports this claim is Ted Gurr's relative deprivation theory. Relative deprivation is the communal experiences of peoples who believe that they are deprived of something to which they are entitled. Further, people join social groups based on what they think they should have in comparison with others, according to their own past or apparent future. This comparison between the individual's expectations and comparing oneself with others in a society entails varying causal mechanisms, but both breed discontent. This theory also reflects the idea of certain religious or ethnic groups' exclusion from political power or economic inequality. According to Bleaney and Dimico (2011), the theory can be captured by using proxies such as ethnic or religious diversity and income inequality, among others, which reflects the opportunities for pursuing reparation by peaceful means. This means that in the case of a certain minority who excessively experience discontent in a society, whether ethno-religious or linguistically, it can lead to social unrest by the group collectively pursuing their cause. These shared grievances promote a group sense of identity and causes a strong sense of in and out-group distinction over time, which in turn leads to politicization and discontent. As pointed out by Taydas Enia and James (2011), armed conflict towards the government is a mode to gain restitution for grievances and modify causes of discontent. However, as the ostensible deprivation increases, correspondingly, the risk of discontentment and civil discord also increases.

The viability approach deals with rebellions that require rebel control of resources, in this case mineral resource, and by foreign support. Le Billon (2001) argued that natural resources could be directly related to armed conflicts. This can either be conflict-motivated by the control of resources and integration of resources to finance the conflict. Further, combinations of geographical locations, e.g. rough terrain that provides secure sanctuary, and an ineffective state, also assist conflict. Buhaug, Gates, and Lujala (2009) argued that geographic features of terrain significantly highlight the incentives for going to war. Lujala's findings revealed rebel access to the location of the natural resources doubled the effects of conflict duration. Further, Fearon and Laitin (2003) argued that factors of terrain, control of resources and foreign support are the main correlates for civil war onset. Moreover, Akcinaroglu and Radziszewski (2005) argued that foreign involvement has a strong link to conflict duration viability. Accordingly, the involvements of foreign states, acting as adversaries to the central government, were found to sustain insurgent activities. In sum, in order for the viability approach to be feasible, it takes into consideration factors that should affect the inception and duration of the conflict before even instigating a conflict.

Postulates

The above sets of theories used by Collier, Hoeffler and Rohner shape the direction of this chapter. Greed (Opportunity), grievance, and viability theories will be used to explain the following postulates:

Topography Indicator

In order for an insurgency to survive, an optimum location is necessary, which government forces would have difficulty in accessing. This has been one of the major criteria for any insurgency to succeed: the topographic location of the rebel camp is critical.

If a province in Mindanao has more than 50% of medium-to-rough terrain, forested lands and mountainous lands, it will have a greater risk of an armed conflict. If these conditions are met *then a province with more than 50% medium-to-rough terrain, mountainous and forested lands is more favorable to the persistence of insurgency groups in an armed conflict.*

Natural Resource Indicator

Throughout history, most armed conflicts have been linked to natural resources. Precious resources, minerals and hydrocarbons have been regularly fought over by many types of insurgents as a means of financing their various activities or as a motivation for violent actions. Similarly, according to Lujala (2010), countries that are abundant with natural resources have the tendency to conduct armed conflict rather than those countries lacking in resources. Lujala further stated that there are two main points why this is so: firstly, easily exploitable natural resources can provide motivation and means for rebel uprisings. Secondly, the success and survival of the rebel groups lies in the accessibility of the natural resource due to the fact that it provides financing. Collier and Hoeffler (2004) as cited by Lujala (2010) argued that rebel groups see natural resources as an alternative source of income. In addition, Le Billon (2001) sees natural resources not only as a means for funding the armed conflict, but also as a means for individual economic growth.

Natural resources have a role in the creation of armed conflict. Many scholars believed that during the post-Cold War period, exploitable natural resources were linked to conflict. Why is a natural resource important for any armed conflict? Rebel groups, as mentioned earlier, need motivation and financing to sustain their cause. Though the cause may be for the common good, in order to sustain the cause, a group needs support. Natural resources can function as the support that could pave the way for groups to survive. Therefore, based on this argument, *richer natural resources in a province are more likely to lead to the persistence of an armed conflict. This indicator will be measured by the presence of mineral and non-mineral resources.*

How do the above theories relate to the hypotheses drawn? Elements from every theory, in one way or the other, have a relationship to and answer the hypotheses. Greed theory emphasizes the relation of resources, where the rebel group could either gain politically or materially. This theory would answer various hypotheses that entail greed, as the main motivation for joining armed rebel groups. Greed and viability theories share some commonalities in terms of control of natural resources as a source of finance. For this chapter, however, greed theory shall primarily answer the hypothesis posted for the natural resource indicator. Meanwhile, viability theory shall be employed to investigate the significance of topography in the persistency of armed conflict in Mindanao.

Greed theory focuses on the natural resource indicator, which I categorize into two types: rich mineral and non-rich mineral resource. Resources are the source of motivation for the rebel group to persist, and as long there are resources that can be exploited, a rebel group will continue to hold on to these resources for they will gain material payoff in the process. These resources are also sources of livelihood to the groups. The level of incomes that can be acquired by the constituents depends also on the richness of resources available in the area. Thus, natural resource indicator can then be linked to poverty and per capita income factors, as it affects the constituents' kind and level of livelihood source.

The viability theory emphasizes the topography indicator, which can be categorized into four distinct types: rough terrain and highly forested terrain; rough terrain and slightly forested terrain; non-rough terrain and highly forested and non-rough terrain and slightly forested. The rough terrain and highly forested indicator is favorable to rebel groups as government forces cannot penetrate insurgents' camps due to inaccessibility and inconspicuousness. On the other hand, the rough terrain and slightly forested indicator means that insurgencies are still viable due to the roughness of the terrain. The government forces, however, may penetrate the rebel camps since forested lands are not densely covered. This combination of roughness of terrain and forest-covered areas means inaccessibility, precluding government services to the communities; thus, in turn, these factors are linked to a weak state capacity indicator, which are in turn connected to poverty and per capita income factors. Meanwhile, the non-rough terrain and highly forested indicator means that agricultural lands, flatlands and woods are one of many sources of income of the communities and are thus it is less likely for an insurgency to occur. Further, the non-rough terrain and slightly forested indicator means more flatlands and agricultural areas to be used to earn income, and thus it is less likely for an insurgency to occur since the areas are visible and accessible. These two latter factors are closely related to generation of income sources, which in turn are linked to poverty and per capita income factors.

What causes an armed conflict: uncovering natural resources and topography

Natural Causes: Topography indicator

According to Weidmann (2009), the impact of territory on conflict should not be underestimated. One of the longest continuous conflicts is to be found in the remote hinterlands in states such as in Myanmar, where the landscape is characterized by rugged mountains and dense tropical forests. Aside from the war in Eritrea that lasted almost three decades, conflict also took place in mountainous areas far from the capital. According to Buhaug, Gates and Lujala, P. (2009), rebel wars are predominantly fought in rural hinterlands that provide protection and tactical advantage. Difficult terrain and porous boundaries are some of the prerequisites to have a successful camp base for any insurgency. As Buhaug, Gates, and Lujala (2009) assert, location matters. Thus, the following hypothesis is generated: *a province with more than 50% medium-to-rough terrain, mountainous and forested lands is more favorable to the persistence of insurgency groups in an armed conflict.*

According to Le Billon (2001), geographic considerations affect the power balance between the rebels and the government. Location determines how the groups strategize the position of their members and occupy in combat. A strategic location determines who has the most advantage in the art of warfare. Rough terrain, for example, offers a good defensive position, which is important to groups with smaller forces. Further, Hensel (2012) argued that topographic location with medium-to-rough terrain, forested lands and mountainous lands has an advantage because control over it brings a military advantage. This very reason is why the MILF chose Camp Abubakar[4] as their main base. Camp Abubakar is located in Maguindanao Province, where nearby forests, lakes and rivers provide natural cover and tracks for the MILF combatants. It also has a good defense system due to fields with tunnels, troughs and furrows. Even the MILF leader Salamat Hashim resided in this camp in a small bungalow house.

While it is true that Mindanao is mountainous and mostly rugged terrain, the government forces are far more advanced and stronger in capacity. During the All-Out-War campaign of President Estrada, Camp Abubakar in Maguindanao fell after two months of encounter with the government forces with air, artillery and commando offensives, on July 9, 2000. In defense, MILF also used guerrillas in black uniforms hidden in trenches. Due to the lack of fighting forces, Alhaj Murad Ibrahim, one of the MILF leaders, withdrew as the 1st Marine Brigade breached the camp's entryway in Matanog, Maguindanao. The strength of the government military forces, despite the overwhelming advantage of the geographical location of Camp Abubakar, did nothing to win the war. Currently, the MILF camps are scattered throughout the ARMM region, most specifically in the Liguasan marshland[5]. The marshland is the crucial point of the larger ongoing-armed struggle, due in part to the protection it offers as a hideaway for conflict. Owing to this, government forces are presently in position within the area to counter any insurgency.

Natural resource indicator

According to Brunnschweiler and Bulte (2009), natural resources have been the main motivation for countries for economic development. However, in the post-Cold War period, the economics of war has shifted and made natural resources a valuable strategic importance.

Collier and Hoeffler, as cited by Lujala (2010) argue that people fight when it pays better than their alternative source of income. Further, according to Lujala (2009) a rebel group that could exploit natural resources may be able to recruit more participants and probably buy more powerful arms. Lujala (2010) strongly emphasized that there are two main arguments why this is so: firstly, easily exploitable natural resources can provide motivation and means for rebel uprisings. Secondly, the success and survival of the rebel groups lies in the accessibility of the natural resource, due to the fact that it provides financing. Similarly, Lujala's (2010) argument postulates that if natural resources have an effect on a rebel group, resources that are located in a conflict zone should have an effect on conflict, leading to the following hypothesis: *richer natural resources in a province are more likely to lead to the persistence of the armed conflict. This indicator will be measured by the presence of mineral and non-mineral resources.*

The study on the relationship of natural resources to conflict is rather recent. Fearon and Laitin (2003) in their study, found that oil-producing countries were more likely to start a civil war. The start of conflict between the forces loyal to Chadian President Idriss Deby and rebel groups who are firm to drive him out of power, for example, revolves around the control of oil resource. On the same note, Collier and Hoeffler (2004) found out that export of primary goods, which includes agricultural produce and natural resource, relates to civil war onset.[6]

The most dominant resource of Mindanao is agriculture, which accounted for more than a third of the Gross Regional Domestic Product (GRDP) in 2000. Muslim Mindanao's economy is highly dependent on the agriculture, forestry and fishing sectors. Among the mostly Muslim areas, only Region 12 appears to be relatively less reliant on agriculture. Is an agricultural resource enough to motivate rebel groups to cause an armed conflict in Mindanao? Ross (2004) cited Collier and Hoeffler (2002b) in arguing that agricultural commodities do not influence any civil war risk.[7] The agricultural sector, although it has the largest share in Mindanao's economy, is not sufficient to fund any rebel secessionism. In Camp Abubakar, before government forces successfully put down the rebellion, a community with abundant agricultural resources could be found inside. However, this could only provide the nutritional needs of the rebels, not arms or defenses. Further, agriculture is very vulnerable to changes in climate and man-made destruction. In 1997-1998, Mindanao was affected by severe drought caused by the El Niño phenomenon, causing a major downfall of the agriculture sector. Agriculture resources cannot sustain a lasting war, let alone four decades of conflict, such as occurred in Mindanao. If the agricultural sector is insufficient as a factor, what then remains that can ignite a conflict in Mindanao? What could be the motivation that can best describe the significance of the quantitative result?

The case of Liguasan Marsh

Liguasan Marsh is an expansive freshwater wetland, the lowest part of a larger watershed region of the Cotabato River Basin. It is located in a lowland area traversed by many streams of water that are surrounded by highlands. This lowland area is called "the land of promise" as it is rich in agriculture, and constitutes a wide green area. Cotabato River Basin is located within three provinces, Maguindanao, North Cotabato, and Sultan Kudarat. Within these three areas the area of conflict is located. According to McKenna (1998), the provincial boundaries for these areas were set in the early 1970s, split off from the original Cotabato Province.

The marshland is the few remaining untapped natural resources of the minority Filipino Muslims. Lacking technical know-how, the residents located in the marshland do not know how to exploit the richness of gas in the area, although some can produce fire by lighting up matches near pockets of gas. The government has mandated the Philippine National Oil Corporation (PNOC) to conduct explorations of natural gas in the area with an estimate of about 1.7 trillion cubic feet. Furthermore, aside from the natural gas, traces of oil deposits were positively identified. Based on the reports of the Department of Agriculture, Petronas Karigali of Malaysia and PNOC started drilling in Maguindanao near the marshland; it was estimated that the area could yield about 117 million barrels of oil.

According to Rosero (2011), MILF Vice Chairman of Political Affairs Ghazali Jafaar claimed that the marshland was the legacy of their forefathers. The MILF will not let go of the mineral-rich ancestral land. During my interview[8] with Eid Kabalu, he said that the natural resource that can be found in the area is so vast that this gave the Moro motivation not to let go of this land. At a recent event, Manlupig, (2012) mentioned that MILF Chair Al Haj Murad Ebrahim has called for the government to suspend the awarding of permits to explore the marshland. If the natural gas and oil in the marshland will be exploited, how much will it generate? In 2008, according to MNLF chairman Nur Misuari, the huge reservoir of natural gas is worth hundreds of billions of dollars (Rosero, 2011). Furthermore, he stated that the Bangsamoro could become one of the richest Moro nations if the marshland is placed under their control. Misuari has told the GMA news network[9] that some American oil engineers informed him about the abundance of natural gases in the area and estimated an amount of $580 billion in revenue from gas extraction once the region is explored, excluding the amount that could be extracted in oil (Rosero, 2011). With this knowledge, the richness of the marshland is enough to finance and sustain the insurgency. As the greed theory suggests, there is enough motivation for rebel groups to struggle for and claim their ancestral land.

During the conduct of my field research, however, various contradictions arose. All of my informants and FGD results agreed, except for one person that shall remain anonymous, who expressed his agreement on the role of natural resource in the conflict, but said that the conflict in Mindanao is not about natural resources. My interviews revealed that the issue is not the richness of the land, but the land itself. At the heart of the issue is the desire to have a separate Islamic nation, and self-determination for the Bangsamoro. The informants further stated that the rebel group does not have enough financial freedom to exploit the natural resources. This can only be a motivation if the insurgents have the means to exploit the land. This revealed that the conflict was sustained by various factors accordingly by the informants.

There is, however, a considerable disagreement between the regression result and the field research conducted.[10] It can be seen that the marshland is a monopoly of the MILF; there are significant data that prove that natural resources have some bearing on the ongoing conflict in Mindanao. If the marshland is not valuable, would the rebel group still be fighting for the ownership of the resources in the area? Eid Kabalu asserts that the MILF's position is not to exploit the natural resources until the conflict is resolved. The MILF camp is now located in the marshland, as Kabalu mentions, in order to use it in their advantage. One of the reasons why the MILF would not let go of the marshland is that they want "to use the marshland for negotiations [a bargaining position] before anything can be resolved; the government should solve the problems Moros are facing first," according to Kabalu.[11]

Lessons learned and concluding thoughts

Not one, but many factors are needed to induce a conflict. MacGinty and Williams (2009) cited Sen's argument that other factors are needed to induce conflict, especially "the illusion of singular identity… in a world so obviously full of plural affiliations" (2006, p. 175). Amartya Sen has a point in saying that poverty on its own is not enough to cause conflict. Accordingly, MacGinty and Williams (2009, p. 29) note that conflicts do not happen solely because a society is "ethnically, racially or religiously fissured". Topography and natural resources are revealed as having a significant relationship to the persistency of armed conflict. This means that the presence of any of these factors can potentially trigger an insurgency if they are not addressed. Governments tend to promote economic developments to address issues to prevent an insurgency; however, they also need to take into account issues related to non-developmental aspects. As Macginty and Williams (2009) argued, conflicts are combinations of factors that are probably not related to each other, but interact somehow to cause an insurgency.

The Mindanao conflict is such a complex issue. Rather than a single theory, combinations of theories can answer to such complexity, as MacGinty and Williams (2009) have argued; there is no universal theory of conflict causation. Each conflict has its own unique cause; it can be similar to other conflicts, but the original cause will always stand out from others. There is no singular cause of conflict; each has different causes that interact with one another, but the strength varies from one cause to the other. Similarly, this chapter has utilized different theories that assist in answering the main question as to the causes of armed conflict in

Mindanao. Unquestionably, there is always a principal cause that starts a conflict that is superior to secondary causes. However, a principal cause cannot start a conflict on its own, but needs other driving factors, be they economic, societal and/or political.

Natural resource and topography indicators, nevertheless, can be a cause of conflict in Mindanao. As has been illustrated above, Mindanao has a rich resource of natural gases, which if exploited, could provide the funding for an armed conflict to persist. As Eid Kabalu asserts, the marshland is the MILF's trump card for bargaining. They will never let the marshland be exploited by the government unless and until the government promises to solve the Moro struggle and give the Moro people the right to own the land they once possessed.

Although there are some disagreements as to natural resources and topography as causes of conflict in Mindanao, this chapter would argue otherwise that these indicators do in fact have a hold on the conflict. They may not be the primary cause of conflict; however, they could trigger another uprising if not given due investigation and taken into account in collective bargaining in the future. The author concurs with Sen's argument that poverty alone cannot cause a conflict, but instead other factors are needed to elevate the struggle leading to violence. Natural resource and topography indicators can be the factors that thrust or elevate any uprising to the next level. This means to say that most conflict analyses solely focus on the ethno-religious or ethno-nationalistic factors, which the researcher has no doubt are among the causes or arousal of conflicts. However, such other factors like national resource and topography are the glue that binds these factors together in inflicting a long struggle. These two factors are contributory in inducing long-term conflicts. The researcher believes that natural resource and topography should not be taken so lightly, but rather, with utmost seriousness, to consider them as an equal to other leading conflict-causing factors.

References

Akcinaroglu, S. and Radziszewski, E. (2005) Expectations, rivalries, and civil war duration. *International Interactions: Empirical and Theoretical Research in International Relations*, 31(4):349-374(26). Retrieved from <http://dx.doi.org/10.1080/03050620500303449> on December 5, 2012.

Amnesty International (2008) Shattered Peace: the human cost of conflict in Mindanao. [Online.] Retrieved from http://www.amnesty.org.nz/files/Shattered%20Peace%20 in%20Mindanao_%20the%20human%20cost%20of%20conflict%20in%20the%20 Philippines.pdf.

Arnado, J.M. and Arnado, M.A. (2004) *Casualties of Globalization:Economic interest, war, and displacement along Ligawasan Marsh, Philippines*. Quezon City: Social Science Research Council Program on Global Security and Cooperation.

Askandar, K. and Abubakar, A. (2009) Resolving the Territorial Issue in the Mindanao Conflict: Challenges for the Civil Society. In Kang, S., McDonald, J.W. and Chaedan, T.Y. (eds.) *Conflict Resolution and Peace Building : The role of NGOs in historical reconciliation and territorial issues*. Seoul, Korea : Northeast Asian History Foundation, 93-115.

Autonomous Region in Muslim Mindanao (ARMM) (n.d.) Historical Background. [Online.] Retrieved from <http://www.armm.gov.ph/history/> on February 6, 2012.

Bleaney, M. and Dimoco, A. (2011) How different are the correlates of onset and continuation of civil wars? *Journal of Peace Research* 48 (2):145-155. doi: 10.1177/0022343310394697

Brunnschweiler, C.N. and Bulte, E.H. (2009) Natural resources and violent conflict: resource abundance, dependence and the onset of civil wars. *Oxford Economic Papers* 61 (4): 651-674. doi: 10.1093/oep/gpp024

Buhaug, H., Gates, S. and Lujala, P. (2009) Geography, rebel capability and the duration of civil conflict. *Journal of Conflict Resolution* 53(4):544-569. doi: 10.1177/0022002709336457

Chiba, A. (2006, May 8-9) Peace and development in Mindanao: Role of alternative learning system/Non-formal education. Peace, security, conviviality. Report of the Seminar Forum, Cotabato City, Mindanao, Philippines.

Collier, P. and Hoeffler, A. (1998) On the economic causes of civil war. *Oxford Economic Papers*, 50, 563-73.

Collier, P. (2000, November) Ethnicity, politics and economic performance. *Economics and Politics* 12:225-45. Wiley Blackwell, vol. 12(3):225-245.

Collier, P. (2000) Economic causes of civil conflict and their implications for policy. In Crocker, C.A. & Hampson, F.O, with Pamela Hall (eds.) *Managing Global Chaos*. Washington D.C.: U.S. Institute of Peace.

Collier, P. and Hoeffler, A. (2004a) Greed and grievance in civil war.*Oxford Economic Papers* 56(2004):563–595. doi:10.1093/oep/gpf064

Collier, P., Hoeffler, A. and Söderbom, M. (2004b) On the duration of civil war. *Journal of Peace Research* 41:253. doi: 10.1177/0022343304043769

Collier, P., Hoeffler, A. & Rohner, D. (2006) Beyond Greed and Grievance: Feasibility and Civil War. *CSAE WPS*/2006-10. [Online.] Retrieved from http://www.csae.ox.ac.uk/ workingpapers/pdfs/2006-10text.pdf on October 13, 2012.

Collier, P., Hoeffler, A. & Rohner, D. (2009) Beyond greed and grievance: Feasibility and civil war. *Oxford Economic Papers* 61(1): 1–27. doi: 10.1093/oep/gpn029

Concepcion, S., Digal L., Guiam, R., De La Rosa, R. and Stankovitch, M. (2003, December.) Breaking the links between economics and conflict in Mindanao. Discussion Paper, presented at the 'Waging Peace' conference, Manila.

Elbadawi, I. and Sambanis, N. (2002) How much war will we see?: Explaining the prevalence of civil war. *Journal of Conflict Resolution*. 46(3) (June, 2002): 307-334. Retrieved from <http:// www.jstor.org/stable/3176229> on October 23, 2012.

Fearon, J.D. and Laitin, D.D. (2003) Ethnicity, insurgency, and civil war.*The American Political Science Review* 97(1) (Feb., 2003):75-90. Retrieved from <http://www.jstor.org/ stable/3118222>on June 23, 2012.

Fearon, J.D. (2004) Why do some civil wars last so much longer than others? *Journal of Peace Research* 41(3):275-301. Retrieved from jpr.sagepub.com on June 23, 2012. doi: 10.1177/0022343304043770

Frey, K. (2004) Liguasan Marsh vulnerability survey. *Notre Dame Journal* 32(3) June 2004.

Gurr, T. R. (1970) *Why Men Rebel*. Princeton, NJ: Princeton University Press.

Gurr, T.R. (2001) Minorities and nationalists: Managing ethno political conflict in the new century. In Crocker, C.A., Osler, F.E. and Aall, P. (eds) *Turbulent Peace: The challenges of managing international conflict.* Washington, D.C.: United States Institute of Peace Press. Chapter 11:163-188.

Hedman, E.E. (2009) The Philippines: Conflict and internal displacement in Mindanao and the Sulu Archipelago. UK: Writenet Independent Analysis (commissioned by United Nations High Commissioner for Refugees, Emergency and Technical Support Service). [Online.] Retrieved from <http://www.refworld.org/pdfid/4a9794482.pdf> on October 22, 2012.

Hensel, P. (2012) Territory: Geography, contentious issues and world politics. In Vasquez, J.A. (ed.) *What do we know about war?* Lanham, MD: Rowman & Littlefield, 3-26.

Humphreys, M. (2005) Natural resources, conflict and conflict resolution: Uncovering the mechanisms. *Journal of Conflict Resolution* 49(4):508-537. doi: 10.1177/0022002705277545

Le Billon, P. (2001) The political ecology of war: Natural resources and armed conflict. *Political Ecology* 20(5):561-584. [Online.] Accessed from <http://www.sciencedirect.com/science/article/pii/S0962629801000154>.

Le Billon, P. (2005) *Fuelling War: Natural resources and armed conflict. The Adelphi Papers* 45(373). [Online] Accessible at <http://www.tandfonline.com/toc/tadl19/45/373#.VRwwS-HPqNF>.London: International Institute for Strategic Studies and Routledge.

Lujala, P. (2009) 'Deadly combat over natural resources: Gems, petroleum, drugs, and the severity of armed civil conflict. *Journal of Conflict Resolution*, 53(1): 50-71. doi: 10.1177/0022002708327644

Lujala, P. (2010) The spoils of nature: Armed civil conflict and rebel access to natural resources. *Journal of Peace Research* 47(1):15-28. doi: 10.1177/0022343309350015

MacGinty, R. and Williams, A. (2009) *Conflict and Development.* Abingdon, Oxon. & New York: Routledge.

McKenna, T. (1998) *Muslim Rulers and Rebels: Everyday politics and armed separatism in the Southern Philippines.* Oakland: University of California Press.

Majul, C.A. (1985) *The Contemporary Muslim Movement in the Philippines.* Berkeley: Mizan Press.

May, R.J. (2002) The Moro conflict and the Philippine experience with Muslim autonomy. Paper for CCPCSAP Workshop, Canberra, September 2002.

Milligan, J.A. (2005) *Islamic Identity, Postcoloniality and Educational Policy: Schooling and Ethno-Religious Conflict in the Southern Philippines.* New York: Palgrave Macmillan.

Milligan, J.A. (2010) The Prophet and the engineer meet under the mango tree: Leadership, education, and conflict in the Southern Philippines. *Educational Policy* 2010 (24): 28.

Regan, P. and Norton, D. Greed, grievance and mobilization in civil wars. *Journal of Conflict Resolution* 49(3): 319-336. doi: 10.1177/0022002704273441.

Rosero, E.V. (2011, August 20.). MILF won't let go of gas-rich wetlands—Wikileaks posting. Retrieved from <http://www.gmanetwork.com/news/story/229965/news/nation/milf-won-t-let-go-of-gas-rich-wetlands-wikileaks-posting>on April 5, 2013.

Ross, M.L. (2004) What do we know about natural resource and civil war? *Journal of Peace Research* 41(3)337-356.

Santos, S.M. Jr. (2005) A holistic perspective on the Mindanao conflict. [Online]. Retrieved from <http://www.aer.ph/pdf/papers/holistic_perspective_on_the_mindanao_conflict.pdf>

Santos, S.M. Jr. (2001) *The Moro Islamic Challenge. Constitutional rethinking for the Mindanao Process.* QuezonCity: University of the Philippines Press.

Sen, A. (2006) *Identity and Violence.* New York: Norton.

Sorens, J. Mineral production, territory, and ethnic rebellion: The role of rebel constituencies. *Journal of Peace Research* 48(5): 571-585. doi: 10.1177/0022343311411743

Taydas, Z., Enia, J. and James, P. (2011) Why do civil wars occur?Another look at the theoretical dichotomy of opportunity versus grievance. *Review of International Studies* 37(5): 2627-2650. [Online.] http://dx.doi.org/10.1017/S026021051100012X

Turner, M., May, R.J., & Turner, R.L. (1992) (Eds.) *Mindanao: Land of unfulfilled promise.* Quezon City: New Day Publishers.

Weidmann, N.B. (2009) Geography as motivation and opportunity: Group concentration and ethnic conflict. *Journal of Conflict Resolution* 53(4): 526-543. doi: 10.1177/0022002709336456

CHAPTER 8

The sun also rises: A nationalist turn in Japanese foreign policy?

H. Steven Green

Prime Minister Shinzo Abe's second term as prime minister coincides with public attitudes of distrust and dislike between the publics of Japan and two of its neighbors, the People's Republic of China and the Republic of Korea. Japan's role in preserving peace in Northeast Asia depends, among other factors, on the attitudes of the Japanese toward their neighbors and their constitution. Does the apparent hardening of attitudes in these three nations reveal Japan's foreign policy is taking a nationalist turn under the Abe administration? This chapter addresses this question through analysis of three related topics: First, we will consider how the so-called pacifist spirit of Article 9 has influenced Japan's defense policies by examining survey data of the Japanese public's attitudes about the role of Japan's Self-Defense Forces from 1955 to the present. Next, we will examine the development of the Self-Defense Forces into arguably the second most powerful military in East Asia after the United States and one of the most powerful armed forces worldwide on the basis of defense spending (Lind, 2004, pp. 92-121; SIPRI, 2013). We will conclude by examining events and public attitudes around current tensions between Japan and South Korea and Japan and China over territorial claims and perceptions of Japan's lack of contrition for past imperialism and military aggression.

Japan's foreign policy and Article 9

Scholars in the constructivist school of international relations claim that anti-militaristic norms have become deeply embedded in Japanese society. Constructivists root the idea of Japan as "first and foremost a cultured, peace-loving nation" in Article 9 of the constitution, which reads:

> Aspiring sincerely to an international peace based on justice and order, the Japanese people forever renounce war as a sovereign right of the nation and the threat or use of force as means of settling international disputes.
>
> In order to accomplish the aim of the preceding paragraph, land, sea, and air forces, as well as other war potential, will never be maintained. The right of belligerency of the state will not be recognized.

Paragraph one can be understood as "no war" and paragraph two as "no weapons." Japan's constitution was written by a team of American officers, scholars and lawyers working under the direction of General Douglas MacArthur. After the US Occupation (1945-1952), Japan pledged to contribute to world peace through a variety of non-military means. The Japanese have never amended their constitution, which constructivists take as evidence for the existence of powerful societal norms against militarism or the use of force in resolving international disputes.

Constructivists believe that norms directly influence a nation's security policies. Thomas Berger (1998) and Peter Katzenstein (1996) claim that domestic as well as international experiences of a country generate societal norms, which in turn determine the permissible list of options for its political leaders. The presence of a norm that considers certain policies unacceptable, such as the use of force to settle international disputes, may constrain state actors. "Whilst this norm might not constrain individual policy-makers to the same degree ... the acceptance of the norm on the popular level acts as a powerful constraint on the government's use of military force as a legitimate instrument of state policy" (Hook, *et. al.*, 2005, p.74).

Berger and Katzenstein argue that the experiences of their government's military aggression leading to crushing defeat forged in the population of Japan a norm against war, or what constructivists call a "culture of antimilitarism." According to Berger, any attempt by the state "to significantly expand ... Japanese defense establishments and international roles foundered on the shoals of domestic opposition" (Berger, 1998, p. 6). Sun-ki Chai emphasizes the constraining effects of Article 9 on would-be Japanese hawks (Chai, 1997). Berger also argues that, unlike citizens in the older democracies of U.K. and the U.S., Japanese remain suspicious of their military, nearly 70 years after the war.

Anecdotal evidence shows this norm of anti-militarism endures. In the words of a 72-year old owner of an antiques and reproduction shop in Tokyo's Roppongi ward, Japan's constitution is a "unique brand." Takeshi Maki told a reporter that, "Despite its cars, electronics and fashion, Japan has one unique brand that you can find nowhere else in the world: its constitution, and in particular Article 9" (Jeffs, 2007). Even a 2004 recruitment poster commissioned by Japan's Self-Defense Forces (hereinafter SDF) appears to have been designed with this peace "brand" in mind. The poster features the 15 teenage members of the all-girl pop-idol singing group Morning Musume in smiles and summer dresses above the proclamation *Isshou-kenme-te, ii-kanji* ("Doing one's best feels good"). Below this exhortation an English message appears in larger print: "Go! Go! Peace!" (*The Japan Times*, 2003).

A review of Japan's foreign and security policy since the end of the Occupation shows that anti-militaristic norms continue, even as the government created and developed a strong defense force. Prime Minister Shigeru Yoshida said the purpose of the SDF was "to defend the peace and independence of the country" when the law for its creation was enacted in 1954 (Dower, 1988, p. 438). Yoshida's decision was influenced by a 1951 meeting between John Foster Dulles and the chief justice of the Japanese Supreme Court, in which it was concluded that "a considerable degree of rearmament was possible within the existing framework of the Constitution" (*ibid.*, p. 439). By 1954 the SDF were formed with the blessings of the Justice Ministry, whose legal brief on the matter concluded that, "To maintain a level of actual power which does not reach 'war potential' and to use this for defense against aggression does not violate the constitution" and that, since the maritime, air and ground branches of the SDF were "not being organized for war purposes it is clear that they are not a military" (*ibid.*, p. 441). Under Yoshida, writes J.W. Dower:

> Article Nine was blown up like a balloon, twisted like a pretzel, kneaded like plasticine. In the end, however, it remained unamended, and its survival was as significant as its mutilation. Even while bending the law to its purposes, the Yoshida group remained sensitive to its ultimate constraints (*ibid.*, p. 439).

Thus, the irony of the formation of what would be called a "military without war potential" is that it actually seems to confirm the existence of an anti-militarist norm. Yoshida's finance minister, Hayato Ikeda made clear to the Americans, in fact, that his government would never support a defense policy that "might infringe on the Japanese Constitution" (*ibid.*, p. 442).

During this period, the government's policies and views were supported by public opinion. A majority of Japanese agreed that Japan needed military forces. In public opinion polls conducted between 1950 and 1957, the percent who responded "Yes" in answer to the question "Does Japan need military forces?" increased from 54% in 1950, to 66% by 1956 and dipped a bit to 64% in 1957, while the percentage of respondents who replied "No" was 28%, 15%, and 17%, respectively (Midford, 2011, p. 59). However, the public did not approve of a "'gradual increase,' 'expansion,' or 'rearmament' of the SDF" during this same period. While 50% did approve in 1950, by 1956 only 37% did and a year later a mere 31% approved of enlarging or increasing the firepower of the nation's new Self-Defense Forces (*ibid.*).

In the 1960s, Prime Minister Eisaku Sato decided to cap spending on defense at 1% of GDP, which remains to this day as an unofficial, but accepted a benchmark by which to measure SDF-related spending. By the conclusion of the 1980s, Japanese officials served as the heads of the World Health Organization, and the UN High Commission for Refugees, which were the highest positions of authority in international organizations ever reached by any Japanese in the post-war era. These positions seem like modest applications of Japanese influence considering that the bubble economy of that decade had many people around the world contemplating, and some even fearing, Japan as a new superpower (Lincoln, 2003, p. 111). Even under the leadership of Prime Minister Nakasone, who famously pledged to U.S. President Ronald Reagan that Japan was an unsinkable aircraft carrier for the United States in its struggle against communism, Japan never sought to participate in international uses of force.

As it had in the first two decades after the war, public opinion in the 1970s and 1980s supported a strong SDF that would remain at home. A survey by the *Mainichi* in 1972 asked respondents to rate whether "various means for Japan's security" were "effective" or "not effective." These means were military, economic and diplomatic, and were considered effective (not effective) by 40% (46%), 75% (11%) and 75% (10%), respectively (Midford, *op. cit.*, p. 61). A 1973 poll by the *Yomiuri Shimbun* newspaper found that only 6.5% of the public believed that SDF activities should not be limited to Japanese territory, territorial waters, or airspace (*ibid.*). Finally, Nakasone's "unsinkable" comment notwithstanding, a Prime Minister's Office (PMO) poll found in 1989 that only 22% of the public supported any role for the SDF in UN peacekeeping operations, compared to 46% who opposed, although 72% did support SDF participation in international disaster-relief operations (*ibid.*, p. 62).

The first test to Japan's official pacifism came in the run-up to the international effort to liberate Kuwait from Iraq in 1990-1991. Facing intense pressure to support a coalition of multinational forces against Saddam Hussein's army, Prime Minister Toshiki Kaifu's government raised taxes to pay for a contribution of $13 billion, the single largest sum of any state in the coalition, although it was delivered after the war had ended. The government and the public were shocked when this contribution was dismissed abroad as mere "checkbook diplomacy" as well as when Japan was excluded from a list of governments thanked by the Kuwaiti government in a full-page *New York Times* advertisement after the coalition had driven out the Iraqi forces. Eventually, in May of 1991, Japan would dispatch minesweepers to the Persian Gulf, which marked the first time since 1945 that a Japanese military vessel was sent outside of Japanese territory or waters. Lee Kuan Yew, the former prime minister of Singapore, publicly fretted that permitting Japan's defense forces to join an overseas campaign was like "giving liquor chocolates to an alcoholic" (Pyle, 1996, p. 164). To assuage fears such as Lee's, "Japanese officials practically repeated a mantra that Japan would never again become an independent military power... Japan would 'learn from the lessons of history,' [and would remain a] 'new-style peace-loving and cultural nation'", according to a Ministry of Finance report in 1990 (*ibid.*).

Beginning in 1992, through lengthy parliamentary deliberation, and against a backdrop of public demonstrations against the decisions, Japan began to deploy its Self-Defense personnel to international peace keeping operations (PKOs), first to Cambodia and then to Mozambique, the Golan Heights, and East Timor. Diet sessions were consumed by debates over whether or not Japanese personnel should be allowed to carry weapons—doing so would violate the Constitution, opponents claimed—and how troops would be allowed to respond if they came under fire. Indicative of the constraints on the use of force even by SDF personnel faced with defending themselves, are comments by then-Post and Telecommunications Minister Jun'ichiro Koizumi to a Cabinet meeting convened after a Japanese member of a UN-led PKO had been fatally shot in Cambodia in May 1993. On the subject of allowing Japanese personnel to use weapons even if only in self-defense, Koizumi reportedly argued, "We should not [make international contributions] to the point where blood starts flowing. If Japan is criticized for that, we should resign ourselves to that criticism" (Yoshida, 2003).

As Table 1 shows, during the build-up to the First Gulf War in 1990, only a small fraction of the public supported an armed role for the SDF overseas. In an opinion poll conducted by the *Nihon Keizai Shimbun* in 1990, a large plurality (48.5%) did not believe it was necessary to dispatch the SDF overseas and 28.4% supported a dispatch only on the condition that the Japanese forces carry no weapons.

Table 1: Opinions on dispatching the SDF overseas.

What do you think about dispatching the SDF overseas?

It is not necessary to dispatch the SDF.	48.5%
As much as possible, the SDF should be dispatched under the condition that they carry no weapons.	28.4%
The SDF should be dispatched overseas carrying weapons.	10.9%
No answer / don't know	12.1%

Reprinted from Midford, 2011, p.71.

A year later, as the Japanese government scrambled to respond to international condemnation for Japan's so-called "checkbook diplomacy," public opinion about the SDF's international role had not changed significantly, as Table 2 shows. According to an *Asahi Shimbun* poll, only 21% supported deployment of the SDF overseas and a meager 5% supported participation in military activities. However, 23% of respondents affirmed they "would recognize a military role under UN command," suggesting there was growing support to participate in internationally sanctioned uses of force so long as Japanese troops were under UN command.

Table 2: Opinions about deploying the SDF overseas

"What do you think of deploying the SDF overseas?"

The SDF should not be deployed overseas.	21%
May deploy to render non-military assistance, such as disaster relief.	46%
Would recognize a military role under UN command, such as participation in a U.N. PKO army.	23%
May participate in military activities such as the Gulf War multilateral army.	5%
Other answers/no answer	5%

Reprinted from Midford, 2011, p. 84.

Support among the Japanese public for SDF participation in non-military, overseas disaster relief operations increased throughout the 1990s. Table 3 shows the results of the Prime Minister's Office surveys asking people's opinion about "SDF participation in overseas disaster relief." In 1991, 54.2% agreed or somewhat agreed with SDF participation, but by 2000 the combined total was 86.3%.

Table 3: "SDF participation in overseas disaster relief"

Date	Agree / Somewhat agree
February 1991	54.2%
January 1994	61.6%
February 1997	78.0%
January 2000	86.3%

Produced from figures cited throughout Midford, 2011, Chapter 6.

As the survey data in Tables 1, 2 and 3 show, despite international criticism for its refusal to send SDF troops into harm's way in the First Gulf War, the Japanese public overwhelmingly favored non-military uses of Japan's armed forces throughout the 1990s. Opinion grew increasingly supportive of SDF participation in disaster-relief operations, while only 1 in 20 believed Japanese troops should be allowed to participate in the First Gulf War alongside other national armies.

Beginning in 2001, public support for SDF participation in overseas operations would grow around non-combative uses of SDF force. The public would remain skeptical of military solutions, despite the policies of its government over the next several years. On September 11, 2001, Prime Minister Koizumi was the first foreign leader to telephone President George

W. Bush to offer condolences as well as to pledge Japan's support for an American military response. Then on October 29th the Diet passed the Anti-Terrorism Special Measures Law that allowed SDF units to deploy to the Indian Ocean as part of a logistical support network for US and multinational forces. Next, in July 2003, the Diet passed the Law Concerning Special Measures on Humanitarian and Reconstruction Assistance to dispatch SDF troops to Iraq to provide logistical support for US and coalition forces on the ground in Iraq. As a result, the Koizumi-led government would dispatch 600 Ground Self-Defense Forces (GSDF) to southern Iraq in January 2004 to help reconstruct an area considered secure and non-hostile (an action that would seem to contradict Koizumi's argument of 10 years earlier to avoid the risk of bloodshed at all costs.)

Despite this historical change in security policy, the Japanese public continued to prefer non-military means to conflict resolution. As we see in Table 4, a majority of Japanese respondents in a 2002 *Yomiuri Shimbun* poll did approve of indirect military support for the United States in international efforts to combat terrorism, but even more approved of non-military means such as helping refugees.

Table 4: "How should Japan cooperate with efforts to combat international terrorism?"
(Multiple answers allowed)

Assistance to refugees	63.3%
Rear-area support for US military and others (medical, transportation, refueling)	57.1%
Reconstruction assistance to Afghanistan	36.5%
Curbing funding sources for terrorists	35.7%

Yomiuri Shimbun, 2002. Produced from figures in Midford, 2011, p.113.

Throughout the period of the Koizumi administration, even as the electorate kept his Liberal Democratic Party (LDP) in power, the public remained reluctant to support war for any reason other than self-defense. As Table 5 shows 47.8% of Japanese believed that "when attacked" war would be "legitimate". When combined with those who believed it was a "somewhat legitimate" reason, self-defense did garner a majority support of 78.1%. The second most-legitimate reason, "prevent genocide in another country," earned a combined total of 50.7 % of responses, and the least legitimate reason for going to war was "when another country is suspected of harboring terrorists."

Table 5: Antimilitaristic attitudes: Legitimate reasons for going to war

Studies of Attitudes and Global Engagement (SAGE) poll, 2004-05

	Legitimate	Somewhat legitimate	Not very legitimate	Not legitimate
Prevent human rights abuses in other countries	8.8%	32.9%	33%	20.3%
Prevent genocide in another country	13.9%	36.8%	25%	18.8%
When another country is suspected of harboring terrorists	7.6%	29.8%	34.8%	22.5%
When attacked	47.8%	30.3%	7.9%	9%

Source: ICU-WSU SAGE Poll, www.wsu.edu/pols/sage/data.htm, Japanese language question 16.

Data in Table 6 affirm the prevalence in Japan of an anti-militaristic norm against the use of force abroad. When asked in 2004 to rank what primary and secondary means Japan can take to respond to international terrorism, overwhelming majorities chose "respond through the UN" (81.4%, combined primary and secondary) and "create new alliance relationships through diplomatic means" (75.8%, combined). Only 5.9% recommend military intervention as a primary means and 31.8% chose it as a secondary means, but the combined total, 37.7% is far behind the next least recommended means, economic intervention.

Table 6: Anti-militarist attitudes: Effective responses to terrorism

"What is the most effective means Japan can take to respond to international terrorism? Choose which of the following means, 1-4, are effective as primary and secondary means."

	Primary Means	Secondary Means	Combined
Military intervention	5.9%	31.8%	37.7%
Economic Intervention	22.2%	31.0%	53.2%
Create new alliance through diplomatic means	38.6%	37.2%	75.8%
Respond through the UN	64.4%	17.0%	81.4%

Source: ICU-WSU SAGE Poll, www.wsu.edu/pols/sage/data.htm, Japanese language question 33.

As Dower wrote of Yoshida's justification for the creation of the SDF, the Koizumi government may have twisted the logic of Article 9 "like a pretzel", but the Constitution remains unamended. A 2007 poll by Japan's largest daily newspaper, the *Yomiuri Shimbun*, showed that only 35.7% of the public supported revising Article 9, even though public approval ratings for Koizumi had been 60% or higher (*Yomiuri Shimbun*, 2007). Taken together, the results in Tables 1-6 demonstrate that, as it has since the 1950s, a societal norm against military solutions to international problems has endured despite state policies that increased the chances that the SDF would become involved in military actions. Even as the Japanese electorate has time and again awarded office to politicians who expand the size and role of the SDF, it has not allowed Japan's leadership to adopt the use of force to settle disputes as the nation's sovereign right.

Japan as a "normal" military power

Despite the prevalence of anti-militarist norms, Japan has developed the second-most powerful military in East Asia after the United States and is among the top eight nations when defense spending is measured (Lind, *op. cit*; SIPRI, *op. cit.*). Whereas constructivists emphasize constraints on Japan's policy-makers, other scholars have highlighted the specific features of Japan's "military without war potential" as proof that, even before the debates of the 1990s, Japan was behaving in accordance with expectations from one branch of the realist school, defensive realism. Offensive realists hypothesize that the anarchy inherent in the international realm drives great powers to seek regional hegemony (Mearsheimer, 2001). Defensive realists argue that states respond to anarchy by strengthening their defense, rather than focusing on offensive capabilities, because expansionism tends to produce counterbalancing coalitions (Waltz, 1979; Snyder, 1991).

The strength of Japan's military power confirms the expectations of defensive realism. Commentators underestimate Japan's military power because they measure it by comparing defense spending as a percentage of GDP across various nations. Japan typically devotes about 1 percent of GDP to its "self-defense" needs, compared to between 1.5 and 3% in other great powers (Lind, *op. cit.*, p. 95). However, this measure is inaccurate since a state with a large economy can produce a large military at a small expense relative to GDP and it is suggested that measuring military power by comparing aggregate defense spending is a better way to grasp the amount of that particular power's resource. On this measure, by 2004 Japan was among the top two or three nations in total defense spending; second behind the United States when measured at market exchange rates; third behind Russia and the US if measured using price purchasing power parity (*ibid.*). By 2013 Japan's ranking had dropped to 7th, tied with Germany for total military expenditures (SIPRI, *op. cit.*).

What kind of bang has Japan gotten for its buck? On the one hand, the SDF has low ground power capabilities but high air and sea power capabilities. Japan lacks airborne and air assault divisions and has no marine corps. It cannot provide airlift or sealift logistics and has no long-range ground attack systems, such as cruise missiles. These kinds of capabilities are offensive so, according to their proponents, their absence adheres to the Yoshida administration's interpretation of a defensive force as consistent with the letter and spirit of Article 9. On the other hand, as Christopher E. Twomey (2000) observes, Japan is secure militarily, even as it describes its power in non-military terms. In order to remain at least rhetorically true to Article 9, Japan relies on euphemisms for much of its military vocabulary, beginning with the term "Self-Defense Force". *The Economist* (2003) dryly notes that the 240,000 men in the Japanese military, whose jobs would seem to be forbidden constitutionally:

> … are not soldiers, you understand, but members of the land, sea and air 'self-defense forces.' Japan does not have tanks… those would sound too much like the sort of thing an army might have. But it does have 'specialty vehicles' which look remarkably like, well, tanks.

The Maritime Self-Defense Force's (MSDF) "disaster relief ship" is really an amphibious assault ship and air defense destroyers are "escort ships" (Twomey, 2000, p.186). By the beginning of the 21st century, Japan's defense, under any name, was world-class. For instance, the MSDF had the largest destroyer force in the Pacific, "centered around four of the most advanced, guided-missile cruisers" in the world; the Air Self-Defense Force (ASDF) possessed several squadrons of F-2 strike fighters, which are the "most capable fighters" in East Asia, after the American planes; and the ASDF's F-2s and F-15s could be armed with both air-to-air and surface-to-air missiles produced in Japan (*ibid.*, pp. 186-187). What's more, the MSDF could deploy 100 P-3C anti-submarine patrol planes in the event of a submarine blockade around the Japanese archipelago plus 100 anti-submarine helicopters. The MSDF can also protect the home islands with a mine fleet larger than that of the United States. It is difficult to refute Twomey's claim that "an adversary's navy entering Japanese waters would suffer dearly, and all but the most capable navies would find themselves outgunned anywhere in the Western Pacific" (*ibid.*).

Japan's defense build-up, coupled with the presence of the US Armed Forces on Japanese soil, reflects a strategy of "buck-passing." Where balancers find allies and confront aggressive states with them, buck-passers "recognize the need to balance against a threat, but they do as little of the required balancing as possible by relying on the efforts of others" (Lind, *op. cit.*, p. 103). Buck-passers do see the need to balance, but also see that doing so can be costly, as a long-term balancing strategy may bleed away manpower and wealth (*ibid.*, p. 104). A strategy of buck-passing transfers some of these costs and risks to other states.

Buck-passing is most likely in states whose "geography or military technology make them less vulnerable to immediate invasion. Buck-passing is also particularly appealing to countries that are relatively secure and to those that have powerful allies that can contain foreseeable threats" (*ibid.*). Japan's security policy in the postwar era matches the expectations of the defensive realists. Following the war, as an island nation quickly redeveloping its industrial base, Japan would not have been an easy target for invasion especially with a superpower offering it protection against shared perceived regional threats. Under the U.S. military umbrella, Japan could obtain protection more cheaply through a strategy of buck-passing than it could have on its own, particularly during the first two decades of redevelopment. According to defensive realists, from the 1950s through the end of the Cold War, Japan was content to remain under the U.S. defense umbrella for security against the USSR, which Japan and the US feared were making hegemonic claims on East Asia (Lind, *op. cit.*; Twomey, *op. cit.*). Enlargements of the JSDF coincide first, during the Cold War with increases in the Soviet threat and then, after the collapse of the USSR, with new expectations from the United States and new threats from North Korean missiles in the 1990s. Since the Cold War's end Japan has pursued a more active role in international security and peacekeeping operations, without replacing its buck-passing strategy (Twomey, *op. cit.*).

In response to the Soviet build-up in the western Pacific that began in the late-1970s, Japan would enlarge the SDF. Following the normalization of relations between China and the U.S., and between China and Japan, the Soviets began a campaign that seemed designed to try to intimidate Japan away from close ties with Beijing and Washington. The USSR dispatched amphibious troops to Shikotan Island, located approximately 75 km from the Hokkaido city of Nemuro. The USSR also deployed SS-20 tactile nuclear missile launchers to eastern Siberia and, in 1985 simulated an attack on Hokkaido. By the end of the 1970s the Soviet Union's Pacific Fleet was the largest of the four Soviet fleets with increased numbers of ballistic missile submarines and surface ships and improved amphibious capabilities (Lind, *op. cit.*, p. 104). The Soviet navy began practicing exercises in the Western Pacific that simulated attacks on Western forces and the air force deployed more MiG-23, MiG-27 and Su-19 aircraft and *Backfire* bombers to bases in eastern Siberia. The Soviets also increased their amphibious capabilities in the Kurile Islands, just off the northern tip of Hokkaido (*ibid.*, p. 107). By the end of the 1970s, Japan and the U.S. had to contend with the fact that the balance of power in Northeast Asia had shifted from their partnership to the Soviets.

Japan did not abandon its buck-passing strategy, but it did adjust to changes in the security environment (while maintaining its position under the U.S. security umbrella) by taking "steps that would transform it into one of the world's major military powers" (*ibid.*, p. 111). The GSDF acquired mobile battle tanks and moved the bulk of its deployments to Hokkaido. The ASDF developed the E-2C Airborne Early Warning Group (AWEG) and purchased F-15 fighters to defend against the Soviet Backfires (Hughes, 2004: 27-28). The MSDF acquired 100 "state-of-the-art" P-3C naval patrol aircraft, *Yushio*-class diesel-electric submarines and four "highly advanced" guided missile destroyers with Aegis radar (*ibid.*).

However, this surge in Japan's military strength did not indicate a break from buck-passing. The additional firepower remained concentrated in and immediately around Japan and was designed to compensate gaps between the U.S. and Soviet strength-levels, inasmuch as the gap directly affected Japan. For example, the explicit purpose of the F-15s was not to intercept *Backfires* bound for the Japanese archipelago, but rather to protect U.S. bases.

From the end of the Cold War through the administration of Jun'ichiro Koizumi in the early 21st century, Japan adjusted to changes in the international system by including SDF forces in both PKOs and non-combatant roles in Iraq, as well as rear-support roles to the U.S. military. Throughout this period, the Japanese public's support for strong defense went hand-in-hand with its preference for non-military and non-combatant roles for the JSDF. In the next section we consider whether additional changes to Japan's official pacifism under Shinzo Abe go hand-in-hand with increased feelings of distrust between Japan and China and South Korea.

Rising nationalism in Northeast Asia?

SDF troops deployed to Iraq in January 2006 were withdrawn in the summer of the same year, yet the government continues to expand Japan's military capabilities. Additional changes to Japan's security policy under the administration of Prime Minister Shinzo Abe correlate with high levels of bad feelings between the publics of China and Japan and Korea and Japan. This correlation raises the question of whether Japan's current security policy reflects an increase in nationalism in Japan.

There are some recent changes to defense policy. For instance, in 2007, during his first term as prime minister, Shinzo Abe oversaw the transformation of the Defense Agency into the Ministry of Defense, indicating an increase in the perceived importance of the JSDF by the government.

At the time of writing, the Abe administration implemented defense-related policies that are unprecedented in the post-war era. At the end of March 2014, Japan lifted a ban on arms exports from Japanese firms, which led to the sale of amphibious U.S.-2 military aircraft to India (*Defense News*, 2014). Japan and India also conducted their first-ever joint naval exercises in the Pacific Ocean and India invited the Maritime Self-Defense Forces to participate in naval exercises with the United States Navy. Furthermore, in August 2014 the Defense Ministry of Japan announced a plan to create a fund to develop military technology through supporting university research projects (*Japan Times*, 2014a). The most controversial defense-related news to date, however, has likely been the administration's proposal (announced on July 1, 2014) to reinterpret Article 9 to allow Japan to exercise a right to collective self-defense (CSD.)

Alongside the changes wrought by Abe, feelings of distrust and dislike are growing between Japanese and Chinese, and between Japanese and South Koreans. In fact, 88% of Japanese "do not trust China" and 79% believe China poses the greatest military threat to Japan of any country or region. (*Yomiuri Shimbun*, 2013). In 2013, for the first time since 1998, a majority of respondents (58%) told the Cabinet Office of Japan survey pollsters they do not "feel close to South Korea" (Stahler, 2013).

It would appear that the Japanese are growing less trustful of China and South Korea while Abe is in office, and at the same time their neighbors seem to dislike Japan in general, and Abe in particular. For instance, 85% of South Koreans and 77% of Chinese view Japan's prime minister unfavorably, while 77% of South Koreans and 90% of Chinese view Japan in general unfavorably (Pew, 2013 pp. 5-6). Many people in China and South Korea feel Japan has not demonstrated sufficient regret for its military actions in the 1930s and 1940s. Large protests in both countries followed Abe's visits to Yasukuni Shrine in 2013, which have been viewed as evidence of the prime minister's support for the wartime roles of the Class A war criminals enshrined there. When asked whether Japan has "sufficiently apologized for its military actions during the 1930s and 1940s," 98% of South Koreans and 78% of Chinese say it has not (*ibid.*, p. 5).

Abe and his Liberal Democratic Party were voted into power, so many Koreans and Chinese view his ascendance to the prime minister's office as an indication of a nascent Japanese nationalism. They do not believe that Japan has demonstrated genuine contrition for imperial aggressions and war crimes committed against their populations between 1910 and 1945 (Korea) and 1932 and 1945 (China) and see his defense policies, as well as comments he has made regarding the war, as reflective of a popular nationalist sentiment. In fact, Japanese support for revising the constitution has been increasing and overlaps with the return of Abe to the prime minister's office. Between 2006 and 2013, support for "changing the Japanese constitution so Japan could officially have a military and declare war" increased from 27% to 36%, while opposition decreased to 56% from 67% (*ibid.*, p. 4).

However, public opinion in Japan does not show obvious signs of resurgent nationalism, or a desire to revise Article 9. The Japanese public does not unconditionally support prime ministerial visits to Yasukuni Shrine. Following Abe's December 2013 visit there, which sparked public and diplomatic protests in Seoul and Beijing, 69.8% of Japanese agreed with the statement that the "Prime Minister should take diplomatic relations into consideration when visiting Yasukuni Shrine" (*Japan Times*, 2013). Although 43.2% thought visits were "good," 47.1% believed they were "not good," and 54.6% felt that "A new shrine to honor war dead should be built" (*ibid*). Nor does the public necessarily support CSD. Public support for the Abe cabinet dropped 5 points at the end of July 2014 to 48%, in the first major poll taken following the proposal for CSD (*Nikkei Asian Review*, 2014). A separate poll shows that 84.1% of Japanese "believes the government hasn't yet provided a sufficient explanation" of why CSD is necessary and 60.2% oppose it (*Japan Times*, 2014 c). Furthermore, although support for revising Article 9 has increased since 2006, as noted above, pro-revisionists still account for only 36% of the public (*Japan Times*, 2014 b). The hurdles to revision are high: Two-thirds of both chambers of the Diet parliamentarians in either chamber would support any revision (*Ibid*). Finally, even as Abe seeks to expand Japan's military capabilities, the SDF struggles to attract reservists. As of August 2014, only 70% of 47,900 reserves desired by the Defense Ministry have been signed up for service (*ibid*). Unlike reservists in the United States, who are sometimes sent into combat, Japan's reservists can reasonably expect to be called to duty only for national disasters. The short supply of reservists during lean economic times suggests nationalist sentiment is less widespread than may be feared from outside Japan. Even the Defense Ministry's goal to fund university research has met resistance at home. Citing militarization of academia during World War II, a group of university researchers has organized a petition opposed to the plan and the University of Tokyo even turned down a request to look for causes behind defects in C-2 transport aircraft (*Japan Times*, 2014 a).

Outside of China and South Korea, Japan remains in good standing with other Asian nations. As Table 7 shows, other Asian nations see Japan favorably. Although super-majorities of South Koreans and Chinese view Japan unfavorably, similar-sized majorities in Malaysia, Indonesia, Australia and the Philippines see Japan favorably.

Table 7: Japan Generally Seen Favorably

	Unfavorable	Favorable
Malaysia	6%	80%
Indonesia	12%	79%
Australia	16%	78%
Philippines	18%	78%
South Korea	77%	22%
China	90%	04%

Source: Compiled with figures from Pew Research Center, 2013: Q9v.

Other Asian views of Shinzo Abe are more positive than negative, as Table 8 illustrates. In South Korea and China 85% have an "unfavorable" view of the prime minister, compared to 15% in Philippines and 9% in Malaysia. Large percentages of people in four of the six countries in Table 8 answered that they "Don't know" Abe, whereas in South Korea and China a mere two- and six-percent, respectively, don't know him.

Table 8: Mixed International Views of Shinzo Abe

	Unfavorable	Favorable	Don't Know
Malaysia	09%	53%	38%
Indonesia	11%	46%	42%
Australia	16%	30%	56%
Philippines	18%	78%	23%
South Korea	85%	12%	02%
China	85%	09%	06%

Source: Compiled with figures from Pew Research Center, 2013: Q43.

Critics worry that exercising a right to CSD will destabilize East Asia. However, both Philippines President Benigno Aquino and Singapore's Foreign Minister K. Shanmugam have publicly expressed support for it (Green and Hornung, 2014). The governments of Indonesia, Malaysia, Thailand, Myanmar, Vietnam and India "have been privately supportive, but more cautious in their public stances" (*ibid.*). China has been involved in contentious disputes with Vietnam, the Philippines, and Malaysia over claims to islands in the South China Sea. Tentative support in the region for Abe's CSD proposal, and the lack of opposition to SDF activities such as Japan's naval exercises with India, possibly reflect the preoccupation of Southeast Asian governments with China's changing role in the region. The CSD proposal may or may not violate Article 9, but in Southeast Asia there seems to be little concern about it as an indicator of Japanese nationalism or a threat. With the exceptions of South Korea and China, Asian populations hold a favorable view of Japan and even of Shinzo Abe. In any case, and as noted above, CSD does not have the support of a majority of Japanese.

Conclusion

The idea of post-war Japan as a nation that embraces the principle of pacifism in international affairs has always been a myth. It has developed a highly potent military and has adopted a strategy of buck-passing, both of which demonstrate that Japan is not becoming a so-called normal military power but, rather, has been one for at least 60 years.

On the other hand, survey data and anecdotal evidence covering the period from 1955 to the present show that the Japanese public remains averse to the use of force for anything except self-defense and humanitarian aid, and is wary of collective self-defense. In this sense, we may say the spirit of Article 9 endures, so long as it is understood as anti-militaristic and not pacifistic. Recent events highlight the continued presence of an anti-militaristic norm. Not even the violent murder of two Japanese nationals could provoke public demands for a military response. After Islamic State militants killed Kenji Goto and Haruna Yukawa in January 2015, Prime Minister Abe announced that he would like to enact legislation allowing the dispatch of JSDF troops to rescue hostages. Although he could not resort to a military solution to this hostage crisis, 51% of Japanese approved of his administration's handling of it, compared to 42% who did not, and 54% approved of his cabinet, a four-point increase over January, compared to just 29% who disapproved (NHK, 2015). Abe also pledged to continue sending humanitarian aid to the Middle East and this non-military policy earned the approval of 65% of Japanese (*ibid.*).

To the extent that there may be increasing nationalist sentiment associated with Japan's security policy, the evidence cited above suggests it is contained to the bilateral relationships between China and Japan, and South Korea and Japan. Negative feelings in these two sets of bilateral relationships notwithstanding, the survey data above demonstrate that the Japanese public does not support deliberately provocative actions toward Japan's neighbors, such as prime ministerial visits to Yasukuni Shrine. If Shinzo Abe is a nationalist, most Japanese are not and their attitudes toward China and South Korea may turn on more inter-governmental dialog, among other things. In March 2015, the foreign ministers of Japan, South Korea, and China gathered for the first time in three years. On March 19 the foreign ministers of Japan and China conducted high-level security talks for the first time in four years. The two sides have discussed the possibility of creating a military hotline and Prime Minister Abe has also promised to affirm previous official apologies for Japan's aggressions in China in the 1930s and

1940s at ceremonies marking the 70th anniversary of the end of World War Two (*The Economist*, 2015). While the Japanese public may not be pacifistic, the Prime Minister will likely keep voters' support, and contribute to maintaining peace in Northeast Asia, if he keeps in mind the anti-militaristic norm within Japanese society.

References

Berger, T. (1998) *Cultures of Antimilitarism: national security in Germany and Japan.* Baltimore, Md: Johns Hopkins University Press

Chai, S. (1997) Entrenching the Yoshida defense doctrine: three techniques for institutionalization. *International Organization* 51(3): 389-112.

Defense News (2014, April 1) Japan Lifts Its Own Blanket Arms Export Ban. [Online] Accessed from <http://archive.defensenews.com/article/20140401/DEFREG03/304010013/Japan-Lifts-Own-Blanket-Arms-Export-Ban> on 5 April, 2015.

Dower, J.W. (1988) *Empire and Aftermath: Yoshida Shigeru and the Japanese experience, 1878-1954.* Cambridge, MA: Harvard East Asian Monographs.

The Economist (2003, July 24) To arms: Japan is starting to take its security responsibilities seriously. High time, too. [Online] Accessed from <http://www.economist.com/node/1940655> on 17 August, 2014.

The Economist (2015). The buds of March, March 28. [Online] Accessed from <http://www.economist.com/node/21647340/print> on 9 April, 2015.

Green, M. and Hornung, J.W. (2014, July 10) Ten myths about Japan's collective self-defense change. *The Diplomat.* [Online] Accessed from <http://thediplomat.com/2014/07/ten-myths-about-japans-collective-self-defense-change/> on 19 August 2014.

Hook, G., Gilson J., Hughes, C.W., and Dobson, H. (2005) *Japan's International Relations: Politics, economics and security.* Okon, UK: Sheffield Centre for Japanese Studies/Routledge Series.

Hughes,. C.W. (2004) *Japan's Re-emergence as a 'Normal' Military Power?* Oxford: Oxford University Press.

International Christian University-Washington State University (ICU-WSU) (2004-2005) Studies of Attitudes and Global Engagement (SAGE) Poll. [Online] Accessed from <www.wsu.edu/pols/sage/data.htm> on 18 August 2014.

The Japan Times (2003, August 9). Go! Go! Peace! The SDF wants you.

The Japan Times (2013, December 29). 69% say Abe should heed fallout from Yasukuni poll. [Online] Accessed from<http://www.japantimes.co.jp/news/2013/12/29/

national/69-say-abe-should-heed- fallout-from-yasukuni-poll/#.U_LIcLySwt0> on 19 August 2014.

The Japan Times (2014 a, August 17). Japan plans fund to develop military technology with universities. [Online] Accessed from <http://www.japantimes.co.jp/news/2014/08/17/ national/japan-plans-fund-develop- military-technology-universities/#.U_K-EbySwt2> on 19 August 2014.

The Japan Times (2014 b, August 19). SDF struggling to attract enough reservists, August 19. [Online] Accessed from <http://www.japantimes.co.jp/news/2014/08/19/national/sdf-struggling-to-attract- enough-reservists/#.U_K81bySwt0> on 19 August 2014.

The Japan Times (2014 c, August 3). 84% of public says explanation of collective defense position unclear: poll. [Online] Accessed from <http://www.japantimes.co.jp/news/2014/08/03/ national/84-public-says-explanation-collective-defense-decision-unclear-poll/> on 19 August 2014.

Jeffs, A. (2007, April 4) 'Don of Roppongi' seeks peace in East Asia. *The Japan Times*. [Online] Accessible from http://www.japantimes.co.jp/community/2007/04/07/general/ don-of-roppongi-seeks-peace-in-east-asia/

Katzenstein, P.J. (1996) *Cultural Norms and National Security: Police and military in postwar Japan.* Ithaca, NY: Cornell University Press.

Lind, J. (2004) Pacifism or passing the buck? Testing theories of Japanese security policy. *International Security* 29 (1): 92-12.

Lincoln, E. (2003, April) Japan: Using power narrowly. *The Washington Quarterly* 27(1): 111-127.

Mearsheimer, J.J. (2001) *The Tragedy of Great Power Politics*, New York: W.W. Norton.

Midford, P. (2011) *Rethinking Japanese Public Opinion and Security: From pacifism to realism?* Stanford: Stanford University Press

NHK (2015, February 9). Support for hostage crisis response. [Online] Accessed from http:// www3.nhk.or.jp/nhkworld/english/news/backstories/20150209.html. on 9 April, 2015.

Nikkei Asian Review (2014, July 28) Public support for Abe cabinet falls below 50%. [Online] Accessed from <http://asia.nikkei.com/Politics-Economy/Policy-Politics/Public-support-for-Abe-cabinet-slips-under-50> on 19 August 2014.

Pew Research Center (2013) *Global Attitudes Project Japan Report Final: July 11, 2013*. [Online] Accessed from <http://www.pewglobal.org/files/2013/07/Pew-Research-Center-Global-Attitudes- Project-Japan-Report-FINAL-July-11-2013.pdf> on 4 April 2014.

Pyle, K.B. (1996) *The Japanese Question: Power and purpose in a new era, second edition*. Washington, D.C.: The AEI Press.

Stahler, K. (2013, December 9) Mutual mistrust: Japanese views of South Korea. *Peterson Institute of International Economics*.[Online] Accessed from <http: //blogs.piie.com/nk/?p=12439> on 4 April 2014.

Snyder, J.L. (1991) *Myths of Empire: Domestic politics and international ambition*, Ithaca, NY: Cornell UP.

Stockholm International Peace Research Institute (SIPRI) (2013) The share of the world's military expenditure of the 15 states with the highest expenditure in 2013. [Online] Accessed from <http://www.sipri.org/research/armaments/milex/milex-graphs-for-data-launch-2014/The-share-of-world-military-expenditure-of-the-15-states-with-the-highest-expenditure-in-2013.png> on 17 August 2014.

Twomey, C.P. (2000) Japan, a 'circumscribed balancer'- building on defensive realism to make predictions about East Asian security. *Security Studies*, 9 (4): 167-205.

Waltz, K. (1979) *Theory of International Politics*. Reading, MA: Addison-Wesley.

Yomiuri Shimbun (2007, April 6th). *Kenpou-no yakuwari kou-hyouka 15-nenkan Kaisei ta-suu* (Fifteen years of evaluating Constitution's role: Majority say "revise".)

Yomiuri Shimbun(2013, February 15th). *Nichi-bei dōmei jūshi tsuyomaru* (Strengthen emphasis on US-Japan alliance.)

Yoshida, R. (2003, December 10) Koizumi's credibility placed on the line. *The Japan Times*. [Online] Accessible from <http://www.japantimes.co.jp/news/2003/12/10/national/koizumis-credibility-placed-on-the-line/#.VX03s0bPrL8>

CHAPTER 9

The Israeli-Palestinian conflict: simulacra of peacemaking

Esta Tina Ottman

Introduction

The search for peace in the Israel-Palestine conflict focuses mainly on peacemaking, despite the fact that over 30 years have passed since 'the end of the peace process'[1], the 1983 Declaration of Principles on Interim Self-Government Arrangements (the 'Oslo' Accords). As far as Israelis and Palestinians are concerned, since then there has been a great deal of process and even less peace, suggesting that answers are likely to lie elsewhere, beneath the layers of process. Specifically, the author argues, it is the strong currents of unresolved collective trauma, continually resurfacing, which hinder all forms of conflict resolution, including the positivist elite Track 1 and Track 2 conflict resolution approaches.

Kelman (1998, p.9) suggests that international conflict *'must be viewed as not merely an intergovernmental or interstate phenomenon, but also as an intersocietal phenomenon'* (author's italics). Historically speaking, the roots of the current conflict lie in the settlement of growing numbers of Jews in Ottoman and Mandate Palestine, producing what we might now consider to be an *intergroup conflict* of 'majorities and minorities' (Fisher, 2000, location 2507-15) based on 'real differences between groups in terms of social power, access to resources, important life values, or other significant incompatibilities' (Fisher, 2000, location 2515-22). Indeed, Fisher (1989) defines conflict itself as social, citing Daniel Katz's 'economic, value and power differences' as 'useful' typologies therein (Fisher, 2000, location 2541-48) and adding 'needs' (a further categorization deriving from the work of Abraham Maslow, Paul Sites, John Burton, Edward Azar and others) and adding the notion that most complex conflicts contain mixtures of such categories. Yet official peacemaking processes have largely approached the Israel-Palestine conflict through the lens of standard 'security dilemma' international relations theory, treating the dispute as an *interstate issue*, notwithstanding the fact that it is 'essentially, an intergroup conflict' as Barak (2005, p.

720) argues. Despite the continuing absence of a United Nations Security Council-recognized state of Palestine, the propensity for all parties (including 'interested outsiders') to adhere to 'hegemonic notions of conflict and peace that stipulated that both were the prerogative of sovereign states' including 'interstate theories of peacemaking' (Barak, 2005, p. 720) is marked.

This chapter considers critically the major processes and initiatives that have taken place since 1991, when the parties commenced an official process of recognition and negotiation. Thus what follows is not merely a critical account of peacemaking in the Israel-Palestine conflict, but an accounting for failures; in some cases, what might have been, with the infuriating luxury of hindsight, and with other lenses of perception.

The discussion will largely be confined to issues concerning Israel and the Palestinians, rather than wider Arab-Israeli processes, and will be organized according to official Track I processes; Track II peace initiatives. The status of official and civil society peacebuilding projects and activities (in the case of the latter, through NGOs, education and outreach, cultural activities, reconciliation and non-violent strategic cooperation) will be dealt with in a subsequent study.

Official Track I processes

Giving any account of peacemaking in the Israel-Palestine requires deep contextualization, but within the constraints of this chapter there are certain discernible milestones; perhaps many of these would have not have occurred without the end of the Cold War, the breakdown of the former Soviet Union and the ending of the bipolar international system.

First contacts

The first Palestinian *Intifada,* a five-year-long civil society-led uprising that commenced in the refugee camps of Gaza in December 1987 and spread to the West Bank including East Jerusalem, employed a range of strategies of non-violent confrontation, with its use of popular committees, and also many episodes of violent resistance. Pappe (2004, p. 235) records that in the first year alone, '400 refugees were killed in clashes with the Israeli army,' while thousands (including many women and children) were injured through beatings and the use of live ammunition and rubber bullets.[2] The solidarity and organizational skills demonstrated by Palestinians unsettled both the Israeli and the marginalized Palestine Liberation Organization (PLO) leaderships (the latter exiled to Tunis since expulsion from Lebanon in 1981). On 31st July 1988, King Hussein of Jordan renounced legal and administrative ties to the West Bank, creating a further vacuum. Thus when the Palestine National Council (PNC) met in Algeria, it attempted to regain the official initiative by declaring a Palestinian state (on November 15th, 1988)[3] and supporting the *Intifada.* The PNC also called for 'an effective international conference on …the question of Palestine, under the auspices of the United Nations and with the participation of the permanent members of the Security Council and all parties to the conflict in the region, including the Palestine Liberation Organization' (UNGA 1988, A/43/827). This marked the first pragmatic acknowledgement of a possible two-state 'partition' solution based on UN Resolution 181, and therefore implicit recognition of Israel (both equally risky positions for the PLO, and in contravention of the Palestinian National Charter). Although the language of the Algiers Declaration was ambiguous on this and on renouncing violence (which had previously led both the Israeli government and the US Secretary of State Kissinger to reject official contact with the PLO) it was sufficient to establish a back-channel for negotiations with the U.S. and led ultimately, to the 1991 Madrid Conference and its antecedents.

Jointly sponsored by the U.S. and the soon-to-be-extinct USSR, the Madrid Conference, hosted in the Spanish capital from October 30, 1991, came to fruition as a result of intensive 'shuttle diplomacy' to the Middle East by US Secretary of State James Baker, following the outbreak of the Gulf War (in which the PLO had disastrously backed Iraq). Israeli Prime Minister Yitzhak Shamir's opening speech at the conference rehearsed a characteristic epic narrative of traumatic Jewish suffering, intertwined with Zionist mythology:

> Jews have been persecuted through the ages in every continent. Some countries have barely tolerated us; others oppressed, tortured, slaughtered and exiled us. This century saw the Nazi regime set out to exterminate us, The Shoah—the Holocaust, the catastrophic genocide of unprecedented proportions … became possible because no one defended us, Being homeless, we were also defenseless …the rebirth of the State of Israel so soon after the Holocaust has made the world forget that our claim is immemorial. We are the only people who have lived in the Land of Israel without interruption for nearly 4,000 years. (Shamir, 1991, pp. 388-389)

This is one of many similar and widely-reported utterances of Israel's politicians, which represent the extensive recycling of traumatic narratives. Without wishing to ascribe complete agency to an elected leader, such patterns of iteration are constantly accessible through media repetition and embedded throughout all stages of the education of secular Israelis.

From the Palestinian delegation, Dr. Hayder Abd el-Shafi offered an eloquent and equally unrelenting portrayal of the collective suffering of the occupied:

> The Palestinian people are one, fused by centuries of history in Palestine, bound together by a collective memory of shared sorrows and joys … We come here wrenched from our brothers and sisters in exile to stand before you as the Palestinians under occupation … We have been denied the right to publicly acknowledge our loyalty to our leadership and system of government. … We

come to you from a tortured land and a proud, though captive people, having been asked to negotiate with our occupiers, but leaving behind the children of the intifada and a people under occupation and under curfew who enjoined us not to surrender or forget. (Abd al-Shafi, 1991, pp. 94-395)

The precedent-setting bilateral talks with Israel and its neighbours Syria, Lebanon and Jordan eventually led to a peace treaty with Jordan, and further talks with Syria; a separate multilateral negotiating track also focused on issues (refugees, water, environment, arms control, economic development) and continued after Madrid until it eventually petered out. Meanwhile negotiations with the 'Palestinian-Jordanian' delegation focused on interim self-government arrangements with the ultimate goal of permanent status talks, a pattern repeated in the later Declaration of Principles on Interim Self-Government Arrangement (the 'Oslo Accords' or DOP) that emerged as a result of more substantive post-Madrid non-public Track II discussions in the Norwegian capital.

While post-Madrid talks were continuing, Deputy Minister of Foreign Affairs Yossi Beilin, (later co-author of the 2003 Geneva Accord peace plan) and Norwegian academic Terje Rød-Larsen put together a clandestine meeting in London for Israeli history professor Yair Hirschfeld and a PLO representative Ahmed Qurei (Abu 'Alaa) with the support of Beilin's opposite number in Norway, Jan Egland. The talks on the notion of an accord continued on in Oslo at Rød-Larsen's Fafo Institute, supported by Shimon Peres (then minister of foreign affairs), who later dispatched further Israeli representatives to contribute to the unofficial talks.

Social and political psychologists Herbert Kelman and Nadim Rouhana additionally provided context towards the Oslo process with a series of more than 30 interactive problem-solving workshops for Israeli and Palestinian Track II leaders in order to change the flow of the 'conflict ethos' (Bar-Tal, 2007). Politically influential 'cadres' of Palestinians and Israelis took part in the workshops from the 1970s to the 1990s (Kelman, 2005) and even after the Oslo Accords, until the second *Intifada*. Yet despite the modest co-acknowledgement of identities and humanities and the notion of a two-state solution, progress was not maintained. A number of interim agreements were signed[4] resulting in the division of the West Bank into areas 'A' (fully PNA-controlled, but only three percent of the territory, although ostensibly 60% PNA-controlled in Gaza), 'B' (jointly controlled by Israel and the PNA, 27% of the territory) and 'C' (solely controlled by Israel, but 70% of the West Bank); meanwhile East Jerusalem remained consigned to 'final status negotiations'. Many theories have been evinced as to the deep deficiencies of the Oslo Accords (Sharabi *et al*, 1997; Karon, 2000; Said, 2000; Shlaim, 2005; Rynhold, 2008; Baumgart-Ochse, 2009; Sela, 2009; Turner, 2012; Clarno, 2013; Elgindy, 2013; Jabareen, 2013; Scheller, Wildangel and Paul, 2013; Shlaim, 2013, Turner and Shweiki, 2014) and the psyches of the leaders themselves (Arafat, the assassinated Rabin and Ehud Barak, whose disastrous premiership contributed to the country's later rightwards swing).[5] Meanwhile all further discursive, therapeutic and conciliatory approaches were abandoned; the limitations of Kelman's approach are evidenced through its inability to achieve longitudinal integration and to mainstream sufficiently throughout all areas of the peace process.

At the time, many Israelis received the process with enthusiasm and optimism; many new projects and joint ventures were launched; it 'seemed to represent the new post-Cold War/ post-Gulf War era, which ostensibly heralded the beginning of a "new world order" under American hegemony' (Sela, 2009, p.105). Later, however, a different story would emerge. The process was one of elites more concerned with formal agreements, and less substantively with sustainable peace rooted in civil society. Hermann (2009) reveals that none of the original architects of the Oslo Accords—who later published various books telling the epic story[6]— mentioned the Israeli peace movement's contribution to the peace process, 'The movement that took as its banner peace with the Palestinians and strove for years to achieve this goal is not given a single line in all of these authoritative accounts of the process, as if the movement had never existed' (Hermann, 2009, locations 151-65). Despite its marginalized status, argues Hermann, the peace movement was responsible for 'influencing the climate of opinion in Israel by persistently putting forward some unconventional and much-contested alternative readings of the conflict, thereby cultivating the ground for the transformation from armed conflict to peace negotiations ... for the strategic policy shift that the Oslo process embodied' (Hermann, 2009, locations 239-51). Moreover, Israeli peace activists, asserts Hermann, were consistently excluded and disregarded in the vital process of peacemaking and peacebuilding.

> Not one Israeli activist as such has ever been invited to join the many Israeli delegations to the peace talks. No representative of the movement participated in the signing ceremonies ... Furthermore, none of Israel's prime ministers who were in office during the relevant era ... ever initiated contacts with the peace movement, let alone used the movement's open channels of communication to the Palestinian side to push the process forward. None of them publicly recognized the movement's activity or acknowledge any contribution that it might have made to the passage from armed conflict to peace negotiations. (Hermann, 2009, Locations 165-79)

Pappe (2004, p.242) equally denounces the Oslo Process for being 'devised' by leaders of the Israeli Zionist left, in particular Yossi Beilin. With hindsight, *Ha'aretz* journalist Ari Shavit asserts:

> When you say 'The Oslo Peace Process' you say 'Yossi Beilin'. Together with the exacerbation of the collapse of the Oslo process, and with the deepening of the violent conflict between Israelis and Palestinians, Yossi Beilin is being perceived by more and more circles [in the Israeli society] as the founding

father of this catastrophe. He is the antihero of invective articles, he is the big villain of the Right's poster boards, he is public enemy number one, the new target of blame for the Palestinian guilt, and for the death of the partner. (Shavit, 2001)

In a series of essays originally written for the Arab and Western press, Said (2000) famously dissected the Oslo process's 'total obliviousness to the interests of the Palestinian people, as well as its enhancement of Israel's position by propaganda and unstinting political pressure' (Said, 2000, p.5). He also railed at the 'cowardly and slavish' failings of the Palestinian leadership who succumbed to the process that brought them only further dispossession, as PM Ehud Barak later continued to build settlements in defiance of the Oslo spirit (Said, p.xiii). As Said (2000), Finkelstein (2003) and Pappe (2004) noted, the agreements deferred all work on substantive issues—Jerusalem, water, reparations, sovereignty, security, land—while the picture became still bleaker for Palestinians.[7] Most surreal of all was the disconnect between 'the rhetoric and the actualities of that peace' (Said, 2000, p.312) in which the existence of a Palestinian people had finally been discovered and acknowledged, but passed over. Like a raging Cassandra, Said made himself extremely unpopular in certain quarters of the Western media for his forthright criticisms of the Oslo Accords and their antecedents, which were treated as 'fact' and thereafter recipient of 'liberal peace' donor schemes.[8]

Like Palestinian intellectual and former Israel Knesset member (now in exile) Azmi Bishara, Said saw potential for reframing the Israel-Palestine conflict through expanding the notion of citizenship. He envisioned a modern, secular nation-state, arguing for a multicultural, multi-ethnic, religiously diverse Palestine, which 'is and always has been a land of many histories', not only Arabs and Jews, but 'Canaanites, Moabites, Jebusites, and Philistines in ancient times, and Romans, Ottomans, Byzantines, and Crusaders in the modern ages', a vision once shared by Jewish intellectuals such as Judah Magnes, Martin Buber and Hannah Arendt before 'the logic of Zionism overwhelmed their efforts' (Said, 2000, p.318).

It was not to be; societies engulfed in repeated patterns of collective trauma require more than semi-committed elite processes to let go of generations of pain, as Beilin reflected: 'After all, we are making an agreement unwillingly. The facial expressions of Yitzhak Rabin and Yasser Arafat when they shook hands [on the White House lawn, September 13, 1993] symbolizes the whole process to this day' (Sharvit, 2001).

After Oslo

For many, the Oslo process ended with the assassination of Israeli premier Yitzhak Rabin on November 4th, 1995; formally, however, its five-year interim period expired (without any sign of a final resolution) on May 4th, 1999. Between July 11th-24th, 2000, a desperate attempt to revive peace process momentum was made by U.S. President Bill Clinton, who convened the newly-elected Ehud Barak and Yasser Arafat at the symbolic site of Camp David, the scene of the peace negotiations between Egyptian President Sadat and Israeli Prime Minister Menachem Begin in 1978. There were radically different perceptions of what was on offer (Pressman, 2003), and in any case the controversial talks did not end in any substantive settlement. Initially, the Israeli account of events prevailed:

> In accounts of what happened at the July 2000 Camp David summit and the following months of Israeli-Palestinian negotiations, we often hear about Ehud Barak's unprecedented offer and Yasser Arafat's uncompromising no. Israel is said to have made a historic, generous proposal, which the Palestinians, once again seizing the opportunity to miss an opportunity, turned down. In short, the failure to reach a final agreement is attributed, without notable dissent, to Yasser Arafat. (Malley and Agha, 2001)

On the table for discussion were yet again, percentages of West Bank land to be returned to the Palestinians, which were described later by the Palestinian side as 'cantonments'; conditions for Palestinian statehood and security (such as maintaining demilitarization); return of refugees and reparations, and Jerusalem. After a further round of talks under EU sponsorship in Taba, Egypt, on 21st-27th January, 2001, a joint statement was issued to the effect that 'Given the circumstances and time constraints [impending Israeli elections], it proved impossible to reach understandings on all issues, despite the substantial progress that was achieved in each of the issues discussed' (according to the joint statement released by Israeli and Palestinian negotiators).[9] Barak's perception of the 'true' Palestinian subtext reveals his existential traumatised pathology:

> What they [Arafat and his colleagues] want is a Palestinian state in all of Palestine. What we see as self-evident, [the need for] two states for two peoples, they reject. Israel is too strong at the moment to defeat, so they formally recognize it. But their game plan is to establish a Palestinian state while always leaving an opening for further "legitimate" demands down the road. For now, they are willing to agree to a temporary truce à la Hudnat Hudaybiyah [a temporary truce that the Prophet Muhammad concluded with the leaders of Mecca during 628–629, which he subsequently unilaterally violated]. They will exploit the tolerance and democracy of Israel first to turn it into "a state for all its citizens," as demanded by the extreme nationalist wing of Israel's Arabs and extremist left-wing Jewish Israelis. Then they will push for a binational state and then, demography and attrition will lead to a state with a Muslim majority and a Jewish minority. This would not necessarily involve kicking out all the Jews. But it would mean the destruction of Israel as a Jewish state. This, I believe, is their vision. They may not talk about it often, openly, but this is their

> vision. Arafat sees himself as a reborn Saladin—the Kurdish Muslim general
> who defeated the Crusaders in the twelfth century—and Israel as just another,
> ephemeral Crusader state. (Morris, 2002)

Bill Clinton was to try one more time before he ended his term of office—after the commencement of the Second 'Al Aqsa' *Intifada* in September 2000—with a series of proposals known as the Clinton Parameters, which covered familiar issues such as Jerusalem, territory, refugees, security and conflict end-point[10]. The Israeli cabinet voted to accept the Parameters, although Barak (also soon to be voted out of office) sent 20 pages of reservations back to Clinton, largely concerning Jerusalem and refugees; on January 3, 2001, Yasser Arafat accepted the Parameters; and that is the last that was heard of them.

The Bush administration's contribution to Israel-Palestinian peacemaking began with the Senator George Mitchell's Sharm El-Sheikh Fact-Finding Report on the worsening of the violence of the Second *Intifada*, published on April 30th, 2001. The report became the basis of President G.W. Bush's Roadmap for Peace.[11]

The Roadmap, under the supervision of the Quartet (the U.S., E.U., Russia and the U.N.) reframed the settlement of the Israeli-Palestinian conflict into three phases, describing itself as 'performance-based and goal driven, with clear phases, timelines, target dates, and benchmarks aiming at progress through reciprocal steps by the two parties' (U.N., 2002). Phase I demanded 'an unconditional cessation of violence', rebuilding and restructuring of security forces, institution building and an 'unequivocal statement reiterating Israel's right to exist in peace and security' from Palestinians; and from Israelis, withdrawal of troops from areas occupied since September 28th, 2002, the usual 'commitment to the two-state vision of an independent, viable, sovereign Palestinian state', a freeze on settlements and improvements of the humanitarian situation. Phase II (envisaged for June-December 2003) provided for a return to Madrid/Oslo working methods: an international conference, multilateral negotiations on substantive issues, while Phase III (2004-2005) foresaw a second international conference aiming at final status agreements and the end of the conflict, including sticking points such as Jerusalem, refugees and settlements.

The Israeli response to the Roadmap was an immediate rejection to settlement freeze and 14 modifying conditions[12]; the autocratic Arafat accepted the appointment of a first-ever prime minister—Mahmoud Abbas (Abu Mazen)—but the process was derailed by another severe outbreak of violence. Islamic Jihad, Hamas, Fatah and the Democratic Front for the Liberation of Palestine (DFLP) then agreed to a *hudna* (temporary cessation of hostilities), which fell apart in August 2003. Thus the Roadmap to nowhere, an imposed but unenforceable process, petered out; in 2004 Arafat died in Paris, permitted to leave his besieged Muqata compound for emergency medical treatment; in 2006, one year after the unilateral Israeli disengagement from Gaza, Prime Minister Ariel Sharon also passed from the political scene, entering a coma after a severe stroke. Meanwhile the 2006 election of Hamas in the Palestinian parliamentary elections began a new round of hostilities with Gaza, culminating in its blockade and Israel's bloody 'Operation Cast Lead' attack on Gaza in December 2008-January 2009 in response to rocket attacks on southern Israeli towns.

Sharon's successor Ehud Olmert pledged to continue the Roadmap, and indeed took part in numerous meetings with Mahmoud Abbas prior to a further peace conference in 2007 hosted by President G.W. Bush and attended by Quartet representatives in Annapolis, Maryland, on the two-state solution and the Jerusalem question. In an unusually unequivocal acceptance of a future Palestinian state for an Israeli prime minister, Olmert was reported to have said, 'I believe that we will be able to reach an agreement [in 2008] that will fulfill the vision of President Bush: Two states for two peoples,' (Benhorin, 2007), while around him coalition partners, such as the ultra-orthodox Shas party, threatened to pull out at the mention of division of Jerusalem (Sela, 2007). The writing was already on the wall for the artificially fast-tracked Annapolis process: a large demonstration of right-wing members of Knesset and Yesha (Judea and Samaria settler movement members) massed in Jerusalem one day prior to the commencement of the conference. A colourful account of the protest shows the extent of in-group fighting at the time, and hence the extent of the challenge of peacemaking in a non-homogeneous Israeli society (Weiss, 2007).

Olmert resigned in 2008; Israel's drift further rightwards was consolidated by the election of pro-settlement Likud party leader Benjamin Netanyahu as prime minister (for a second term of office) and the appointment of the ultranationalist Avigdor Lieberman as foreign minister, who declared the Annapolis process non-binding and moribund, saying 'Those who want peace should prepare for war and be strong' (Sofer, 2009).

Finally, it is important to note that not all Track I peace initiatives were U.S. or Quartet sponsored: at various times both Egypt (pre-revolution) and Turkey (prior to PM Erdogan's tough stance with Israel's killing of nine Turkish Gaza-bound activists aboard the Mavi Marmara in 2010) have attempted limited mediation in the Israel-Palestine conflict. Moreover, a Middle East regional discourse process was launched in 2002, with the Saudi Peace Initiative, proposed by then-Crown Prince Abdullah (also known as the Arab Peace Initiative). Adopted in Beirut in March 28, 2002, at the Council of the League of Arab States, and re-endorsed in 2007 at the Arab League's summit in Riyadh, the proposal (still on the table) calls for Israel's withdrawal to all 1967 borders; a Palestinian state in the West Bank and Gaza Strip; and a 'just solution to the Palestinian refugee problem … in accordance with U.N. General Assembly Resolution 194' (Council of the League of Arab States, 2002). Unsurprisingly, successive Israeli prime ministers have officially rejected the plan (while some Israeli politicians privately appreciated Saudi goodwill). Meanwhile the Palestinian Authority (but not Hamas) has supported it.

Track II peace initiatives

This section will examine three non-state peace proposals launched by Israeli and Palestinian leading politicians, the Geneva Accord[13], the People's Voice Plan and the Elon Peace Plan, now known as the Israeli Initiative, *HaYozma HaIsraelit*[14] (all 2003), and finally describes the Kairos initiative of Palestinian Christians in 2010.

These are not the sum of all peace proposals that have ever been promulgated post-Oslo, but they have been selected as the most prominent. None of the proposals were formally adopted, but primarily they can be regarded as peacebuilding initiatives: their function was not only to suggest a way out of intractable conflict, but also to raise awareness in Israeli society, and hope in Palestinian society for an end to conflict.

The Elon Peace Plan (aka the Israeli initiative/ the Right Road to Peace)

Whether or not this controversial plan qualifies as a 'peace plan', other than by virtue of its name, is debatable, due to its association with Moledet.[15] Moledet is the Israeli political party most associated (along with even further right proto-fascist party Kach, founded by Rabbi Meir Kahane) with the notion of promoting 'transfer' of Palestinian Arabs to countries outside of Palestine. The plan was the brainchild of West Bank settlement resident Rabbi Binyamin (Benni) Alon, who served at the time of its instigation (2002) as tourism minister.[16] The proposal envisaged that Jordan would become the new Palestinian state, and that the West Bank and Gaza should be officially annexed to the state of Israel, with Arab Palestinian population at first receiving Jordanian citizenship and later being encouraged to relocate to 'Jordan is Palestine'.[17] Refugee camps in neighbouring countries were to be dismantled, and their populations absorbed by those countries (such as Lebanon and Jordan). The notion of 'Jordan is Palestine' did not find favour with Crown Prince Hassan, who reportedly met with Alon (Arutz 7 Israel National News, 2004) and it was downgraded in later versions of the plan.

The promotional discourse for the 'moral, practical and simple' Elon Peace Plan claims that "the Oslo dream has become a nightmare" and that it has:

> … not brought about peace but rather a whirlpool of blood …Neither have the Palestinians reaped any benefits from the Oslo Agreement. Poverty and suffering and a regime that employs terrorism against its own citizens [the PA] are the net results of the Oslo approach. (Elon, n.d.)

The unsuspecting consumer of the proposal literature may be struck by the concern for 'the human tragedy' of Palestinian refugees, a key element of the plan, which aims at 'a **humanitarian** solution to the Palestinian problem, instead of a **political** one' but soon learns that it is equivocated by the notion of Jewish refugees, made homeless by World War II and by Arab governments on the establishment of the state of Israel:

> With the establishment of the State of Israel, hundreds of thousands of Arabs were displaced and since then have remained homeless. The Palestinian refugee camps in the West Bank and Gaza are not their homes, but rather temporary stations.
>
> The question that remains open is not whether they will return to their homes. They will not return to their homes, just as Jews will not return to Poland, Iraq or Morocco. The question is how to rehabilitate and resettle them in spite of the fact that they have been uprooted from their homes.
>
> Amazingly, this question has hardly been asked. For many years, Israel preferred to ignore the refugee problem in the hope that in time, it would resolve itself. Successive governments have chosen to stick their heads in the sand when faced with the looming fear of the refugee issue. (Elon, 2008)

For now the uninational proposal remains one of the less well-known peace plans, but a review of its newsletters at the plan's website (http://www.israelinitiative.com/)reveals that it has made some inroads in gaining support (and possibly funding) with certain kinds of American Christian Zionists.[18]

The People's Voice

Officially presented at a Tel Aviv press conference on June 25th 2003, the People's Voice (in Hebrew, the National Consensus) was the work of former Shin Bet chief Ami Ayalon[19] and Palestinian intellectual Sari Nusseibah. The Ayalon-Nusseibah proposal recommends a 'two-states for two peoples' solution, based on an adherence to 1967 borders in principle with some land-swap possible exchanges included, and some geographical unspecified connection linking the non-contiguous Gaza and the West Bank; Jerusalem as a shared capital of both states, and Palestinian refugees controversially returning to the demilitarized Palestinian state. Equally controversial is the notion that Israel is the state of the Jewish people (a notion that the PA currently refuses to endorse) while Palestine would be the state of the Palestinian people. The plan is more often referred to in its absence, being a one-page document that did not have further development.

The Geneva Accord

The Geneva Accord, funded and supported by the Swiss Foreign Ministry, is the most developed of all the Track II peace plans, taking into account the work done on other peace initiatives. The 47-page Accord was ceremonially launched in Geneva by Israeli politician Yossi Beilin (also involved in the Oslo DOP, mentioned above) and Palestinian Authority politician Yasser Abed Rabbo on 1st December 2003 after 36 months of discussion.[20]

The negotiators of the Geneva Accord realized the importance of marketing the Accord (it was translated into major languages spoken in Israel and mailed to the entire population) and moreover, it continues to be refined and developed; in September 2009, for example, the Geneva Initiative published a further series of 13 annexes on key issues.[21] Essentially the Accord provides a two-states-for-two peoples solution, similar to other peace plans (excluding the Elon Peace Plan), but is far more detailed and comprehensive, and provides for full settlement of the conflict rather than interim stages (such as the DOP) or goal-driven deadlines (like the Roadmap). The Accord does not, however, decide the fate of Palestinian refugees, although it offers limited return (but not right of return) for some refugees, and defers to UN Resolution 194 in principle, which offers refugees a choice between return or compensation; the mere notion of partial acquiescence on refugee return was much criticized by the Israeli right. A major 'concession' of the Accord—again much criticized by the Israeli right and in particular the late PM Sharon himself—is the ceding of the Temple Mount to Palestinian control, although the Jewish Western Wall would remain under Israeli supervision.

Reaction to the Geneva Accord ranged from cautiously positive (the U.S. government welcomed the Accord while preferring its own official interstate Roadmap that had Israeli governmental support) to highly critical: Palestinian Arabs living in Israel did not feel included; Hamas and Islamic Jihad openly opposed the Accord; there were questions about a peace plan funded by foreign governments (the Japanese as well as the Swiss were rumoured to have been involved); the Israeli right, especially PM Sharon, attacked the plan for ceding 'Greater Israel'. Former Russian refusenik and prisoner of conscience, then Israeli minister for Jerusalem and Diaspora Affairs Natan (Anatoly) Sharansky complained:

> This gang seems to have forgotten, or hasn't yet understood, that as much as we long and hope for peace, it is not a value that stands by itself. It is an essential condition for the existence of a country that wishes to live, but it isn't the goal. It was not for the sake of peace that the State of Israel was established, and it was not because of peace that millions of Jews gathered here.
>
> Nor was it peace for which the Jewish people prayed for thousands of years. The Jewish people prayed for Jerusalem. Because of Jerusalem, the Jewish

people returned to Israel from the four corners of the earth, for it they were willing to make all the necessary sacrifices. For that same dream of a thousand generations – "next year in rebuilt Jerusalem." (Sharansky, 2003)

Above all, the formulators of the Accord were compelled to defend the fact that they had produced what appeared to be an official document with no official status and no government mandate:

> The Geneva initiative is a model, not a formal document between governments. It is a proposal for a permanent agreement, agreed upon by the two sides. Two things make it special - it delineates the end of the conflict and does not leave any question marks over anything. All the details, down to the last, have been resolved and neither side has any more demands. (Mitzna, 2003)

Abdel Monem Said, who attended the signing ceremony of the Accord, wondered 'what [has] happened to the Geneva Accord':

> Somehow, what was said in Geneva was so different from reality that it made people adhere more adamantly to what they had known. It is also likely that during the past three years of violence, Palestinians and Israelis discovered about each other things that made them skeptical about accepting yet another moment of idealism. The dreams of Oslo were still present in their minds, and they still recalled how those dreams were shattered on the walls of closures, home demolitions, settlement building and Apache attacks on the one hand, and suicide bombings on the other.

> All this may be true, but it is more likely that the historians will find guidance in other explanations, paramount of which is that the prevailing talk in Geneva about both parties having reached a point of fatigue was not true. Both Palestinians and Israelis still have enough of a reserve of animosity and enough energy to prolong the conflict, or at least enough to prevent the implementation of the Geneva Accord. The truth of the matter is that there are not only huge strategic reserves of accumulated hatred and abhorrence, but also other alternatives viciously nurtured by major political powers that mobilized all forces to resist the agreement in Geneva. (Monem Said, 2004)

The Kairos Initiative

Last but not least, the Kairos ('moment of truth' in ecclesiastical Greek) Document was launched in Bethlehem on December 11th, 2009, by an ecumenical group of Palestinian

Christians who wished to appeal to the wider Christian and international community about the situation of the Occupation.

The document details the painful and humiliating 'reality on the ground' of Palestinians under occupation, separated into cantonments, divided by the separation wall, and by emigration, refugeeism and 'internal [Fatah-Hamas] conflict'. It asks rhetorically what the 'international community … the political leaders in Palestine, in Israel and the Arab world' are doing, and explains the Church's involvement in the assertion, 'The problem is not just a political one. It is a policy in which human beings are destroyed, and this must be of concern to the Church' (Kairos Palestine, 2009). Noting the 'diverse' responses of Palestinians, the document dismisses 'negotiations: that was the official position of the Palestinian Authority, but it did not advance the peace process' and also 'armed resistance' which Israel merely used 'as a pretext to accuse the Palestinians of being terrorists and was able to distort the real nature of the conflict, presenting it as an Israeli war against terror, rather than an Israeli occupation faced by Palestinian legal resistance aiming at ending it' (Kairos Palestine, 2009). The document also emphasizes the special 'universal' role of the birthplace of Jesus, and reaffirms the historic connection of Palestinians to their land and the 'injustice' of exile.

Although steeped in collective trauma, the document purports to carry a message of hope for 'resolution … as indeed happened in South Africa and with so many other liberation movements in the world'. Against the 'sin' of occupation, it offers the right to nonviolent resistance through supporting campaigns and boycotts:

> We say that our option as Christians in the face of the Israeli occupation is to resist. Resistance is a right and a duty for the Christian. But it is resistance with love as its logic. It is thus a creative resistance for it must find human ways that engage the humanity of the enemy. (Kairos Palestine, 2009)

The plan does not offer strategic details for the political resolution of the conflict, different from other civil society/Track II proposals, but is more a call to action and an appeal; it has been endorsed by many Christian groups worldwide, and by South African anti-apartheid campaigner Archbishop Desmond Tutu, who offered support and solidarity (Tutu, 2009).

Conclusions, and an update

The above sections have attempted a critical analysis of Israel-Palestine Track I and Track II peace initiatives that began with mutual acknowledgment in Madrid, and expanded to envisage increasingly comprehensive and detailed political settlements. Regrettably, these have produced little peace, two bloody Gaza wars (2008-2009 and 2014, with response-reaction attacks in between) and at the time of writing, it seems that indeed, there is little possible way ahead.

Imposing a framework of peace, without deep recognition of responsibility for historical issues, cannot hold.

Notwithstanding, with little to lose, PA President Mahmoud Abbas attempted his own new strategy to create a framework by turning to the international community. On 31st October 2011, the PA was accepted as a full UNESCO member, but in December 2014 the UN Security Council rejected a Palestinian draft resolution 'that would have affirmed the "urgent need" to reach within 12 months a peaceful solution to the situation in the Middle East and would have paved the way to a Palestinian state with East Jerusalem as its capital', hence by implication permitting Palestine to move beyond observer status to full membership at the UN (UN News Center, 2014). Undeterred, the PA succeeded in April 2015 in attaining membership of the International Criminal Court (ICC, a body that is not recognized by Israel). Its prosecutor, Fatou Bensouda, launched a preliminary investigation into the possibility of war crimes committed by Israel during its Operation Cast Lead war on Gaza in 2014, which may take into account the publication of two reports (A/HRC/29/52 and A/HRC/29/CRP.4) on the war by the UN independent commission of inquiry issued in June 2015.[22] This process is still underway.

Meanwhile, on the ground, few changes are to be observed. As Sam Bahour wrote eloquently wrote (in 2011 when President Abbas commenced his UN maneouvres) 'The world seems to be in deep, collective amnesia. We have been here before … It's wake-up time' (Bahour, 2011). He reminds us of Palestinian trauma, 'Palestinians do not forget so easily. The deep wounds they carry, of dispossession since the violent creation of Israel in 1948, military occupation since 1967 and non-stop institutional discrimination against Palestinians inside Israel, have never had a chance to heal. … The facts on the ground are bitter, very bitter' (Bahour, 2011).

Likewise, much has been written on how Israelis continue to maintain their own consensus narratives of '2000 years of exile' and persecution as a form of Reichian body armour against the claims of Palestinian collective trauma; as a traumatized society, Israel 'is therefore very dangerous' (Kahan, 2015). After all this time, focusing on a new peace process (with the emphasis on process, rather than on peace and a 'just and sustainable resolution') may have little impact. The clock of history cannot be turned back to 'challenge the legality of UN Partition Plan Resolution 181 instead of seeking membership based upon it' (Bahour, 2011). Possibilities for successful peacemaking formulae must be sought through alternative approaches.

References

Abd el-Shafi, H. (1991) Speech at the Madrid Peace Conference (October 31, 1991). In Laqueur, W. and Rubin, B. (eds.) *The Israel-Arab Reader: A Documentary History of the Middle East Conflict* (6th edition). New York and London: Penguin Books.

Arutz 7 Israel National News (2004, 17th August) Benny Elon Presented "Jordan is Palestine" Plan to Prince Hassan. [Online] Accessed from http://www.israelnationalnews.com/News/News.aspx/67417#.TuTVinLjowA on 19th August 2004.

Bahour, S. (2011) Illusionary peace negotiations can only lead to a hallucinated peace. The Economist 's debate on Middle East peace, 'This house believes that bilateral Israeli-Palestinian negotiations are not currently a viable way to reach a two-state solution', October 17th, 2011 [Online]. Accessed fromhttp://www.economist.com/debate/days/view/769 on October 20th, 2011.

Barak, O. (2005) The failure of the Israeli-Palestinian peace process, 1993-2000. *Journal of Peace Research,* Vol. 42, No. 6 (November 2005): 719-736.

Bar-Tal, D. (2007). Sociopsychological Foundations of Intractable Conflicts. In*American Behavioral Scientist* 50(11) July 2007:1430-1453. Sage Publications, doi: <10.1177/0002764207302462>

Baumgart-Ochse, B. (2009) Democratization in Israel, politicized religion and the failure of the Oslo peace process. *Democratization,* 16:6: 1115-1142, DOI: 10.1080/13510340903271761

Beilin, Y. (1999) *Touching Peace: From the Oslo Accord to a Final Agreement.* London: Weidenfeld and Nicolson.

Benhorin, Y. (2007, 27th November) Israelis, Palestinians agree to launch peace talks.*YNet News.* [Online]Accessed from http://www.ynetnews.com/articles/0,7340, L-3476404,00. html on 20th January 2008.

Clarno, A. (2013)Securing Oslo: The dynamics of security coordination in the West Bank. *Middle East Report 260.* [Online] Accessed from <http://www.merip.org/mer/mer269/securing-oslo> on 2nd February, 2014.

Council of the League of Arab States (2002), Beirut Declaration on Saudi Peace Initiative-28-Mar-2002. (English translation.)[Online] Accessed from the Israel Ministry of Foreign Affairs website, <http://tinyurl.com/o5oc9so> on 4th November 2011.

Dana, T. (2015) The Structural Transformation of Palestinian Civil Society: Key Paradigm Shifts, *Middle East Critique*. DOI: 10.1080/19436149.2015.1017968

Elgindy, K. (2013, September 13th) Oslo's 20-year legacy of failure lives on. Al Jazeera English. [Online.] Accessed from <http://america.aljazeera.com/articles/2013/9/13/oslo-s-20-year-legacyoffailureliveson.html> on 4th October 2013.

Elon, B. (n.d.) The Israeli Initiative - Personal Message. [Online] From the website of The Israeli Initiative, http://www.israelinitiative.com/rewr-true/language-en_us/PersonalMessage.aspx, accessed 5th November 2011.

Elon, B. (2008) Rehabilitation of the Palestinian Refugees: A New Israeli Approach. [Online] Accessed from http://www.israelinitiative.com/rewr-true/language-en_us/Principle-33/Father-108/PrinciplesSub.aspx on 5th November 2011.

Finkelstein, N. G. (2003) *Image and Reality of the Israel-Palestine Conflict* (2nd edition). London & New York: Verso Books.

Fisher, R.J. (2000) Intergroup Conflict. In Deutsch, M., Coleman, P.T. and Marcus, E.C. (eds.) *The Handbook of Conflict Resolution: Theory and Practice* (2nd edition) [Kindle Edition]. San Francisco: Jossey-Bass.

Hermann, T.S. (2009) *The Israeli Peace Movement: A Shattered Dream* [Kindle edition]. Cambridge: Cambridge University Press.

Jabareen, H. (2013) 20 years of Oslo. *Journal of Palestine Studies*, 43(1) (Autumn 2013): 41-50. [Online] Accessed from http://www.jstor.org/stable/10.1525/jps.2013.43.1.41 on March 11th, 2014.

Kahan, H. (2015, June) 'A traumatized society is dangerous.'Mondoweiss: The war of ideas in the Middle East (website). [Online] Accessed from http://mondoweiss.net/2015/06/traumatized-society-dangerous on August 5th, 2015.

Kairos Palestine Document (2009) A moment of truth: A word of faith, hope and love from the heart of Palestinian suffering. [Online] Accessed from http://www.oikoumene.org/en/folder/documents-pdf/Kairos%20Palestine_En.pdf on 15th February 2011.

Karon, T. (2000, October 20) Ten reasons the Peace Process is all but dead. *Time* magazine. [Online.] Accessed from <http://content.time.com/time/nation/article/0,8599,58303,00.html> on 12th July 2015.

Kelman, H.C. (1998) Social-psychological contributions to peacemaking and peacebuilding inthe Middle East. *Applied Psychology: An International Review.* Vol. 47(1): 5-28.

Kelman, H. C. (2005) Interactive Problem Solving in the Israeli-Palestinian Case: Past Contributions and Present Challenges. In R. Fisher (Ed.), *Paving the way: Contributions of interactive conflict resolution to peacemaking.* Lanham, MD: Lexington Books, 2005.

Malley, R. and Agha, H. (2001, 9th August). Camp David: The Tragedy of Errors. *The New York Review of Books.* [Online] Accessed from http://www.nybooks.com/articles/archives/2001/aug/09/camp-david-the-tragedy-of-errors/ on 27th September 2011.

Mitzna, A. (2003, 16th October) They are afraid of peace. *Ha'aretz*[Online].Accessed from<http://www.haaretz.com/print-edition/opinion/they-are-afraid-of-peace-1.102885> on 7th November 2011.

Monem Said, A. (2004, 2nd November) What happened to the Geneva Accord? *Ha'aretz* [Online] Accessed from http://www.haaretz.com/print-edition/opinion/what-happened-to-the-geneva-accord-1.113686 on 5th November, 2011.

Morris, B. (2002, 13th June) Camp David and After: An Exchange (1. An Interview with Ehud Barak). *The New York Review of Books.* [Online] Accessed from <http://www.nybooks.com/articles/archives/2002/jun/13/camp-david-and-after-an-exchange-1-an-interview-wi/>on 10th November, 2011.

Pappe, I. (2004)*A History of Modern Palestine: One Land, Two Peoples.*Cambridge: Cambridge University Press.

Pressman, J. (2003) Visions in Collision: What Happened at Camp David and Taba? *International Security* 28(2) (Fall 2003): 5–43. [Online] Accessed from http://belfercenter.ksg.harvard.edu/files/pressman.pdf on 20th September 2011.

Rynhold, J. (2008) The failure of the Oslo Process: Inherently flawed or flawed implementation? *Mideast Security and Policy Studies* No. 76:1-26.

Said, E. (2000) *The End of the Peace Process: Oslo and After.* London: Granta Books.

Scheller, B., Wildangel, R., Paul, J. (Eds.) (2013, December) 20 years since Oslo: Palestinian perspectives. *Perspectives* 5. Tunis, Beirut and Ramallah: Heinrich Boll Stiftung. [Online] Accessed from https://www.boell.de/sites/default/files/perspective_issue5_decembre_2013.pdf on January 14, 2014.

Sela, N. (2007, 27ᵗʰ November) Yosef: Shas will quit government if J'lem divided. *YNet News.* [Online] Accessed from http://www.ynetnews.com/articles/0,7340, L-3476045,00.html on 20ᵗʰ September 2008.

Sela, A. (2009) Difficult dialogue: The Oslo Process in Israeli Perspective. [Online] *Macalester International,* 23: 105-138. Accessed from <http://digitalcommons.macalester.edu/macintl/vol23/iss1/11> on 7ᵗʰ November, 2011.

Shamir, Y. (1991) Speech at the Madrid Peace Conference (October 31, 1991). In Laqueur, W. and Rubin, B. (eds.) *The Israel-Arab Reader: A Documentary History of the Middle East Conflict* (6ᵗʰ edition). New York and London: Penguin Books.

Sharabi, H., Finkelstein, N.G., Tamari, S., Abdel Shafi, H., Drake, L. &Sharoni, S. (1997) *Oslo's Final Status and the Future of the Middle East.* Washington, D.C.: The Center for Policy Analysis on Palestine.

Sharansky, N. (2003, 16ᵗʰ October)Temple Mount is more important than peace. *Ha'aretz* [Online]. Accessed from <http://www.haaretz.com/print-edition/opinion/temple-mount-is-more-important-than-peace-1.102869> on 8ᵗʰ November, 2011.

Shavit, A. (2001, June 15ᵗʰ) Interview with Yossi Beilin on the Oslo Peace Process. *Ha'aretz.* [Online]. Accessed from <http://middleeast.atspace.com/article_250.html>on 17ᵗʰ September, 2011.

Shlaim, A. (2005) The rise and fall of the Oslo Peace Process. In Fawcett, L.(ed.) *International Relations of the Middle East,* Chapter 11.Oxford: Oxford University Press, 241-61.

Shlaim, A. (2013, September 12ᵗʰ) It's now clear: the Oslo peace accords were wrecked by Netanyahu's bad faith. *The Guardian.* [Online] Accessed from <http://www.theguardian.com/commentisfree/2013/sep/12/osloisraelrenegedcolonialpalestine> on September 13ᵗʰ, 2013.

Sofer, R. (2009, 1ˢᵗ April) Lieberman: Concessions won't bring peace.*YNet News.* [Online] Accessed from <http://www.ynetnews.com/articles/0,7340, L-3695840,00.html> on 2ⁿᵈ April, 2009.

Turner, M. (2012)Completing the Circle: Peacebuilding as Colonial Practice in the Occupied Palestinian Territory. *International Peacekeeping* 19(5) November 2012: 492-507. Accessed from https://www.aub.edu.lb/ifi/international_affairs/unaw/Documents/events/Mandy_Turner_IPK_Vol19_No5_November2012.pdf on 14ᵗʰ June, 2015.

Turner, M. and Shweiki, O. (2014) *Decolonizing Palestinian Political Economy: Dedevelopment and beyond.* Basingstoke: Palgrave Macmillan.

Tutu, D. (2009) Statement to be read out in Bethlehem on 11 December 2009. [Online] Accessed from <http://www.kairospalestine.ps/sites/default/Documents/Letter%20 from%20Archbishop%20Desmond%20Tutu.pdf>on 3rd November, 2011 [dead link] Available from <https://www.svenskakyrkan.se/default.aspx?id=584938>

United Nations General Assembly (1988) A/43/827 S/20278, 18 November 1988: Agenda Item 37, The Question of Palestine. Letter dated 16 November 1988 from the Deputy Permanent Observer of the Palestine Liberation Organization to the United Nations addressed to the Secretary-General. Annex I and Annex II: Political Communique. [Online] Available at <http://unispal.un.org/UNISPAL.NSF/0/6EB54A389E2DA6C6852560DE0070E392> [accessed on 10 July 2010].

UN News Center (2014, December 30th) UN Security Council action on Palestinian statehood blocked. Accessed from http://www.un.org/apps/news/story.asp?NewsID=49709#. VcI0i_l-qVA on January 2nd, 2015.

United Nations Press Centre (2002) A performance-based roadmapto a permanent two-state solution to the Israeli-Palestinian conflict. [Online]. Accessed from <http://www.un.org/ media/main/roadmap122002.html> on 2nd November 2011.

Weiss, E. (2007, 26th November) Jerusalem: Thousands rally against Annapolis. YNet News. [Online] Accessed from http://www.ynetnews.com/articles/0,7340, L-3475956,00.html on 28th November, 2007.

CHAPTER 10

The Yamba Dam: Conflict and consequences for a rural community

Hugh Palmer

> *"Considering that 80% of the people in the reservoir area are opposed, the dam definitely can't be built... we can defeat this dam." Yasuhiro Nakasone, Prime Minister of Japan 1982-1987, speaking in 1966 to a group of anti-dam petitioners.*(Shimazu and Kiyozawa, 2011, p. 35)

In 1952, the village of Kawarayu, Gunma prefecture, was growing in population and prosperity. The village had been famous for its hot springs, but relatively remote until a railway was pushed through the rugged Agatsuma gorge and began bringing tourists to the community northwest of Tokyo. In the summer of that year, an official from the Ministry of Construction (hereafter, MOC) called a village meeting and told the villagers: "A dam is going to be built here...this village will be completely flooded" (Hagiwara, 1996, p. 1). It eventually became clear that the reservoir formed by the Yamba Dam would submerge the homes of 1,170 people in Naganohara district, including those of all 623 residents of Kawarayu.

Local reaction forced the state to close its offices in the town, and for over a decade little more was officially announced about the project. By the mid-1960s it was widely assumed by locals that the dam project was dead. In 1965, however, the government announced that the dam project would proceed. During the intervening years, the state had been dealing quietly with a number of problems, one of which was the extremely high acidity of the water in the Agatsuma River. Its likely effects on a concrete dam had been pointed out by locals; officials decided that a water treatment plant would solve the problem (Aldrich, 2008, p. 100).

Opposition to the dam was strongest in Kawarayu. In the months following the re-announcement, an anti-dam citizens group, *Kiseidomei*, was formed, headed by a prominent hot spring hotel owner, Tomijiro Hida. The group lobbied legislators, held demonstrations, and organized repeated petitions to national diet politicians in Tokyo (Gorton, 1997, p. 42). In July 1966, 200 townspeople were bused to Tokyo to present a petition to Gunma's most powerful national politician, Finance Minister Takeo Fukuda. The minister told his visitors, "We don't need to include funds for investigating Yamba dam implementation in next year's budget. I am the finance minister, so even if the estimate is attached, it will be eliminated. You don't need to worry." (Shimazu and Kiyozawa, 2011, p. 34). Another diet member from Gunma, Yasuhiro Nakasone, was more explicitly supportive, saying, "Considering that 80% of the people in the reservoir area are opposed, the dam definitely can't be built. I'm opposed to building this unnecessary, ineffective dam... if you are united and join hands with us, we can defeat this dam". The petitioners went back to Gunma believing they had been promised support, but were surprised when the following year's budget included 80 million yen for preparatory work on the Yamba dam project (*ibid.*, p. 35).

For three years preparatory work by the MOC and Gunma prefectural government continued, while Hida's group continued to oppose the dam, and other smaller groups sought guarantees of greater compensation. In March 1969, a group of senior diet members visited Hida's hot spring hotel in an effort to persuade the anti-dam group to accept the prefecture's proposals. The senior official present waited for some initial heated exchanges to die down, then stood and made a proposal: "If you make a statement recognizing the prefecture's reconstruction study, I'll take responsibility on behalf of the Liberal Democrat Party (LDP) to promise that you will receive assistance and not be victimized". After 10 hours of heated give and take, at four in the morning a distressed and exhausted Hida agreed to make a statement accepting a MOC proposal to conduct a study on "the resettlement of residents in new villages and the reconstruction of livelihoods" (Shimazu and Kiyozawa, 2011, p. 41).

The next day, the LDP prefectural diet assembly applauded Hida as he read a short prepared statement that agreed to allow the prefecture and ministry to conduct the study, while including some qualifying language:

> ... we may be forced to go back to the drawing board, depending on whether or not we can agree and verify exactly what you will do to reconstruct the livelihoods of those residents whose land, homes and livelihoods will be destroyed by the dam project... the Prefecture and the MOC must absolutely promise that on all points they will inform your group and gain its agreement in all aspects relating to the project (*ibid.*).

Hida is said to have wept in frustration after returning to a friend's house that evening (*ibid*). The statement, even with its concessions to the anti-dam group, was a turning point for state efforts to proceed with the project. From this point on momentum began to slowly shift towards the pro-dam residents of the town, and to the MOC and the government, which had the resources and patience to wait for sentiment to shift and use the time to tackle the technical difficulties of building a dam in a highly active geothermal area.

Dams and the MOC

The Yamba dam became one of the most contentious dams in Japan partly because the struggles took place over such a long period, partly because it is situated in an area of remarkable beauty and historical and cultural interest, and partly due to its cost. It is by some accounts the most expensive dam in Japan's history. The official cost of the project is 460 billion yen (approximately five billion USD) although other sources put the likely total cost of the project at between 800 and 900 billion yen (Miyaharada, 2010, cited in Chakraborty, 2013).

Dams have been called "the cornerstone of Japan's construction state" (Aldrich, 2008, p. 96). Although sometimes contentious, dams are typically in remote, thinly-populated areas where residents rely on public construction projects for jobs and therefore have difficulty mobilizing opposition. Furthermore, older Japanese can recall disasters such as the floods that killed 1100 people when Typhoon Kathleen caused rivers to burst their banks in 1947. Although floods of this magnitude have become rare as almost all rivers have been dammed or modified, the argument that dams are necessary for flood protection still has resonance for many Japanese. While Japan's population was still growing, dams could also be promoted as necessary to ensure water supply to large cities.

Prior to the late 1960s, only one dam project attracted enough opposition to cause significant delay for the MOC and attract national attention. The Matsubara and Shimouke dams submerged the homes of 480 families, but one prominent local was wealthy and resourceful enough to disrupt plans for a decade by organizing sustained and sometimes violent resistance. This dam, however, was the exception; in most cases a combination of hard and soft social control tactics were sufficient to persuade affected residents to accept government conditions (*ibid*. p. 102). Aldrich found that size and population density of a town were important factors in the planning process for the MOC when considering potential dam sites:

> Larger towns generally have lower population densities (and) they may find it hard to rally local officials to take collective action...villages that experience a burst in population, finding it difficult to maintain the social networks and ties that facilitate collective action, are less able to present a united front against siting, and their resistance is more likely to fragment under pressures such as offers of compensation... (*ibid*, p. 44)

The communities affected by the Yamba dam fit this profile. Naganohara town and Kawarayu are separated from each other and from other affected communities by steep terrain, so that a driver following route 145 along the Agatsuma gorge sees a series of villages separated by narrow passes rather than a single, contiguous town. The "burst of population" criteria would have been met by almost any town in Japan in the early 1950s, but besides the typical postwar population growth, the area experienced a change in community climate as the new train line brought in tourists and income to a specific section of Naganohara's community: hotel owners in Kawarayu, and other owners of tourist-related businesses such as restaurants and inns (Gorton, 1997, p. 41).

It is questionable whether the farmers in the area shared in this new affluence. A 1965 questionnaire of residents of the planned reservoir area highlighted differences in attitudes between hot spring villagers and farmers; 101 Kawarayu residents were opposed to the dam and 11 were in favor, but in the nearby farming village of Kawarahata only three people were opposed, with 58 in favor (Shimazu and Kiyozawa 2011, p. 30). Compared to hotel, shop, and restaurant owners, people in farming communities seemed to be either more prepared to leave their land and accept compensation, or less inclined to believe the dam could successfully be opposed. Some pro-dam residents were characterized as renters or people with bad business locations (Gorton, 1997, p. 49). Long-term residents and business owners in Kawarayu tended to be more attached to the land or relatively affluent, and in the case of hot spring hotel owners, their business was associated with a specific area, making it difficult to relocate. The nature of civil society in a community has been found to be the most important factor for the state when choosing sites for nuclear power plants (Aldrich, 2008, p. 38) and although this appears to play less of a role in dam site selection, the quality of community solidarity in Naganohara district may have been significant both in the selection of the site and in how local opinion divided largely by area and socio-economic group.

The fact that dams announced during the post-war period were almost always completed as planned with little or no delay gave the MOC the ability to pressure residents of areas subsequently announced as dam sites. As construction of a dam, once announced, came to be seen as inevitable, uncooperative locals faced the risk of having their land forcibly purchased at prices determined by the state, so for some it was seen as wiser in the long term to cooperate with the government. One Kawarayu resident was told by a ministry official, "There has never been a dam project that has been stopped, even if local residents opposed its construction" (Shimazu and Kiyozawa, 2011, p. 39).

Many hard social controls are available to authorities wishing to site an unpopular facility in a given area. Public works projects in rural areas provide much-needed jobs, and the ability to cut funds for these gives the state a powerful tool. Excluding individuals from participation in irrigation and water resource projects is another tactic available to the state. Localities that refuse to accept facilities such as dams can be punished by cutting spending on other construction and maintenance projects that provide jobs for many residents. Several Japanese villages that publicly refused to accept dam sitings have faced administrative pressure, losing promised funding and construction assistance (Aldrich, 2008, p. 45; *ibid.*, p. 111).

As well as the "stick" of denial of funds and services, the ministry could also use the "carrot" of offering compensation to affected residents. One MOC official stated, "Once you solve the compensation problem the dam is 80% built." However, if monetary inducements failed to persuade residents to move, the final tactic of forced expropriation was available. Beginning in the early postwar period the state "... began to rely on the coercive tool of land expropriation to site dams... should bargaining over compensation break down, state officials could always rely on the tried and true tool of eminent domain"(*ibid.*, p. 103; *ibid.*, p.100).

The MOC and its even larger successor, the Ministry of Land, Infrastructure and Transport (MLIT), have a history of announcing projects with little or no prior notice or explanation, and then limiting public access to information about them, justifying this in one case by arguing that full disclosure would be "bothersome to the public as a whole" (*ibid.*, p. 112). The announcement of the Yamba dam itself without any prior explanation was consistent with this policy, as was the use of bureaucratic language to describe the assessment process which gave the villagers the impression that there was a possibility the dam would not be built (Gorton, 1997, p. 46). One early dam opponent in Kawarayu would write:

> ... notification of government's decisions, made with little consideration for the people living there, was common practice... (on the surface) the state won't force the project on us. They will put pressure on us and wait for the locals to wilt (Hagiwara 1996 cited in Nakazawa, 2012).

Until the 1990s disputes over dam construction tended to be local issues, which were given little attention by national media outlets. Nor was there any sustained national media coverage of the anti-dam movement and the issues involved in dam construction. This began to change after the 1980s, as some Japanese citizens began to question whether all the dams being planned were necessary. By the turn of the century, Japan was entering a period of depopulation, and water supply was no longer a pressing issue for most cities (Chakraborty, 2013). Disastrous floods had not occurred for decades, partly because so few unmodified rivers were left. The taxes which paid for expensive public works projects mostly originated from voters in large cities, and some civic leaders in these cities no longer saw the value in their residents' taxes being used to pay for dams. In the case of the large Tokuyama and Kawakami dams, Nagoya and Nishinomiya city withdrew from the projects (*ibid.*). In 2000, an anti-dam governor of Nagano prefecture, Yasuo Tanaka, was elected and began canceling dam projects, in one case even canceling a dam which had already been partly paid for with public funds. (*ibid.*)

Tanaka's anti-dam policies offended many powerful interests in Nagano and in the giant successor to the MOC, the "mega-ministry" MLIT. By the time Tanaka's difficult governorship ended in 2006, it was doubtful his activist policies could be sustained. His successor as governor was seen as having a better relationship with MLIT and a more flexible attitude to dam construction. One observer described the problem faced by Tanaka and other elected leaders opposing dams:

> [Successful opposition to dams] has only come from extraordinary individuals with strong independent vision, or in cases where local opposition was so strong that it could not be overridden. In general, governors are not key actors in basin governance policymaking, and they often find it extremely hard to override the combined interests of state level policymaking bodies such as the MLIT and regional level construction lobbyists, who share a close relationship based on mutual benefit. (Chakraborty, 2013).

Partly because of these factors, the post-1980s anti-dam movement has been largely urban-based. Local opposition in the rural communities where dams are sited has been affected by depopulation and the vulnerable economies of small towns. Rural areas like Naganohara have become even more dependent on public works projects than in the postwar boom years. As one small construction company owner in Naganohara put it: "I'm not wedded to the idea of building a dam here, but we need the public works to keep everyone employed" (Fackler, 2009). By the turn of the century, depopulation was seriously affecting most small towns away from the main population centers of Japan, and public works projects became a way for aging and shrinking communities to maintain enough of a tax base to survive.

Kawarayu was affected by the rural downturn even more than other small towns because many residents, sensing that the dam would eventually be built, were accepting compensation and moving out of the area. Farmers had difficulty once neighbors relocated because it took entire communities to maintain the irrigation ducts used for rice farming. One farmer did not want to leave the family home where as a three year-old he last saw his father, who died in World War II. After many of his neighbors left however, he decided he had little option but to follow them (*ibid.*). As the number of residents steadily fell, businesses suffered. Some hotels began to spend less money on upkeep or maintenance, affecting visitor numbers further. One hotel owner who had opposed the dam with his father began to believe the dam was inevitable, leading to a confrontation and split with his father after he tore down the anti-dam poster in front of the hotel (Gorton, 1997, p. 34).

Describing how local communities can be persuaded to accept development projects and, in his phrase "become project promotion agents for the state agenda," Nakazawa (2010) references sociologist Takashi Machimura's concept of "development subjection" in which in his view:

... rather than using blatant candy and whip methods such as violence and intimidation, threats or large-sum compensation, it is more effective and long-lasting to set a scene where opponents make the moves and become flag bearers for the power... making all talks proceed rapidly. (Nakazawa, 2010)

Residents of Naganohara and Kawarayu did not accept the Yamba dam "rapidly". The process took decades, but by most accounts community attitudes were shifting gradually in the 1970s. One prominent hotel owner, Yoshio Hagiwara, led one of the first anti-dam groups, but by the mid 1970s he was regarded as neutral and becoming more responsive to the idea that the community had more chance of surviving if it could negotiate the best possible compensation plan from the government before agreeing to move (Shimazu and Tomizawa, 2011, p. 43).

Similarly, when Tomijiro Hida was elected mayor of Naganohara in 1974, it meant that the leader of the main opposition group was now mayor of the largest town in the district, but Hida's actions over the next eleven years indicate that he recognized long term political, economic and population trends were working against the anti-dam movement. The mayor won delays by stalling tactics, while town officials and residents used the time gained to make over fifty research trips to other communities which had been relocated by dams. The information collected on the serious social and economic damage these communities had suffered helped Hida prepare bargaining points for negotiations with the state. In February 1985, Naganohara presented a 478-item list of reconstruction demands to the prefecture (Gorton, 1997, pp. 47-48).

Later that year, the mayor and the prefectural governor finally concluded a memorandum on a "livelihood reconstruction" plan for residents of the dam area. For previous dams, relocated residents had often been moved to unfavorable locations. Under the 1985 plan, Kawarayu village would be moved higher up the valley slopes to a new site as close as possible to the original location. Since no flat land was available there, hillsides would be bulldozed away to make a site for the new village, which would be on the shore of the newly created lake. The onsen's[1] spring water would be piped underwater and uphill to the new village, where it was hoped most of the hot spring hotels would relocate. A total of eight road and rail bridges would be built to connect the villages separated by the lake and improve access to the town, and many other infrastructure improvements would be made (ibid.). For the dwindling group of locals still actively opposed to the dam, the writing was now on the wall, and in 1992 Kawarayu's anti-dam group formally ended its opposition activities.

The attempted cancellation of 2009

In the 2009 national election, the opposition Democratic Party of Japan (DPJ) campaigned on a platform which promised to cut wasteful public works projects, taking as its campaign slogan "People, Not Concrete". Identifying the Yamba dam as the most egregious of these projects, the DPJ promised to cancel the dam when elected. Urban voters responded and swept the party and new Prime Minister Yukio Hatoyama to power in a landslide, ending 60 years of near-continuous LDP government. Most foreign media tended to see the change of power as a turning point. The unelected power of the ministries—especially the gargantuan MILT—might now be reined in by elected representatives. As one of his first acts in office, the new MLIT minister, Seiji Maehara, announced the suspension of the Yamba dam project, as the first step towards canceling it.

"Construction freeze on Japan Dam marks end of era" was one headline typical of the tone of foreign media coverage at the time (Alabaster, 2009). Even some Japanese observers sensed real change. Takayoshi Igarashi, a professor of politics at Hosei University stated: "What's happening at Yamba Dam is actually a revolution in the way Japan is run...this would end Japan's structure of dependence on public works and central planning" (Fackler, 2009). Other observers were more cautious, however; one suggested that "Hatoyama's true battle once in power will not be with his political rivals, but with the bureaucrats who dominate the higher echelons of the Japanese system" (Carter, 2009).

A week after taking office, the new minister went to Naganohara. Maehara's visit was sensitive; it came just days after the suspension of the dam project. A meeting with locals had been planned, but this had to be canceled. Media reported that locals "refused to meet with [the minister] on the grounds there was nothing to negotiate as the decision had already been made" (Alabaster, 2009). At a news conference in the town hall, Maehara stated that the roads and bridges under construction would still be finished, but that the dam would be canceled, and that his ministry was reviewing 143 dam projects. While he spoke, residents gathered outside, and "Quickly rebuild livelihoods, quickly finish the Yamba Dam" was posted on the building in large letters. Naganohara Mayor Kinya Takayama, once opposed to the dam but now furious at another governmental change of direction, told the media, "The delay has been the cause of huge bother for local people... if the dam gets canceled, how are we going to eat?" (*ibid.*) Yoji Hida, son-in-law of the man who led opposition to the dam for two decades, told reporters: "We don't really mind whether they stop construction on the dam or not, we just want our new life." Hida had taken over the family hotel in Kawarayu, and was now chairman of a group backing the dam project (*ibid.*).

The Japanese press, which had offered some criticism of the dam prior to 2009, now began to see the story in different terms: as big government bullying a small town. The DPJ faced a wave of news coverage sympathetic to the town and highly critical of the government. The bad press came from across the political spectrum; when Maehara later refused to speak to reporters from the right-wing *Sankei Shimbun*, which had referred to him 16 times in five months as "*Iudakebancho*" ("juvenile gang leader who is all mouth"), he was condemned for this by the left-wing *Tokyo Shimbun* (Cucek, 2012). The government was also under pressure from prefectural governments downriver (Tokyo, Saitama, Ibaraki and even distant Chiba) which had been pressured to contribute to the project by the MOC. The ministry had obtained compliance by telling the prefectures it could not guarantee their water supplies if the dam were not built (Brasor 2010). The likelihood of having to pay compensation to these prefectures meant that canceling the dam was likely to prove more expensive than completing it.

The government began to exhibit signs of internal conflict and indecision. Within a year, Hatoyama had lost the prime ministership, and Maehara had been moved to the Foreign Ministry. Their successors lasted no longer. As prime ministers came and went yearly, MLIT ministers came and went even faster. Chakraborty (2013) characterizes the advantage possessed by holders of long-term unelected power (in this case, bureaucrats) over holders of short-term elected power such as ministers and governors: "In this scenario of rapid changes in the top political leadership, or the incumbent parties, the only continuity in the policy mechanism is the bureaucracy." One effect of this imbalance in long-term, well-coordinated power was that ministers did not have adequate time to learn their jobs, and therefore came to rely on their official staff rather than try to effect change.

In late 2011, the fourth MLIT minister in eleven months, Takeshi Maeda, called a news conference to announce that the dam would after all be built. Stating that the dam was needed to prevent floods and other disasters, he added, "It's regrettable the result turned out to be different from what our campaign pledges promised" (Japan Times, December 23 2011). A state-ordered review set up to advise on the project's future before Maeda's final announcement had been seen by one dam opponent as an early negative sign: "Just as we worried, it was packed with scholars who support dams... now things are the same as they were under the LDP. The bureaucracy decides everything" (Mure, 2012).

The last political obstacles to completing the dam were now gone, and the LDP's landslide win in the 2012 national election brought a new government and a renewed commitment at the highest level to large construction projects as a way to keep the economy moving, this time without even pro forma political opposition. New Prime Minister Abe's economic growth policy emphasized anew the building of roads, dams and levees nationwide to "protect the nation from natural disasters" (Asahi Shimbun December 26, 2012). By 2014 nearly all the associated road, rail, residential and other infrastructure at the Yamba Dam site was at or near completion.

However, the projected completion date of the entire project has continued to be repeatedly set back. In 1997, completion was projected to be in 2006, but by 2013 the completion date had been set back for the fourth time, to 2019 (Newsonjapan.com, August 4, 2013).The long delay in starting construction of the dam seems remarkable in view of its relatively modest size (it is only the tenth largest dam in Japan by reservoir volume) and is difficult to attribute entirely to anti-dam activism. Technical difficulties relating to the unstable nature of the site may be a contributing factor. The region around the dam has been repeatedly subject to volcanic activity and has experienced landslides as recently as 2007. The potential effect of millions of tons of water on a hydro-thermally active valley that has highly permeable soil concerns some observers, who question the safety of this site (Masano, 2008). The long delay could be seen as a responsibly cautious interval to ensure every possible precaution is taken to ensure the site is stable before filling the reservoir, or (more speculatively) as evidence of ministerial cold feet, because of the possibility of a dam collapse if volcanic activity increased. In any event, as long as the dam continues to be under construction, jobs and government money continue to flow into the area. Even if technical problems continue, this will provide an ongoing source of jobs and income by keeping construction companies busy. One hot spring owner describes the dam as "like a drug that is making us addicted... the money keeps pouring in every year to build things for us" (Fackler, 2009). One unstated function of the dam has already been fulfilled, even if the reservoir is never filled: it has provided hundreds of jobs for people working for construction companies.

Present state of site

The new Kawarayu site is about half a kilometer from the old one, on a ledge carved out of the hillside overlooking the valley. Two hot spring inns were operating there in late 2014. These were the only survivors of the 18 hotels operating in Kawarayu in 1980 (Shimazu and Tomizawa, p. 11). Residents indicated to the author that it is doubtful more will be built. The new Kawarayu Onsen railway station is several times the size of the old one that will be submerged, although the population it will serve has been dropping since the 1980s. By one account, approximately half the village has abandoned the area altogether (*Yomiuri Shimbun*, 13 January 2005). The last operating hot spring inn on the old Kawarayu site closed its doors in June 2014, by which time nearly every structure on the original village site was demolished or empty.[2]

Although it seems unfair to judge the new site in its incomplete state, it is noticeable that despite its small area, the new village has many blocks of unused land even though nearly all residents have relocated. Looking down from the site at the valley floor, local anger at the 2009 "infrastructure but no dam" compromise announced by then-minister Maehara becomes easier to understand. Without the lake, the village looks out over an unfinished construction site and the demolished homes of the old villages, and there is no lakeshore frontage to provide a touristic focal point. The assurance that the new site would maintain the character of the village and its value as a tourist destination helped persuade some residents to relocate during the long negotiations of the 1970s and 1980s. In its present state, however, the village has limitations as a tourist attraction.

Further up the valley, Naganohara town is mostly above the level of the reservoir and will not be submerged. The district population of 5,600 is down from 7,200 in 1980. A single convenience store and a small shopping park are at a crossroads at the far western end of town, located more conveniently for drivers passing through than for the increasingly elderly residents. The newer infrastructure appears to be almost all associated with transportation—roads, rails, bridges, stations and tunnels. As a result, the town is easier to reach than it once was, but also easier to bypass without stopping. Between the town and Kawarayu is a new highway rest stop with a dam information booth featuring a mural which emphasizes the flood protection function of the dam and depicts a history of the project, ending the narrative in 2008, just before the DPJ came to power.[3]

The new bridges crossing the heights have not hidden the valley's still considerable natural beauty, much of which will be obliterated when the dam is built. However, access to some areas began to be restricted in 2014. At one of the most scenic stretches of the gorge, a popular hiking path ran right past the dam site. When this path was suddenly closed to the public without prior notice in March 2014, it seemed a strong indicator that dam construction was about to proceed. A sign at the path gate stated "Closed for the winter season", although the closure happened in spring, well after the snows. Five months before the closure, the author asked staff at the dam information booth when the path would be closed, and was told that it hadn't been announced. To check, the staffer left the information desk and returned with an older colleague who was cautious but apparently trying to be helpful. When the author asked about a hike in the spring, she implied the path would be open: "... if you can't walk it this year, it's beautiful in spring..." These staffers (themselves locals) seemed genuinely to want to provide this information, but did not appear to have access to it. A later visit to the booth by a Japanese assistant produced no more specifics, but did elicit some cautiously-worded hints about disagreements among local residents regarding compensation. The question of how much compensation was paid to which residents is a highly sensitive one, which locals are naturally unwilling to discuss with the author or anyone else, but anecdotal evidence suggests a division exists between locals living outside the reservoir zone and those who were relocated, such as the remaining residents of Kawarayu, who were moved to the new site at great expense, and whose new homes, many with solar panels on the roofs, are conspicuously larger and better-appointed than most other houses in the district.

The effect of the dam has been to divide the community, cause many people to leave the area, and to change the economy from one based on farming and hot springs into one that depends largely on construction. More than 20 construction companies in Naganohara employ about 400 people, or at least 10 percent of working-age residents. (Fackler, 2009) The leaders of the district, who might have been working in agriculture or running a hotel in the 1960s, are now more likely to make their living in a construction-related business. Though there is little overt local enthusiasm for the dam itself, it was these economic changes, and the sacrifices made by residents in giving up their land and relocating after extremely hard-won concessions, that contributed to the hostile local reaction to the abortive 2009 attempt to cancel the dam.

The outcome for the careers of the two most powerful LDP politicians in Gunma contrasts with the dam's effects on the communities within the reservoir area. Both went to the top, former Finance Minister Takeo Fukuda becoming prime minister of Japan in 1978, and Yasuhiro Nakasone doing so in 1982. Nakasone, the most senior LDP member to oppose the dam, suffered no apparent lasting political consequences from his early opposition. A change of heart had become obvious by 1970, when he began openly distancing himself from dam opponents (Brown, 2011, p. 66). This appears to coincide with a change in his political fortunes. Having been out of cabinet for seven years, he was appointed transport minister a year after the failure of the dam opponent's 1966 petition to Tokyo (described earlier). From the time Nakasone ended his criticism of the dam, his career appeared to accelerate and maintain a steady rise until he became prime minister.

With all its difficulties, Naganohara district has in some respects survived the nation-wide rural depopulation trend more successfully than many similar communities. Even in Japan's premier hot spring town of Kusatsu, a 20-minute drive away, derelict hotels could be seen in 2015. Other rural towns lacking high-profile tourist attractions have fared considerably worse. Given the social, economic and demographic circumstances existing in Gunma in the last quarter of the 20th century, it is difficult to make a convincing case that the anti-dam group might have sustained its opposition successfully for much longer than it did. How locals will view the environmental destruction the dam will bring once it is built remains to be seen, as does its safety and long-term economic benefit. A utilitarian view might be that Naganohara has, for the time being, avoided the fate of many similar communities by the use of pragmatic and politically astute civic activism. This activism did succeed in extracting substantial compensation from the state, although what amount of compensation would have made good for the four decades of uncertainty, disruption and dislocation locals endured is difficult to say. In any event, the highly questionable utility of the dam does not seem adequate compensation to the broader public for the loss of environmental and cultural value represented by the Agatsuma Gorge and the towns that once thrived there.

References

Alabaster, J. (2009, 24th September) Construction freeze on Japan dam marks end of era. The Huffington Post. Accessed from <http://www.huffingtonpost.com/huffwires/20090924/as-japan-frozen-dam/>

Aldrich, D. (2008) *Site Fights: Divisive facilities and civil society in Japan and the West.* Ithaca, New York: Cornell University Press.

Association for Concerned Citizens for Yamba Dam Project. (n.d.) About Yamba dam. Retrieved from <http://www.yamba-net.org/eng/>

Brasor, P. (2010, April 11th) Public works project has DPJ in a dam mess. The Japan Times. Accessible at <http://www.japantimes.co.jp/news/2010/04/11/national/media-national/public-works-project-has-dpj-in-a-dam-mess/>

Brown, P. (2011) Dam Japan No More! A Half Century of Planning and Protest. Proceedings paper of the seminar "The Environmental History of Europe and Japan", 7-11 September, 2010, published by the Oxford-Nagoya Environment Seminar, Nagoya University Graduate School of Environmental Studies. Accessible at <http://yamba-net.org/wp/wp-content/uploads/2013/07/Env-Hist-PCB-Dam-Japan-No-More1.pdf>

Carter, P. (2009, 1st September) Yukio Hatoyama does the impossible. . . now for the difficult part. The Daily Telegraph. Accessible at <http://tinyurl.com/o8swvxj>

Chakraborty, A. (2013) Developing rivers—how strong state and bureaucracy continue to suffocate environment-oriented river governance in Japan. *SAGE Open,* Accessible at<http://sgo.sagepub.com/content/3/4/2158244013501329>DOI:10.1177/2158244013501329

Cucek, M. (2012) Politics and society in comic verse – Senryu of March 3, 2012. Shisaku. Accessed at <http://shisaku.blogspot.jp/2012/03/poetry-of-everyday-part-ii-senryu-for.html>

Fackler, M. (2009, 15th October) Japan rethinks a dam, and a town protests. The New York Times. Accessible at<http://www.nytimes.com/2009/10/16/world/asia/16dam.html?pagewanted=all&_r=0>

Gorton, M.E. (1997) *Damming the Agatsuma River: An exploration of Changing Space and Place in Kawarayu, Japan.* University of Montana.

Hagiwara, Y. (1996) *The Yamba Dam Conflict* (yanba damu no arasoi). *Tokyo:* Iwanami Shoten.

Japan Press Weekly (2012, 5th December) Stance towards public works questioned in General Election. Accessible at <http://www.japan-press.co.jp/modules/news/index.php?id=4669>

Masano, A. (2010, 4th January) The immense cost of Japanese dams and dam-related landslides and earthquakes. (damu to chisuberi ni ryohi sareru kyo hi masa no atuko). The Asia-Pacific Journal 1-2-10. Accessible at <http://www.japanfocus.org/-masano-atsuko/3280>

Miyaharada A. *(2010) Even then, the Yamba dam should not be built.* (sore to mo yanba damu wa tsukutte ha ikenai). *Tokyo, Japan: FuyoshoboShuppan.*

Mure, D. (2012, 12th December) Japan dam debacle shows DPJ's failings.*Financial Times.* Accessible at <http://www.ft.com/cms/s/0/0bebe938-42b6-11e2-a3d2-00144feabdc0.html#axzz3dEjqKjsP >

Nakazawa, H. (2010, 22nd July)Political studies of power through Yamba: Regional development sites and the state. *The Yomiuri Shimbun.* Accessible at <http://www.yomiuri.co.jp/adv/chuo/dy/research/20100722.html>

Shimazu, T. and Kiyosawa, Y. (2011) *Yamba Dam: Its past, present and future (yanba damu, kako, genzai, soshite mirai).* Tokyo: Iwanami Shoten.

CHAPTER 11

Language choice and political preferences in Ukraine: Can language unite the nation?

Bogdan Pavliy

Introduction

It cannot be denied that the language choice has been an important attribute of political life in Ukraine. However, the national and social identity of each individual matters even more than linguistic choice. Laitin (1998) states that social identities are "built from available categories that both divide and unite people in society," and mentions "inter alia national identities, racial identities, religious identities, and hometown identities" Laitin (1998, p. 16). I would add to these categories linguistic identities. Language and language choice as an element of the linguistic identity can unite or divide people in different regions of the nation. It "influences perception, thought, and, at least potentially, behavior" (Holmes 2008, p.336). Because of that, language can be a very convenient tool for manipulating people and communities in their political choices.

On the other hand, while the language of the members of a community might affect their political preferences, language choice could not be called the key marker of the national identity in Ukraine (Kuzio, 2001). It was often debated in the parliament if Ukraine should cling to one official language (Ukrainian), or have two official languages, or make Russian a regional language. "The notion of the existence in an individual of two native languages as harmful has deep roots in nationalist thoughts on the connection between language and nation," (Bernsand, 2001, p. 42). No wonder that nationalist and right-center parties (Batkivschyna [Fatherland], Svoboda, Udar) favored Ukrainian-only language policies. Leaders of parties with their electorate in the east and south (Party of Regions) supported the idea that Russian should be a regional language. Communists insisted on Russian as a second official language.

Language in Ukrainian politics

During its independence, Ukraine has had two laws on languages. Until 2012, Ukraine had the 1989 law, "On the languages in the Ukrainian SSR". When Yanukovych and his Party of Regions reached the peak of its power in 2012, they adopted a new law, "On the principles of the state language policy" (informally, "Kolesnichenko-Kivalov law", after the name of its authors). According to this law, if the percentage of representatives of a national minority in an administrative district exceeds 10% of the total population of the district, the language of the minority should be granted the status of a regional language. As the law should enable Russian to become an official regional language in southern and eastern regions of Ukraine, nationalist and centrist parties strongly opposed it. There were fights in the Ukrainian Parliament and protests in the streets, but finally, the Party of Regions pushed the vote ahead of schedule, and in July 2012, the law was adopted. Later it was signed by President Viktor Yanukovych and came into force on August 10, 2012.

Since then, Russian has become a regional language in the oblasts (administrative regions) of Odessa, Mykolaiv, Kherson, Dnipropetrovsk, Zaporizhzhia, Donetsk, and in the cities of Odessa, Mykolaiv, Kherson, Dnipropetrovsk, Zaporizhzhia, Kharkiv, Luhansk, Krasny Luch and Sevastopol (Pavliy, 2014, p. 213).

While the adoption of the new language law has created a lot of controversy in political circles, on a social level things have not changed much. As Bilaniuk (2005) describes it: "It was expected that everyone living in Ukraine should know both languages at least passively. By the year 2000 in Kyiv [Kiev], it generally became culturally correct to treat language in public as transparent, reacting neither positively nor negatively to language choice" (p. 177). This situation can be seen not only in Kyiv, (Kiev) but in all major cities of Ukraine. While there is a big difference between the linguistic preferences of the communities of Western and South-Eastern Ukraine, the language division in most oblasts of central Ukraine is not that clear. Language-switching there takes place not only in big cities, but also in small towns or villages. It happens also in many oblasts of southern and eastern Ukraine (except Donetsk oblast, Luhansk oblast and the Autonomous Republic of Crimea). As Bernsand (2001) explains:

> As regards language relations on the regional level, the main dividing line is traditionally drawn between a mainly Ukrainian-speaking western Ukraine and the predominantly Russian-speaking eastern and southern parts of the country. Although this to some extent is a fair description it should not be accepted without some qualifications. In eastern and southern Ukraine during the 19th and 20th centuries uneven status relations made peasants change to Russian in an effort to adjust to city life. The predominance of Russian, which has been strengthened by migration from central Russia, is not, however, complete. In the

oblasts of Charkiv, Sumy, Dnipropetrovs'k and Zaporizhzhia code-switching between Ukrainian and Russian is more common in informal domains than is the use of only one language, and there is still a not insignificant number of people in this area who claims to speak only Ukrainian.

In large areas of western Ukraine, where historically more favourable conditions existed for the spread of Ukrainian national consciousness, Ukrainian clearly predominates, even if Russian is quite widespread in urban centres.(p. 42)

Language and electoral choice

According to the last census, which was held in 2001, the percentage of those whose mother tongue is Ukrainian totals 67.5% of the population of Ukraine (2.8 percentage points more than in 1989) and the percentage of those whose mother tongue is Russian totals 29.6% of the population.

The division by the language spoken by the two major ethnic groups can be seen from Table 1.

Table 1: Language spoken by the two main national groups

	Ukrainian speakers	Russian speakers	speak another language
Ukrainians	85.2%	14.8%	0
Russians	3.9%	95.9%	0.2%

Source: 2001 census, http://2001.ukrcensus.gov.ua/eng/results/general/language/

It should be said that from this data we cannot get the whole picture of the diversity of language choices, because there are many people who use Surzhyk (a mixture of Russian and Ukrainian) as a first language. Moreover, people get used to a constant switching between languages. The same person can speak Ukrainian with his family and friends, Russian with colleagues and clients at work, and Surzhyk with his mother-in-law from a distant village.

The language preferences among the different regions of Ukraine vary drastically. That is why it was very convenient for political parties and candidates in presidential and parliamentary campaigns to tackle the language issues. It could help them to raise their popularity among certain regions or regional communities. Language choices of politicians often depend on the region or community of their audience. Moreover, when a politician comes to the rival region, he/she can easily switch the language used for the audience, adjusting to the needs of his/her prospective voters, as Polese (2011) comments:

The national language of political speeches is Ukrainian and even non-Ukrainian speakers, at official occasions, make an effort to speak Ukrainian (or something they believe is Ukrainian), when addressing the country on national events. However, when targeting a specific public, they might take the liberty to use Russian. This is the case of many politicians willing to gain support in regions where Russians are the majority. President Yanukovich's discourses in his native Donetsk are often in Russian, and even a Ukrainian speaker such as former President Yushchenko, when addressing eastern regions on national TV during the Orange Revolution in 2004, used Russian instead of Ukrainian in an attempt to convince them he was not anti-Russian. (p. 46)

A more recent example is the inauguration speech of President Petro Poroshenko, in which he used both Ukrainian and Russian. Most of his speech was in Ukrainian, but while addressing his words to compatriots from Donetsk and Luhansk, he switched to Russian.

Electoral sympathies of voters during 2000-2012

From the beginning of 2000, the electoral sympathies of voters can be clearly divided into two major categories: pro-European and pro-Russian. Although the boundaries on a regional level are blurred, on a national level, each time we can see the same border that separates the electorate. This is not only a political, but also a historical phenomenon: Ukraine is split into two parts--Western and South-Eastern-- pro-European vectored and pro-Russian vectored. Parties used these two vectors to gain or maintain the sympathies of their voters, and it made the Europe/Russia division even more vigorous and the borderline between the supporters of different political vectors more stable. By analyzing the following electoral maps of the supporters of Yushchenko (pro-European course) and Yanukovych (pro-Russian course) in the 2004 elections, which led to the Orange Revolution, we can see that although the borderline itself is constant, voters in the "border zones" or oblasts near the borderline, do not have as strong preferences for candidates as voters in oblasts further from the borderline.

There was another phenomenon, which we cannot see from the maps, but its presence in Ukrainian politics until 2013 was obvious. Whoever was elected as a president or whichever party took political leadership, they inevitably became neither pro-European, nor pro-Russian, but rather pro-Ukrainian.

Yanukovych and his government was not an exception. Soon after his inauguration, he proclaimed the course to Europe to be an important element of his politics. In this sense, Yanukovych became "neither pro-Russian nor pro-European, but pro-Ukrainian", as Jofre M. Rocabert (2010) notes:

As any political actor, Ukrainian elites will remain as long as they can in the most advantageous place, which is right now a loose equilibrium between the two poles. Of course, I am not denying that the profound division of the country makes the government more sensitive to the side it identifies with, but besides that, there are facts no government can overlook, such as the EU being the first commercial partner.

Electoral maps

Now let us analyze the maps of the electoral support in presidential elections in 2004, parliamentary elections in 2007, presidential elections in 2010 and parliamentary elections in 2012. Although we already have the data on presidential elections in 2014, I would abstain from considering it, because in my opinion, it should be analyzed together with the data on parliamentary elections 2014, which were scheduled in autumn 2014 at the time of writing.

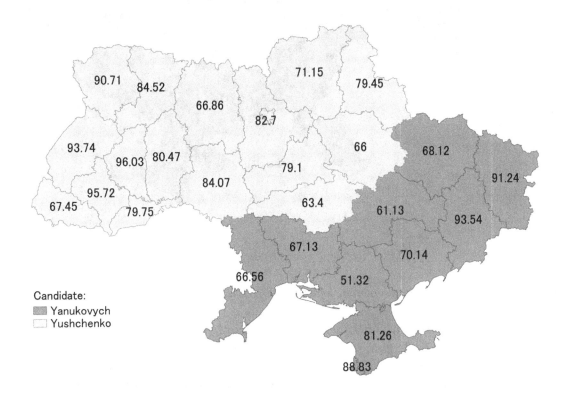

Map.1. Results of the presidential elections in 2004

On Map.1, the two electoral "border zone" oblasts, where Yuschenko was victorious in general, but had the lowest percent of voters comparatively to the other oblasts, are Poltava and Kirovograd (66% and 63,42% respectively). The same percentage of voters have supported Yanukovych in the oblasts on the other side of the "border zone": Kherson (51,32%), Dnipropetrovsk (61,14%), Odesa (66,56%), Mykolaiv (67,13%), Kharkiv (68,11%).

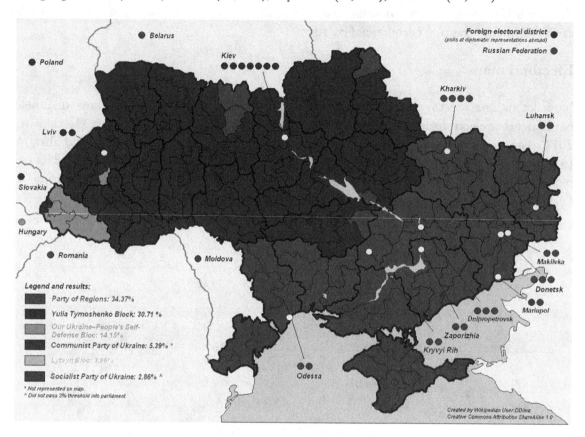

Map.2. Results of parliamentary elections 2007

Source:http://thepolitikalblog.files.wordpress.com/2010/08/ukraine-2007-parliamentary-election.png >

The same border is seen at the parliamentary elections in 2007 (Map.2). Here, we can see that the pro-Russian Party of Region, which was led by Yanukovych, gained victory in the same oblasts of South-Eastern Ukraine, while the pro-European Yuliya Tymoshenko Bloc together with Our Ukraine-People's Self-Defense Bloc won in almost all regions of Western and Central Ukraine.

In the presidential elections in 2010 (Map3), the two electoral "border zone" oblasts, where Tymoshenko won in general, but got the lowest percent of voters, are again Poltava and Kirovograd (54.2% and 54.7% respectively). In addition, in the oblasts won by Yanukovych, again he achieved the lowest percentage of support: in Kherson he won 59.8% of the vote, and Dnipropetrovsk 62.7% of the vote. This time, more than 70% in Odessa, Mykolayiv and Kharkiv voted for Yanukovych, mainly because of the strong antipathy and aversion to Tymoshenko and her politics in these oblasts rather than their support of Yanukovych.

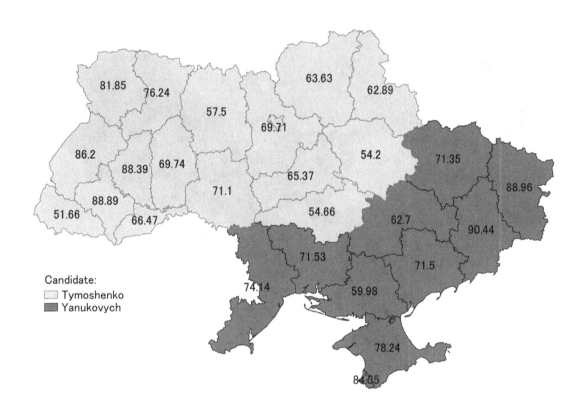

Map. 3. Results of presidential elections 2010

In the 2012 parliamentary election (Map.4), the two electoral "border zone" oblasts, which gave the Tymoshenko-led Batkivschyna party the lowest support among the winning oblasts, were again Poltava (30.13%) and Kirovograd (32.15%). Furthermore, the Yanukovych-led Party of Regions again received the lowest percentage of support in Kherson (29.38%), and Dnipropetrovsk (35.79%). This time, the Zakarpatska oblast in western Ukraine also voted for the Party of Regions (30.94%), which was unusual for that oblast. One of the reasons was the strong impact of the local administration, which decided to support the Party of Regions. Another reason for the relatively lower support for Batkivschyna (27.69%) may have been the dislike of Tymoshenko, and the popularity of the Udar party (20.02%), which occupies the same niche in the political spectrum.

Map.4. Results of parliamentary elections 2012

As for the electoral support in "border zone" oblasts, we can conclude that these oblasts are pivotal for victory in presidential and parliamentary elections. The next step would be to consider the language situation in these borderline regions.

Language border

Here is the data from the 2001 national census on native language by oblasts:

1) Two oblasts from the pro-Ukrainian vote side of the borderline

According to the 2001 Ukrainian governmental census[1], the language breakdown for Poltava is Ukrainian – 90% and Russian – 9.5%:

The percentage of those whose mother tongue is Ukrainian totals 90% of the population of the region; this is 4.1 percentage points more than in 1989. The percentage of those whose mother tongue is Russian totals 9.5%of the population. Compared with the data of the previous census this index has decreased by 3.7 percentage points. The proportion of other languages, specified like mother tongue, during the period that has passed since the previous census has decreased by 0.4 percentage points and accounts for 0.5%. (State Statistics Committee of Ukraine, 2001)

With regard to Kirovograd, Ukrainian language speakers number 88.9%, and Russian speakers constitute 10% of the population (State Statistics Committee of Ukraine, 2001).[2]

2) Oblasts on pro-Russian vote side

In Dnipropetrovsk, Ukrainian speakers constituted 67% of the population, in contrast to the Russian speakers, who made up 32% of the population (State Statistics Committee of Ukraine, 2001).[3]

Kherson's Ukrainian speakers numbered 73.2%, while Russian speakers accounted for 24.9% of the population, as the 2001 State Census affirms:[4]

The proportion of those whose mother tongue is Ukrainian totals 73.2% of the population of region, this is 5.5 percentage points more than in 1989. The percentage of those whose mother tongue is Russian totals 24.9% of the population. Compared with the previous census data, this index has decreased by 5.5 percentage points. The proportion of other languages, specified like mother tongue, during the period that have passed since the previous census remained at the previous level 1.8%. (State Statistics Committee of Ukraine, 2001)

The State Census for 2001 describes Mykolaiv's Ukrainian speakers as numbering 69.2%, and Russian speakers constituting 29.3% of the population:[5]

The proportion of those whose mother tongue is Ukrainian totals 69.2% of the population of the region, this is 5 percentage points more than in 1989. The percentage of those whose mother tongue is Russian totals 29.3% of the population, Compared with the data of previous census, this index has decreased by 4.5 percentage points. The percentage of other languages, specified like mother tongue, during the period that has passed since previous census has decreased by 0.5 percentage points and accounts for 1.5%. (State Statistics Committee of Ukraine, 2001)

For Kharkiv, Ukrainian speakers counted for 53.8% of the population, and Russian speakers 44.3%:[6]

> The proportion of those whose mother tongue is Ukrainian totals 53.8% of the population of Ukraine, this is 3.3 percentage points more than in 1989. The percentage of those whose mother tongue is Russian totals 44.3% of the population. Compared with the data of previous census, this index has decreased by 3.8 percentage points. The proportion of other languages, specified like mother tongue, during the period that have passed since previous census has increased by 0.5 percentage points and accounts for 1.9%. (State Statistics Committee of Ukraine, 2001)

Odessa's Ukrainian speakers were 46.3% and Russian speakers 41.9%:[7]

> The proportion of those whose mother tongue is Ukrainian totals 46.3% of the population of Odessa region. The percentage of those whose mother tongue is Russian totals 41.9% of the population. Compared with the data of previous census, this index has decreased by 5.2 percentage points. The percentage of other languages accounts for 11.8%. (State Statistics Committee of Ukraine, 2001)

As we can see, in all the electoral "border zone" oblasts, the majority of people are native Ukrainian speakers. Yet if we continue to study the data on the oblasts that are further from the border zone, we would note the following: in Zaporizhzhia, for example, Ukrainian speakers make up 50.2% of the population, while Russian – 48.2% (State Statistics Committee of Ukraine, 2001).[8] However in Donetsk, Ukrainian speakers are in the minority 24.1%, and Russian speakers in the majority at 74.9% (State Statistics Committee of Ukraine, 2001).[9] The trend is similar in Luhansk, where 30% are speakers of Ukrainian and 68.8% are speakers of Russian (State Statistics Committee of Ukraine, 2001).[10]

Furthermore, in the Autonomous Republic of Crimea, Ukrainian speakers decline to a mere 10.1%, while Russian speakers number 77%, and speakers of Crimean-Tatar are 11.4% of the population (State Statistics Committee of Ukraine, 2001).[11]

As we can see from the above, except Zaporizhzhia, all the South-Eastern regions further from electoral border have a considerable balance in favor of Russian as a native language; in the most extreme case of Crimea, only 10% of the population indicated Ukrainian as their mother tongue. In Donetsk only 24%, and in Luhansk 30%—less than one third of population—considered Ukrainan their native language. Thus we can see that the borders by native language and electoral choice do not match.

vote for pro-Russian candidate
vote for pro-European candidate

Recent changes

Ukraine became an independent state 23 years ago. Before that, for more than 300 years, it belonged to either Russia as a republic or to "Soviet Russia" (USSR). Even after gaining independence in 1991, Ukraine as a state remained unstable. It was split between two political and cultural spaces: European and Russian. Until 2013, all presidents of Ukraine built their politics on keeping equilibrium between Russia and the EU. In November 2013, President Viktor Yanukovych—who had promised a Ukrainian association with the EU—could not withstand the pressure of Russia, and changed the vector of his politics, making a dramatic turn back. It has led to the ongoing uprising in Ukraine, which turned into revolution and the defeat of the Yanukovych government.

After that, Russia broke its obligations to protect Ukrainian territorial integrity, and occupied and annexed the Autonomous Republic of Crimea. Russia has also supported the separatist movement in the Donbas (Donetsk and Luhansk oblasts) region of Ukraine. To fight the separatists, the Ukrainian government started the Anti-Terrorist Operation (ATO), which has continued since April 2014. By the end of August 2014, it had become clear that unless Russia started military aggression into Ukraine, the separatist state would be completely defeated in the ATO by Ukrainian forces. To intensify its pressure on Ukraine, Russia has chosen direct military aggression and, seemingly, escalation of the conflict, which may lead to an open war in the future. Antonova and Gaudichet (2014) describe the situation on September 2nd, 2014:

> On the ground, Kiev said its forces south of the rebel hub of Luhansk were forced to retreat from the local airfield and a nearby village after withstanding artillery fire and fighting a Russian tank battalion."There is direct, overt aggression against Ukraine from the neighboring state," Ukraine's President Petro Poroshenko said. The retreat marked the latest setback for Ukrainian troops, which had been closing in on rebels in Donetsk and Luhansk until about a week ago, when the insurgent opened a new front in the south.

Conclusion

As we can see from this research along with recent events, Russian plans of annexing parts of Ukraine have spread primarily to the regions with a high percentage of native Russian speakers, which Russia considers to be a part of "Russkiy mir" (the Russian world). The annexation of Crimea, followed by separatist movements and war in Donetsk and Luhansk oblasts, proved to be successful for Russia at the time. Yet at the same time, the fact that Odessa and Kharkiv (where the percentage of Russian native speakers is relatively high) did not show much vigor for separatism, I presume, surprised Russia.

Kuzio (2001) suggests that "when states are close in language and culture this can often produce more—not less—conflict over national identity," (p. 361). Although this was said about Belarus and Russia, the same can be said about the eastern part of Ukraine, which Russia now calls "Novorossiya" (New Russia), where pro-Ukrainian volunteer battalions consist mostly of Russian speakers. During this period of conflict between the separatists and Russian military forces, it has become clear that Russian-speaking Ukrainians should not be automatically considered as pro-Russian. The more we insist that language is a decisive factor for national identity, the further we get into discussions and turmoil, which have nothing in common with the real unity of the nation.

That is why Kuzio (2002) insists that both "Ukrainization" and "Russification" should not be prioritized in the language policy in contemporary Ukraine (pp. 196-197). Moreover, as

Russian-speaking people should not be identified as "pro-Russian" or in any way disloyal to Ukrainian independence; Ukrainian-speaking people should not be considered to be ultra-nationalists, ultra-right or "banderivtsy" (after Ukrainian hero Stepan Bandera [1909-1959], who fought for the independence of Ukraine from the USSR).

It cannot be denied that the language problem was at the epicenter of Ukrainian politics since the first day of independence. However, the good news is that nowadays not so many people pay much attention to the language of the candidates for presidential or parliamentary elections. They care about the content much more. Frye (2014), in his recent research on election sympathies in Ukraine, describes the situation as follows:

> I found that while a voter's ethnicity and language influenced a hypothetical vote choice, a candidate's language and ethnicity were far less relevant. Russian and Ukrainian voters were not much moved by learning that a candidate was Russian or Ukrainian or was a native speaker of Russian or Ukrainian. Far more important was whether a candidate favored an economic policy orientation toward Russia or Europe.

Now Ukraine has a unique chance to become an officially recognized part of Europe. People have struggled for that, and hopefully the president of Ukraine, Petro Poroshenko, and the current Ukrainian government will be wise enough not to lose the opportunity this time. The road to Europe is not easy. It is still unclear whether Ukraine can remain within its borders as a state, or is bound to be divided into two or more smaller states, some of which may be assimilated by Russia. The resolution of Ukraine's linguistic problems can be postponed until due time. The best development in this unstable period of Ukrainian history would be if the nation united and consolidated regardless of the language choice of its citizens.

References

Antonova, M., and Gaudichet, N. (2014, 2 September) "No military solution" to Ukraine crisis, UN chief warns.*Yahoo News*.ARetrieved from <http://news.yahoo.com/kiev-warns-great-war-russia-forces-retreat-170207035.html> on 2nd September, 2014.

Bernsand, N. (2001). Surzhyk and national identity in Ukrainian nationalist language ideology. *Berliner Osteuropa-Info*, 17. Retrieved from <http://www.oei.fu-berlin.de/media/ publikationen/ boi/boi17/11_bernsand.pdf> on 2nd September, 2014).

Bilaniuk, L. (2005) *Contested tongues: Language politics and cultural correction in Ukraine*. Ithaca: Cornell University Press.

Frye, T. (2014, 27 August) For Ukrainian voters, key is policy preferences, not native language or ethnicity, of candidates. *The Washington Post* [Online]Retrieved from <http://www. washingtonpost.com/blogs/monkey-cage/wp/2014/08/27/for-ukrainian-voters-key-is-policy-preferences-not-native-language-or-ethnicity-of-candidates/> on 2nd September, 2014).

Holmes, J. (2008) *An Introduction to Sociolinguistics (3rd Edition) (Learning About Language)*. Harlow: Pearson Education Limited.

Kuzio, T. (2001) Identity and nation-building in Ukraine: Defining the 'Other'. *Ethnicities,* 1: 343-365.

Kuzio, T. (2002) *Ukraine: State and Nation Building*. Routledge Studies of Societies in Transition, 2nd edition. New York: Routledge.

Laitin, D. (1998) *Identity in Formation: Russian-Speaking Populations in the Near Abroad*. Ithaca: Cornell University Press.

Pavliy, B. (2014) The abolition of the 2012 language law in Ukraine: was it that urgent? *Bulletin of Toyama University of International Studies Faculty of Contemporary Society*, Vol.6:. 207-216.

Polese, A. (2011) Language and Identity in Ukraine: Was it Really Nation Building? *Studies of Transition States and Societies (Studies of Transition States and Societies)*, Issue: 3.3,: 36-50.

Rocabert, J.M. (2010, 28 November) "New government in Ukraine: pro-Russian or pro-European? How should Europe approach Ukraine and its new leader?" *Thenewfederalist. eu: Webzine of the Young European Federalists.*, [Online] Retrieved from <http://www.

thenewfederalist.eu/New-government-in-Ukraine -pro-Russian-or-pro-European> on 24 Aug 2014.

State Statistics Committee of Ukraine. All-Ukrainian population census (2001). Всеукраїнський перепис населення 2001|English version|Results|General results of the census: Language. Retrieved from <http://2001.ukrcensus.gov.ua/eng/results/general/language/> on 30 Aug 2014. Linguistic composition of the population: Results by regions available at: <http://2001.ukrcensus.gov.ua/eng/results/general/language/Dnipropetrovsk/> ; <http://2001.ukrcensus.gov.ua/eng/results/general/language/Poltava/>;<http://2001.ukrcensus.gov.ua/eng/results/general/language/Kirovohrad/> ; <http://2001.ukrcensus.gov.ua/eng/results/general/language/Kherson/> ; <http://2001.ukrcensus.gov.ua/eng/results/general/language/Kharkiv/> ; <http://2001.ukrcensus.gov.ua/eng/results/general/language/Mykolaiv/> ; <http://2001.ukrcensus.gov.ua/eng/results/general/language/Odesa/>; <http://2001.ukrcensus.gov.ua/eng/results/general/language/Zaporizhzhia/> ; <http://2001.ukrcensus.gov.ua/eng/results/general/language/Donetsk/> ; <http://2001.ukrcensus.gov.ua/eng/results/general/language/Luhansk/> ; <http://2001.ukrcensus.gov.ua/eng/results/general/language/Crimea/>.

Wagstyl, S., and Olearchyk, R. (2010, 8 February) Likely victor faces power struggle in Kiev. *Financial Times* [Online] Retrieved from <http://www.ft.com/intl/cms/s/0/1015c1f0-14dd-11df-8f1d-00144feab49a.html#axzz3CbKuBG4H> on 1st September,2014.

Zhurzhenko, T. (2010) *Borderlands into Bordered Lands: Geopolitics of Identity in Post-Soviet Ukraine*. Stuttgart: ibidem-Verlag

CHAPTER 12

Multiculturalism: Misconceptions, misunderstandings and the current state of affairs

Daniel Warchulski & Zane Ritchie

Introduction

Many contemporary Western nations are culturally plural societies, defined as nations whose populaces are from different ethnic and cultural backgrounds living together within a shared social and political framework (Brooks, 2002). In the future, more and more nations will likely join them; the estimated number of international migrants in 2013 was approximately 232 million, an increase of 77 million or 50 percent from 1990 (United Nations, 2013, p.1).

Whether through immigrant and refugee movements, slavery, or colonisation, modern western societies now include mutually co-existing groups with different ethnic, religious, and, cultural backgrounds. This coexistence has not always been peaceful; numerous instances exist where cultural differences have been perceived as a contributing factor to discrimination, tensions, and conflicts between majority and minority groups, and between immigrants and native-born individuals living together within a shared space. Many states have coped with pluralism through the implementation and adoption of multiculturalism and multicultural policies (hereinafter MCP). It is widely accepted that MCPs are a suitable mechanism for addressing inequalities associated with former systems of organizing and dealing with cultural diversity, inequalities which were often based on unequal and hierarchical relationships between groups (Kymlicka, 2012). A solid body of empirical evidence has emerged to support the benefits of multiculturalism as an approach for managing cultural diversity (Leong, C.H. and Liu, J. H., 2013, p. 661).

Despite the benefits attributed to multiculturalism throughout most of its short history in managing culturally diverse societies, there has recently been a backlash against MCPs by some policy-makers, commentators, and researchers, and it could be argued that a retreat has been declared. This has been further perpetuated by negative reporting by various media sources and commentators. In this regard, the Netherlands serves as the prototypical example of a backlash against MCPs. Similarly, the leaders of Germany, France, and Britain have been associated with statements that multiculturalism has been unsuccessful in their countries because it leads to segregating and separating groups, rather than integrating them (Edmonton Journal, February 13, 2011).

The perception exists that while there are benefits associated with multiculturalism, there are many fundamentally challenging issues that are difficult, if not impossible, to overcome. As such, multiculturalism and MCPs continue to be the subject of a range of criticisms which often call for abandoning MCPs in favor of more coercive policies held to promote assimilation and civic integration. A frequently heard criticism of multiculturalism is that it ignores the importance of universal human rights by undermining liberal values leading to, for instance, the oppression of women, while promoting cultural isolation, thereby causing minority groups to lead "parallel lives", which in turn creates obstacles to integration (Kymlicka, 2012; Bloemraad and Wright, 2014). Additionally, there is a fear that multiculturalism leads to ethnic enclaves and ghettos that have the effect of undermining integration. There is concern that an emphasis on diversity promotes isolation rather than unity, and undermines collective identity and action while creating an obstacle to social ties with those outside the ethnic enclave and prevents majority-language learning and meaningful socio-economic integration (Koopmans, 2010).

Conversely, proponents of MCPs often assert that multiculturalism and MCPs play a key role in the integration of minority and marginalized groups into a host culture by removing some of the systematic barriers and social exclusionary processes that impede full and meaningful participation in society, including the mitigation of processes that are responsible for inequities and discrimination associated with an individual's or group's racial, religious, and ethnic origins (Hyman et al., 2011). It is contended that "when discourse and policy valorize and accommodate cultural specificity, members of minority communities will feel increased connection to and engagement in the polity and society where they live" (Bloamraad and Wright, 2014, p. 293).

In light of a supposed retreat from multiculturalism and MCPs in some nations, it seems pertinent to examine some of the issues associated with perceptions of what multiculturalism entails, since much of the concern and backlash against it appears to be associated with definitional and conceptual misunderstandings. Furthermore, it is important to assess the evidence concerning multiculturalism's recent retreat. A central concern is whether there is actually a retreat from multiculturalism and MCPs or not.

It could be argued that many misunderstandings regarding multiculturalism stem from the multidimensional and complex nature of what it involves. Many of the definitional and conceptual issues are attributable to defining multiculturalism in a simplistic and inaccurate manner. Further, many of the criticisms made of multiculturalism lack empirical support and tend to be overstated without adequate justification. When one investigates the nature of the retreat from multiculturalism and MCPs, it becomes evident that much of what has been stated is misleading. In this article, we seek to examine some definitional and conceptual ideas of multiculturalism. Some common criticisms will be briefly addressed followed by an evaluation of the perceived retreat from multiculturalism and MCPs in relation to the current reality. Finally, a short case study will be presented exploring the Canadian model which can serve as evidence in support of a positive view of multiculturalism given Canada's long-standing experience with MCPs.

Definitional misconceptions and criticisms

The concept of multiculturalism has been understood in quite diverse ways. Academics, commentators, and politicians have all defined multiculturalism according to their own understanding and beliefs, which has contributed to a lack of definitional clarity regarding what multiculturalism entails. Accordingly, it is pertinent to outline a framework that encompasses ways that multiculturalism has been defined, while describing some of the main criticisms made against it.

Within the literature, multiculturalism can be examined using either a research or social construct framework (Long and Liu, 2013). With respect to a research framework, Berry (2013) asserts that from an analytical perspective, multiculturalism consists of three related and overlapping hypotheses:

1. The multicultural hypothesis postulates that mutual respect, cross-cultural sharing, and acceptance of culturally diverse and minority group members is strongly related to one's socio-economic status.
2. The integration hypothesis proposes that for immigrant and minority groups, as an adaptive approach and for the maintenance and enhancement of one's personal socio-psychological well-being, concurrent contact and engagement with the dominant culture(s) is necessary.
3. The intergroup contact hypothesis stipulates that positive intercultural interactions and relations are best achieved through intergroup contact and through relations that are carried out in non-threatening, intimate, and equitable environments.

As a social construct, multiculturalism has been enumerated in a variety of ways. Early on, Berry et al. (1977) classified the concept according to three levels: demography, ideology, and policy. More recently, Bloemraad and Wright (2014) identify a fourth dimension – multiculturalism as public discourse. This refers to the "discourse adopted by governments or institutions to signal recognition and valorization of diversity" which "finds reflection in symbolic acts or pluralism language without necessarily being tied to laws or institutional support" (p. 299). For instance, when German Chancellor Merkel denounced multiculturalism by asserting that it has "utterly failed", and that it promotes "parallel societies" (Winter, 2015), her opposition can be seen as a symbolic one that is opposed to the celebration of diversity and tolerance. However, while this view holds some validity, multiculturalism as public discourse is generally concerned with changing symbolic hierarchies and initiating a policy of equality between minority and dominant groups that opposes coercive orientations such as assimilation (Bloemraad and Wright, 2014).

For some, multiculturalism is perceived as a descriptive term that is largely concerned with demographic diversity or pluralism. From this perspective, a multicultural society is one that is "represented by distinct ethno-cultural groups living together in a given geography" (Leong and Liu, 2013, p. 658). Although some of the debate deals with involuntary migration movements, most of the issues focus on immigrant populations and their descendants. Here, calls to abandon multiculturalism in favor of more coercive policies are generally associated with ethnic, racial, and religious diversity within a demographic space (Bloemraad and Wright, 2014). Much of the literature tends to emphasize how demographic diversity can challenge and potentially weaken social cohesion, social capital, or support for a welfare state (Harell and Stolle, 2010). However, many of these claims are exaggerated and there are plenty of examples of multiculturalism being seen as beneficial. For instance, according to Johnson and Soroka (1999), diversity can have a positive effect on social capital within a society including an increased level of trust and gains in other civic orientations. Bloemraad (2010) came to a similar conclusion noting that MCPs have positive outcomes with respect to minorities' political participation and social capital.

From an ideological perspective, multiculturalism is conceived from respect for liberal values. Conceptualizations here take into account "the prevalent political and religious ethos, which may include injunctions on the degree of tolerance and mutual respect, and allowance for ethno-cultural groups to maintain their heritage culture that is normative" (Leong and Liu, 2013, p. 658). Furthermore, according to Kymlicka (2012), ideological conceptions of multiculturalism are part of a larger post-war era human rights revolution involving racial and ethnic diversity which contributes to a process of democratic "citizenization" that turns into relations of liberal democratic citizenship thereby, among other things, transforming both vertical relationships between groups and the state and horizontal relationships among members of different groups. Put another way, multiculturalism is premised on and constrained by liberal-democratic constitutionalism and respect for principles of human rights that seek to challenge illiberal practices and traditional ethnic and racial hierarchies. Within this ideological perspective, multicultural theorists tend to negatively appraise some forms of classical liberalism from a normative concern for equality and justice that is based on outcomes, as opposed to similarity of treatment (Kymlicka, 2001; Bloemraad and Wright, 2014).

Based on this brief overview, it is clear that descriptions of multiculturalism and MCPs require a broad definition that takes into account the multitude of ways in which they are depicted. In this regard, Rosado (1996) provides a relatively broad and comprehensive characterization whereby multiculturalism is referred to as a "system of beliefs and behaviours that recognizes and respects the presence of all diverse groups in an organization or society, acknowledges and values their socio-cultural differences, and encourages and enables their continued contribution within an inclusive cultural context which empowers all within the organization or society" (p. 2). Thus Rosado's classification is quite thorough since it accounts for the ideological and policy components of multiculturalism, and to a lesser degree, public discourse.

While some conceptions of multiculturalism are derived from the multidimensional and overlapping framework described above, the term is often diluted and many of the criticisms made against multiculturalism are premised on a simplified or inaccurate understanding. According to Kymlicka (2012, pp. 4-7), much of the post-multicultural literature has characterized multiculturalism inaccurately as nothing more than a feel-good celebration of ethno-cultural diversity that encourages citizens to accept and embrace the spectrum of customs, traditions, cuisine, and music that exist in multi-ethnic cultures. Kymlicka goes on to point out that many critiques of multiculturalism and MCPs are premised on this celebratory model, including the following:

1. It ignores or trivializes issues of political and economic inequality such as problems of unemployment, segregation, poor educational outcomes, poor language skills, and political marginalization. These problems cannot be resolved simply by celebrating and focusing on cultural differences.
2. The focus of celebrating some cultural practices is potentially dangerous since not all customs practiced by a group are worthy of being celebrated or legally tolerated. For instance, forced marriage can be counter to norms and laws. To avoid controversy, there's a tendency to place emphasis on inoffensive practices which runs the risk of trivializing cultural differences while ignoring real challenges that differences in cultural or religious beliefs can pose.
3. The celebratory model can encourage the belief that groups are sealed and static, each reproducing their own distinct practices. Multiculturalism may encourage the sharing of customs, but assuming that each group has its own unique customs and practices overlooks processes of cultural adaptation, mixing, and emerging commonalities, thus possibly reinforcing perceptions of minorities as eternally "other." Consequently, this can result in strengthening of prejudice and stereotyping, which can lead to the polarization of ethnic relations.

4. This model can potentially reinforce power inequalities and cultural restrictions within minority groups which, in turn, ignores the ways that many traditional practices are often challenged by internal group members. Accordingly, it can imprison people in "cultural scripts" that they are not permitted to challenge or dispute.

In determining the validity of claims made by the celebratory model and the criticisms made with reference to it, it is necessary to examine the Western experience of multiculturalism and MCPs. However, for now it can be argued that the celebratory model of multiculturalism is inaccurate for three main reasons:

1. The notion that multiculturalism is mainly about symbolic cultural politics is misleading because MCPs combine cultural, political, economic, and social dimensions whereby policies are concerned with minorities' access to political power and economic opportunities such as affirmative action, funding, and access to citizenship. In these cases, MCPs are concerned with political participation, economic redistribution, and cultural recognition.
2. The claim that multiculturalism is not concerned with liberal practices and universal human rights is inaccurate since multiculturalism is itself a human-rights-based movement that condemns and challenges illiberal practices that infringe on human rights. For instance, no Western democracy has exempted minority groups from constitutional norms by allowing practices such as forced marriage or cliterodectomy.
3. The belief that multiculturalism denies the reality of cultural fluidity and change is misleading because multiculturalism-as-citizenization is a transformative experience for minority and majority groups alike. It requires both groups to engage in new practices by entering new relationships and embracing new discourses which in turn transform identities.

(Kymlicka 2012/2007)

Before moving on to examine MCPs in relation to the fears and recent retreat from multiculturalism by some countries, it is worthwhile to briefly explore the validity of a key condemnation of multiculturalism, which is that through its support for diverse identities, support for collective action and institutions will be impeded, thereby causing isolation. On this topic, Miller (2000) points out that individuals must feel a sense of connectedness and common identity and bond, which leads to political participation and a concern for the welfare of others. Taking this argument further, Barry (2001) asserts that to avoid cultural segregation, some form of cultural assimilation is necessary because some multicultural programs can inhibit people in minority communities from forming bonds with the broader society outside their ethnic community. This, he believes, involves more than a legal concept of citizenship; it instead requires a connection and commitment to a liberal and redistributive state. Additionally,

Joppke (1999) lends support to Barry's contention by suggesting that when state resources are directed to the protection and promotion of minority group cultural practices, there is a greater likelihood that minority communities will spend more time within their own groups, with the result that less time will be spent with the majority group. It is suggested that this presents a major obstacle to integration since minority and majority communities are likely to remain isolated from each other.

In contrast to this view, proponents of multiculturalism submit that it is an important means of connecting ethnic minority groups to the majority community and to the state. Taylor (1994) suggests that rather than having an isolating effect, MCPs can have a positive role in affecting the manner in which minority groups see themselves in relation to the state and as such, can facilitate in the creation and maintenance of environments that allow minorities to integrate. Similarly, Kymlicka (2001) points out that MCPs can play a pivotal role in helping members of ethnic-minorities integrate and participate to the same degree as the majority community in political, social, and economic activities through various forms of accommodation.

An investigation of various countries' experiences with multiculturalism is warranted, since empirical evidence remains scarce with virtually no reliable cross-national studies attempting to isolate the effects of MCPs (Boemraad and Wright, 2014; Kymlicka, 2012). In this regard, examining MCPs with respect to claims made for a retreat from multiculturalism may help to determine whether or not there has been a broad decline.

A retreat from multiculturalism and MCPs?

Given the negative reporting in the media, and critical statements made by political figures, it is reasonable to state that there is an increasingly negative perception of multiculturalism among the public in many western countries. In particular, MCPs are perceived as failing both minority and majority groups and as such, there are continued calls to abandon multiculturalism as a policy for dealing with cultural pluralism. The Dutch case has come to be seen as a cornerstone of the narrative for failure and retreat. Similar views have been expressed in France, Germany, and more recently Britain. These views are reflected by a recent Council of Europe report of its 47 member states which concluded that "what had until recently been a preferred policy approach, conveyed in shorthand as 'multiculturalism' has been found inadequate" (Council of Europe, 2008, p. 9).

Given the negative assessments of multiculturalism in many European countries, one must ask whether there is any justification for such views, since there is a lack of reliable empirical evidence in this area and as such, many of the claims made pertaining to the effects of multiculturalism and MCPs must be treated cautiously. In one of the few cross-national studies that attempts to test and isolate the effects of MCPs from other factors, Kesler and

Bloemraad (2010), after surveying 19 countries, found that MCPs have a positive effect on social capital and political participation. Other cross-national studies largely support this view. For instance Weldon (2006), concludes that MCPs have been beneficial in reducing prejudice in Western Europe. Similarly, Koopmans and colleagues (2012) identify policies measuring cultural pluralism across ten European countries, with the results indicating a consistent increase from 1980 to 2002, with a relative degree of stability from 2002 to 2008.

In addition, Banting and Kymlicka (2013) have created a more comprehensive MCP index that measures eight types of policies from 21 nations at three points in time – 1980, 2000, and 2010, analysis of which confirms that they remain firmly established, and are expanding in some cases. (see Appendix for the complete MCP Index). The average score for European countries shows a steady increase with the average rising from 0.7 in 1980 to 2.1 in 2000 and 3.1 in 2010. Additionally, the overall average for all countries likewise confirms a pattern of growth in MCPs. Only Italy, Denmark, and the Netherlands show a decrease – with the Dutch case being the only dramatic drop. Twelve countries, including Belgium, Sweden, Finland, Spain, and Portugal, have witnessed an expansion in MCPs. It should also be noted that Australia and Canada continue to maintain their supportive attitude towards MCPs. Based on this evidence, one can conclude that perceptions of a retreat do not reflect the reality and are perhaps nothing more than a rhetorical backlash.

While the use of indices provides some compelling evidence to support the notion that multiculturalism continues to thrive and has shown a modest growth, some degree of caution is warranted. Recently, the use of indices has been contested by some and criticisms have alleged that measuring and quantifying MCPs is not necessarily an accurate reflection of day to day experiences with multiculturalism. For example, Voyer (2013) questions the use of indices since they are potentially incapable of measuring and capturing the complexities of "everyday multiculturalism", which is concerned with the daily interactions between groups, individuals, and policies. Still, the criticisms of policy indices are few, and overall, indices are quite beneficial since they provide much needed empirical evidence in the study of multiculturalism and allow researchers to operationalize terms such as "accommodation" and "integration". It could be argued that much of the evidence is somewhat inconclusive and future research will likely be necessary to confirm these findings, since much of this research examines general trends, and country-specific circumstances may differ on some issues. Notwithstanding these concerns however, there is a growing body of evidence pertaining to some countries' experiences with MCPs which suggests that under appropriate circumstances they are beneficial.

In spite of the evidence indicating expansion of multiculturalism, political figures and the media continue to contribute to a perception of a backlash and a retreat. It is likely that part of the answer for this apparent paradox lies in the tendency of some politicians to avoid the use of the term "multiculturalism", while at the same time continuing with policies that promote pluralism and accommodation. In the case of German Chancellor Merkel, the declaration of a retreat is somewhat baffling since Germany has never been a country that widely embraced any forms of meaningful MCPs. In other countries, as a public discourse, the narratives for advancing multiculturalism have taken on terms such as *diversity, civic integration, inter-culturalism,* and *community cohesion* without affecting actual policies (Bloemraad and Wright, 2013; Kymlicka, 2012). In these cases, there appears to be a strengthening of civic integration measures which emphasize the importance of integration, and which are entirely compatible with strong forms of multiculturalism and MCPs, as is the case with the Canadian model of multiculturalism (*Ibid.*). Although there is some recent concern that multiculturalism may be experienced differently by immigrants in countries with similar policies since some civic integration policies can be more coercive than others (Goodman, 2010), it is reasonable to argue that much of the rhetoric regarding a retreat in multiculturalism and MCPs is misplaced. An examination of the Canadian model and experience with multiculturalism can serve to highlight the evidence supporting the view that MCPs are beneficial.

Multiculturalism in Canada

Canada was the first Western country to adopt and implement an official government policy of multiculturalism and continues to be the only country that has enshrined this policy in its constitution. Beginning in 1971, Canada adopted various policy measures in an effort to deal with immigrant and minority groups in an equitable manner. Berry (2013) suggests that Canadian multiculturalism has always sought to promote a combination of elements in an effort to help ensure integration and equitable access for all members of society, including a shared national identity, equitable participation, intercultural dialogue, and the valorization of diversity. Many countries that have implemented MCPs have attempted to replicate aspects of the Canadian model. In this regard, Canadian multiculturalism was imitated, marketed, and exported worldwide with varying levels of success (Kymlicka, 2004).

In institutionalizing multiculturalism, it could be argued that Canada retains the strongest basis for cultural diversity and inclusion of any western country. For instance, in its constitution, which was amended in 1982 to include the Canadian Charter of Rights and Freedoms, article 27 asserts that all members of society are guaranteed rights "in a manner consistent with the multicultural heritage of Canadians." Additionally, other legislative provisions, including the 1988 Multiculturalism Act and the 1995 Employment Equity Act, provide further legislative protections and statements of Canada's commitment to a diverse, equitable, and inclusive society for all.

The intent of Canada's MCPs is the integration and inclusion of all groups and individuals through mechanisms that ensure equality of opportunity and treatment (Ley, 2007). Canada's multiculturalism progressed through three developmental stages beginning with *demographic multiculturalism*, moving onto *symbolic multiculturalism* (that included grants and support for cultural programs and events), finally culminating in *structural multiculturalism*, which presently includes items of anti-racism policy, employment equity, equal treatment before the law, education and immigration policy, and redress for past and present discrimination (*Ibid.*). This progression has been decribed as evolving through three developmental phases: the *incipient stage* (pre-1971), the *formative period* (1971 - 1981), and the *institutionalization period* (1982 to the present), which in 2010 culminated in the introduction of three new goals to meet some of the contemporary challenges facing multiculturalism (Dewing, 2013). These, under the umbrella of the Multiculturalism Program, included the following broad objectives:

- to build an integrated, socially cohesive society;
- to improve the responsiveness of institutions to meet the needs of a diverse population; and
- to actively engage in discussions on multiculturalism and diversity at an international level.

(*Ibid.* at p. 8)

Accordingly, it can be suggested that Canada's MCPs support the integration and participation of minorities by removing barriers to allow and promote economic, political, and social participation of all groups.

However, as discussed previously, some concerns have been expressed that multiculturalism can undermine solidarity, common identity, and sociopolitical integration (Bloemraad and Wright, 2014). Within this context, examining the evidence pertaining to Canada's lengthy experimentation with multiculturalism can provide some important insights about potential adverse effects of MCPs. Given that Canada has had the longest and most extensive experience with multiculturalism, any undesirable effects should surface there first.

In examining the Canadian experience, research seems to indicate that despite difficulties, multiculturalism has had predominantly positive effects. This research suggests that in Canada, the process of minority and immigrant integration has been successful relative to the experience of other countries, and that MCPs play a positive role in this process (Kymlicka, 2010b) Specifically, recent studies and research indicate the following:

- There is a high level of mutual acceptance and identification among immigrant and minority groups with native-born Canadians.
- Compared to every other Western democracy, political integration in Canada is highest with naturalized immigrants more likely to participate in the political process as voters, party members, and candidates – making Canada's political process inclusive.

- The children of immigrants in Canada have better educational outcomes than in any other Western democracies.
- Compared to Europe, there is an almost complete absence of immigrant and minority ghettos.
- Multiculturalism plays a constructive role in enabling healthy processes of individual acculturation.
- At the institutional level, MCPs play an important role in creating more inclusive and equitable public institutions.

(Ibid.)

Despite these findings, critics have disputed the notion that MCPs are responsible for this success, arguing that other factors can help explain this comparative success of integration. It has been suggested for instance, that Canada's immigrants are more highly skilled than in other countries and that MCPs make an insignificant contribution to the successful integration of immigrants and minorities and perhaps even hinder it (Goodhart, 2008). However, in one of the few studies that attempts to isolate the effects of MCPs, Bloemraad (2006) shows that they do in fact have a range of positive effects. In her study, Bloemraad compared the integration experiences of two virtually identical Vietnamese immigrant groups in Boston and Toronto. In comparison to the immigrants in Boston, the Vietnamese group in Toronto was able to participate and integrate more quickly and successfully into various Canadian institutions as a result of MCPs. Further, the same study showed similar results for the two cities' Portuguese communities (ibid).

In spite of Canada's overall positive experiences with multiculturalism, the authors are by no means advocating that other countries pursue the Canadian model of MCPs, since each country has its own unique history, culture and political system, and these may not always be suited to the introduction of the multicultural model adopted by Canada. For instance, it has been suggested that as a settler society the Canadian model has had relative success, whereas countries in Europe may face issues that are substantially different than those in Canada, and therefore need to be cautious in the manner that MCPs are adopted and implemented (Bloemraad and Wright, 2014). Nevertheless, there is substantial evidence to suggest that Canada's MCPs have played a positive and crucial role in promoting integration, mutual understanding, and social cohesion through individual-level effects on attitudes, identities, and society-level effects on institutions (Kymlicka, 2012).

Conclusion

Based on this overview of some of the current research on MCPs, we can conclude that multiculturalism continues to offer valid solutions for the issues involved in culturally plural societies. Although not without difficulties, multiculturalism has proven to be more appropriate than previous systems of dealing with cultural diversity and pluralism. This, in part, explains its continued expansion against a rhetorical narrative of retreat.

It should be observed that some legitimate concerns and challenges remain for countries wishing to implement MCPs. Evidence suggests that multiculturalism may be more likely to be successful in settler societies, such as Canada, where it can be more closely tied to fluid conceptions of national identity, than in some European countries where notions of nationhood are likely to be more rigid and enshrined. Studies of immigrant youth support this view whereby national and ethnic identities are positively correlated in settler societies such as Canada, Australia, and New Zealand, and tend to be negatively perceived in some European countries (Berry, 2013).

In this respect, while multiculturalism remains a viable option for most countries, its successful implementation is likely to be dependent on a variety of factors. When countries and immigrants respect human rights, economic contributions, diversity of immigrant groups, border control, and desecuritization of ethnic relations as important (Kymlicka, 2012), MCPs have been successfully implemented. This is evident when looking at the experience of Canada, where most of these conditions are present and multiculturalism thrives.

References

Banting, K. & Kymlicka, W. (2013) Is there really a retreat from multiculturalism policies? New evidence from the multiculturalism policy index. *Comparative European Politics* 11(5): 577-598.

Barry, B. (2001) *Culture and Equality: An Egalitarian Critique of Multiculturalism.* Cambridge: Polity Press.

Berry, J. W. (2013) Research on multiculturalism in Canada. *International Journal of Intercultural Relations* 37(6): 663-675.

Berry, J. W., Kalin, R., & Taylor, D. (1977) *Multiculturalism and ethnic attitudes in Canada.* Ottawa: Ministry of Supply and Services.

Bloemraad, I., & Wright, M. (2014) "Utter failure" or unity out of diversity? Debating and evaluating policies of multiculturalism. *International Migration Review* 48(1): 292-334.

Brooks, S. (Ed.) (2002) *The challenge of cultural pluralism.* Westport: Praeger.

Council of Europe (2008) *White Paper on Intercultural Dialogue: Living Together as Equals in Dignity.* Strasbourg, France: Council of Europe.

Dewing, M. (2013) *Canadian Multiculturalism, Background Paper.* Ottawa: Library of Parliament.

Edmonton Journal (February 13, 2011). Accessed August 2014 from: http://www.edmontonjournal.com/opinion/Multiculturalism+failure+Europe/4273602/story.html

Goodhart, D. (2008) Has multiculturalism had its day? *Literacy Review of Canada* 16(3): 3-4.

Goodman, S. W. (2010) Integration requirements for integration's sake? Identifying, categorizing and comparing civic integration policies. *Journal of Ethnic and Migration Studies* 36(5): 753-772.

Harell, A., & Stolle, D. (2010) Diversity and demographic politics. *Canadian Journal of Political Science* 43(2): 235-256.

Hyman, H., Meinhard, A. and Shields, J. (2011) *The role of multiculturalism in addressing social inclusion processes in Canada.* Canadian Multicultural Education Foundation.

Johnson, R., & Sorokan, S. (1999) *Social Capital in a Multicultural Society: The Case of Canada.* Paper presented at the 1999 Annual meeting of the Canadian Political Science Association, June. Sherbrooke, Quebec.

Joppke, C. (1999) *Immigration and the Nation-State: The United States, Germany, and Great Britain.* New York: Oxford University Press.

Kessler, C. & Bloemraad, I. (2010) Does immigration erode social capital? The conditional effects of immigration-generated diversity on trust, membership, and participation across 19 countries, 1981-2000. *Canadian Journal of Political Science* 43(2): 319-347.

Koopmans, R. (2010) Trade-offs between equality and difference: Immigrant integration, multiculturalism and the welfare state in cross-national perspective. *Journal of Ethnic and Migration Studies* 36(1): 1-26.

Kymlicka, W. (2004) Marketing Canadian multiculturalism in the international arena. *International Journal* 59: 829-852.

Kymlicka, W. (2007) *Multicultural Odysseys: Navigating the New International Politics of Diversity.* Oxford: Oxford University Press.

Kymlicka, W. (2010a) Testing the liberal multicultural hypothesis: normative theories and social science evidence. *Canadian Journal of Political Science* 43: 257-271.

Kymlicka, W. (2010b) *The Current State of Multiculturalism in Canada and Research Themes on Canadian Multiculturalism, 2008 – 2010.* Ottawa: Citizenship and Immigration Canada.

Kymlicka, W. (2012) *Multiculturalism: Success, Failure, and the Future.* Washington, D.C.: Migration Policy Institute.

Leong, C. H. and Liu, J. H. (2013) Whither multiculturalism? Global identities at a cross-roads. *International Journal of Intercultural Relations* 37: 657-662.

Ley, D. (2007) Multiculturalism: A Canadian defence, working paper series. *Research on Immigration and Integration in the Metropolis* 7(4): 1-20

Miller, D. (2000) *Citizenship and National Identity.* Cambridge: Polity Press.

United Nations, Department of Economic and Social Affairs, Population Division (2013) *International Migration Report 2013.* New York, N.Y.: United Nations.

Voyer, A. M. (2013) *Strangers and Neighbors: Multiculturalism, Conflict, and Community in America.* New York, NY: Cambridge University Press.

Weldon, S. (2006) The institutional context of tolerance for ethnic minorities: A comparative multilevel analysis of western Europe. *American Journal of Political Science.* 50(2): 331-349.

Winter, E. (2015) Rethinking multiculturalism after its "retreat": lessons from Canada. *American Behavioral Scientist* 59(6): 637-657.

APPENDIX

MCP Index (Reproduced from Banting and Kymlicka, 2013).

	1980	2000	2010
Canada	5	7.5	7.5
Australia	4	8	8
Austria	0	1	1.5
Belgium	1	3	5.5
Denmark	0	.5	0
Finland	0	1.5	6
France	1	2	2
Germany	0	2	2.5
Greece	.5	.5	2.5
Ireland	1	1.5	3
Italy	0	1.5	1
Japan	0	0	0
Netherlands	2.5	5.5	2
New Zealand	2.5	5	5.5
Norway	0	0	2.5
Portugal	1	2	3.5
Spain	0	1	3.5
Sweden	3	5	7
Switzerland	0	1	1
United Kingdom	2.5	5.5	5.5
United States	3	3	3
European average	.7	2.1	3.1
Overall average	1.29	2.71	3.48

Countries could receive a total score of 8, one for each of the following 8 policies: (a) constitutional, legislative, or parliamentary affirmation of multiculturalism at the central and/or regional and municipal levels and the existence of a government ministry, secretariat, or advisory board to implement this policy in consultation with ethnic communities; (b) the adoption of multiculturalism in school curriculum; (c) the inclusion of ethnic representation/ sensitivity in the mandate of public media or media licensing; (d) exemptions from dress codes; (e) allowing of dual citizenship; (f) the funding of ethnic group organizations or activities; (g) the funding of bilingual education or mother-tongue instruction; and (h) affirmative action for disadvantaged immigrant groups.

ENDNOTES

Chapter 1: How Do Japanese Elementary School Children Perceive Peace and War? Changes in Children's Perceptions Through English Lessons on Land Mines and Peace

1   A number of studies on students' perception of war and peace through social studies or extra curricula activities (i.e. field studies, school excursions) are reported. For example, reports by Nagoya University School of Education–affiliated upper and lower secondary school (Yagi and Hiramatsu, 1991; Maruyama, 1993), Kyoto University School of Education–affiliated Momoyama Elementary School (Murakami, 2013) and so on. As shown in the study of Murakami (2013), experiences of war in Hiroshima, Nagasaki, and Okinawa have greatly influenced peace education in Japan, which also affected international peace education practice in the 1970s (Vriens, 1999).

2   A foreign language to be taught does not have to be English but English is taught most commonly in Japan.

3   In A. Raviv, L. Oppenheimer, and D. Bar-Tal, D. (1999) How children understand war and peace- A call for international peace education, San Francisco, US: Jossey-Bass Publishers, p. 7.

4   In A. Raviv, L. Oppenheimer, and D. Bar-Tal, D. (1999) How children understand war and peace- A call for international peace education, San Francisco, US: Jossey-Bass Publishers, p. 7.

5   The fourth through sixth graders are divided into two groups for the English class. The author teaches one of the groups mainly with fourth and fifth graders. The other class is taught by a native speaker of English.

6   L.J.A. Vriens, (1987) Pedagogiektussenvrees en vrede: Eenpedagogischetheorie over uredesopvoeding [Pedagogy between fear and peace: A pedagogical theory of peace education]. Thesis, Utrecht University. Antwerp, Belgium: InternationaleVredesinformatiedienst.

Chapter 2: The Media Literacy Deficit in Japan: Exploring the Link Between Digital Citizenship, Cultural Diversity and Critical Thinking

1   There is also a lag of two decades between the adoption and implementation of media literacy policies in public schools in Western contexts such as the implementation of the Media Literacy: Resource Guide into Ontario, Canada's public school curriculum in 1989 and the publication of this 2010 article.

Chapter 3: Toward a Utopian peace education

1   Galtung's (1975) observation that "it is hard to be all-out against peace" and that it often serves to obtain consensus remains true (p. 109).

2   For a helpful overview, see Bloch's (1995) introduction, available at <https://www.marxists.org/archive/bloch/hope/introduction.htm>. Accessed on 19 June, 2015.

3   Jameson (2005: xvi) adapts Sartre's *anti-anti-communist* slogan, which served as a way of navigating between flawed communism and worse anti-communism, into a strategy for those utopists who refuse to give up on the power of utopia.

Chapter 4: Education and spaces of, for, and by Ainu: Lessons from the 2013 New Zealand Ainumosir Exchange Program

1   Traditionally ainu/aynu words are not capitalized.

2   See, for example <http://www.teataarangi.org.nz/?q=about-te-ataarangi>

3   A marae is a complex of buildings on grounds that belong to a particular Māori tribe and is a place of spiritual refuge.

Chapter 5: Towards the location of a dynamic learning environment

1   Due to his serious concern about this situation, in 1998 David Adams created an alternative news service dedicated to disseminating encouraging news stories about developments in the promotion of peace and human rights around the world. 'The Culture of Peace News Network' can be found here: <http://cpnn-world.org>

2   Dear Short-sensei, I watched the movie "13 Days". Why are we fighting? Why are we always doing wars? We humans are always in a state of war aren't we? For example, in the cases of the Crimean peninsula or in Donetsk. Why are we always fighting wars? And why is James-sensei studying Peace Studies? Aren't we all living in a condition that isn't peaceful? Russia and ISIS (aren't Iraq and Syria in a kind of state of

ultra-nationalist war?) aren't they in a state of right-leaning war? Sensei is studying Peace Studies. But isn't that just idealism? (I watched the movie "13 Days". Why are we fighting? Why are we always doing wars?[sic] Bokutachi wa itsumo senso jyotai ni arimasu yo ne? Tatoeba Crimea hanto no ken ni shitemo, Donetsk no ken ni shitemo. Doshite watashitachi wa itsumo senso wo suru no? Soshite, doshite Short-sensei wa "Heiwa Gaku" wo benkyo shiteru no? Bokutachi wa itsu datte heiwa dewanai jyotai no naka de ikiteru jyanai ka? Russia mo ISIS mo (Iraq to Syria no kokusui shugi mo senso wo hiki okoshiuru sonzai jyanai ka) mo, migi yori de senso wo hiki okoshiuru sonzai jyanai ka? Sensei wa heiwa gaku no benkyo wo shiteru. Sore te riso shugi jyanai desu ka?)

You teach me "Peace Studies", but is this only idealism?

Realistically there's no chance of peace. Why do you continue as a teacher of Peace Studies? I'm sure that I've made many mistakes in this, but I'd really like James-sensei to tell his opinion directly to us students. I appreciate that what I've said is impolite, but please could you do this. I really hate this condition of wars happening around the world. (Genjistuniheiwananantearienai. Nandeanatawaheiwagaku no sensei de aritsutsuketeirundesuka? Goji datsujiwaooi to omoimasuga, zehi James-sensei nisochokunaiken wo watashitachiseitoniokikasekudasai. Bushitsuke de reigiganatteinai no mojyujyushochidesu. Zehiyoroshikuonegaishimasu. Sensogaokoteiruima no jyokyowabokuwahontoniiyadesu. K.N.)

3   A detailed account of the preceding decision-making process and content of this course is given in Short (2013), 'Curriculum development in peace-related learning within the Japanese higher education sector: The structure and content of a new one year undergraduate course in Peace Studies', Toyo University Law Faculty Journal, vol. 57, no. 2, pp. 1-32.

4   Barash, D. and Webel, C. (2008) Peace and Conflict Studies, 2nd edition, SAGE Publications.

5   Matsuo, M. (1995), 'Peace Studies in Japan: The Current State', Journal of International Development and Cooperation, vol. 1, no. 1; Matsuo, M., (2001), 'Whither Peace Studies? Fragmentation to a New Integration?', Journal of International Development and Cooperation, vol. 7, no. 2.

6   A specific breakdown of the data from the formal class evaluations of the academic years 2012-2013 and 2013-2014 can be obtained from the author on request.

7   The author would like to take the opportunity to express his gratitude to the magnanimity and understanding shown by the American students Ms. B, Ms. O and Ms. W, and Mr. G, Mr. N and Mr. W during the 2013-2014 academic year.

8   These adjustments were not pre-planned strategies, but approaches that were adopted as the course progressed in circumstances where they were deemed appropriate.

9   Data available from the author on request, see Note 13 above.

10 "I'm not all that good at English, but there was a real difference between some students' English ability and so some of the discussions with the exchange students were a real struggle." ("Eigo wo rikai suru no wa taihen de sono bubun wa muzukashikata desu ga, jyugyou naiyo wa kyomi bukai mono ga ooku hokano hito no iken nado ironna kangaekata ga mi ni tsuita to omoteimasu. Moto sekai wo shiru hitsuyo ga aru to kanjimashita.")

"This was one of the only classes that I could take together with foreign exchange students and as I wanted to improve my English it was good for me. However, at times the content of the class was difficult and there were occasions when I couldn't join in the discussions. But getting to know lots of things that I hadn't known before was good." ("Ryugakusei to isho ni jyugyo ga ukerareru yuitsu no jyugyo datta node eigo ryoku wo nobashitai jibun ni totte wa yokatta. Shikashi jyugyo no naiyo ga tama ni muzukashiku, tama ni giron dekinai koto mo atta. Demo shiranai koto wo takusan shirete yokatta desu.")

"There were lots of opportunities to think about things that I don't normally think about, even if I knew a little about them, and things that I didn't know very much about, so I really learned a lot. I had thought that international peace was a really distant thing, but after studying this I think that it is a much closer thing to me." ("Fudannakanakakangaenaikoto, tashoshiteitemo, fukakuwashiranaikotonitsuitekangaerukikaigatakusanari, totemobenkyoninarimashita. Kokusai heiwanantetoidekigoto da to omotemashitaga, kore wo kikakeni, mijikanikangaeru you ninarimashita.")

11 The evaluation questionnaires were designed only for the Japanese students. It goes without saying that the author regards the input of foreign exchange students as extremely valuable and has therefore submitted a request to Toyo University that an English version of the questionnaire be prepared for future sessions.

12 In most cases the difficulties that arose within group discussions alluded to above by the Japanese students came about as a result of language difficulties and not a lack of effort on the part of the American students to facilitate them.

13 It goes without saying that the author is far from enamoured by this timetable change since one group of students has been effectively denied the opportunity of studying the course, and those who are currently studying it have been denied the opportunity of studying in cooperation with their colleagues from overseas. As a consequence of this, a formal request has been submitted to the Kyoumuka that henceforth Peace Studies should be taught during the afternoon so that it will no longer clash with the foreign language students' obligatory Japanese classes which always take place in the morning.

14 For this purpose the author has hitherto made use of Toyo University's common access website ToyoNet-Ace. His colleague from the United States also recommends the Microsoft 'Slide Share' service.

15   This is the motivation behind the author's formal request to the Kyoumuka described above.

Chapter 7: Natural resource and topography: Rethinking the cause of conflict in Mindanao

1   Certain groups would mean unscrupulous persons, politicians and businessmen who took advantage of the people's low economic state in the island.

2   For this chapter, civil war, armed conflict and rebellion are used interchangeably. Others may argue about such distinctions, but these concepts involve actions and violence against an established authority collectively.

3   The authors, Collier and Hoeffler, later changed this approach to a broader notion called "opportunity" in their paper entitled "Greed and grievance in civil war", *Oxford Economic Papers,* 56:4 (2004), pp.563-95.

4   Camp Abubakar was later called Camp Iranun by President Gloria Macapagal-Arroyo in 2005 as it became a 'zone of peace'.

5   More detailed information about the marshland is in the Natural Resources section of this chapter.

6   According to Collier and Hoeffler, primary commodity exports tend to increase the dangers of civil war. The data suggests that the state's dependence on natural resources has a significant influence on the likelihood of the commencement of civil war. However, many researchers pose a challenge to the findings of Collier and Hoeffler, stating that the share of primary commodity exports in GDP nor its square is remotely significant.

7   M.L. Ross (2004) 'What do we know about Natural Resource and Civil War?' in the *Journal of Peace Research,* Volume 41, number 3, May, cites P. Collier and A. Hoeffler (2002b), 'The Political Economy of Secession', manuscript, 30 June, pp. 346.

8   Interview was conducted on August 2012 to identified informants in various locations in Mindanao.

9   GMA News is one of the leading networks in the Philippines bringing news and current affairs to the country.

10   Due to limitations of this particular paper, the researcher cannot detail his methodology and results, but that further publications of the whole research work will do so. This chapter is a snapshot of the full research project.

11   Interview was conducted on August 2012 to identified informants in various locations in Mindanao.

Chapter 9: The Israeli-Palestinian conflict: simulacra of policymaking?

1   Edward Said (2000) vilified the Oslo Accords in his collection of essays, The End of the Peace Process—Oslo and After, London, Granta Books.

2   A breakdown of data is given by B'tselem, the Israeli Information Center for Human Rights in the Occupied Territories http://old.btselem.org/statistics/english/First_Intifada_Tables.asp

3   See Letter dated 16 November 1988 from the Deputy Permanent Observer of the Palestine Liberation Organization to the United Nations addressed to the Secretary-Generalhttp://unispal.un.org/UNISPAL. NSF/0/6EB54A389E2DA6C6852560DE0070E392

4   Listed variously by the Palestinian Society for the Protection of Human Rights and the Environment in 1998 as 'the Protocol on Economic Relations which formed annex IV of the Gaza -Jericho agreement signed in Paris on 29th April 1994 (The Paris Protocol), Agreement on the Gaza Strip and the Jericho area signed on 4th May 1994 in Cairo (The Cairo Agreement), Agreement on Preparatory Transfer of Powers and Responsibilities signed at Erez on 29th August 1994 (The Erez Agreement), Interim Agreement on the West Bank and Gaza Strip signed on 28th September 1995 (The Taba Agreement), Agreement on the Temporary International Presence in the city of Hebron signed on 9th May 1996 (TIPH Agreement), Protocol Concerning the Redeployment in Hebron signed on 7th January 1997 (The Hebron Protocol)' ('Five years of Oslo: The Continuing Victimisation of Human Rights' <http://www.jnul.huji.ac.il/ia/ archivedsites/gushshalom010204/www.gush-shalom.org/archives/oslofive.doc>)

5   Yossi Beilin, interviewed by Ari Sharvit, attempted to claim that procrastination put paid to the Oslo peace process, together with extremist opposition on both sides: 'The biggest mistake was to adopt the interim settlement model put forward way back, by [PM Menachem] Begin. From the beginning I thought that those five years would not make us and the Palestinians better friends, so I tried to persuade both Rabin, Peres and the Palestinians to move quickly to a permanent settlement. It's possible that this could not have been done immediately in 1993, but in my opinion it was possible back in 1995 to reach an agreement on the basis of my understandings with Abu Mazen. The time that has passed since then has only enabled the extremists on both sides to badmouth one another and to claim that there is no partner.'

Beilin also alleged that Palestinian 'incitement' during Barak's term as prime minister, as a result of the unopposed expansion of settlements, put paid to the process: 'But there were two other important mistakes, particularly in the term of Barak's government. One mistake was that we didn't treat the incitement problem as seriously as it deserved. I admit that I did not take into consideration the gravity of Palestinian incitement. I was too liberal on that subject. The second mistake was the settlements. Because we all believed that peace was just around the corner, we did not devote enough attention to the fact that in the Barak period the number of settlers increased by 12 percent. I think that my and my colleagues' silence in the face of the expanding settlements was a mistake.' Interview with Yossi Beilin on the Oslo Peace Process by Ari Shavit (Ha'aretz, June 15, 2001) reproduced at http://middleeast.atspace.com/article_250.html.

One of Israel's negotiators in Oslo, the late Ron Pundak, writing in 2001 (From Oslo to Taba: What Went Wrong? in Survival: Global Politics and Strategy, 43:3, 31-45, DOI: 10.1080/00396330112331343035), confirms 'the opportunity for peace did in fact exist, but that it was squandered due to the misperception of each of the sides regarding the real interests of the other party, and to the faulty implementation and management of the entire process. ... The average Palestinian in the West Bank and Gaza continued to experience humiliating treatment, new settlements were established both on and off expropriated land, and the general perception was of continued occupation. ...'

'The version of events, which was fed to the Israeli public during Barak's tenure, was different from the reality on the ground. The "Oslo years" under Barak did not see the end of the Israeli occupational mentality, did not enable real Palestinian control over the three million citizens of the PA, did not bring an end to building in the settlements or to the expropriation of land, and did not enable economic growth in the territories. In addition, Barak's repeated statements that he was the only Prime Minister who had not transferred land to the Palestinians raised questions for many about his sincerity. The suspicions increased once it became clear to the Palestinians that Barak would not transfer the three villages on the outskirts of Jerusalem (Abu Dis, Al Eyzaria and Arab Sawahra) to PA control after both the Government and the Knesset had approved the transfer.'

Pundak gives a graphic description of the mounting conditions of repression: 'closures which were interpreted as collective punishment; restrictions on movement which affected almost all Palestinians; a permit-issuing system which mainly hurt decent people already cleared by Israeli security; mistreatment at IDF and Border Police checkpoints often aimed, on purpose, at PA officials; a dramatic decrease in employment opportunities in Israel, leading to increased unemployment and the creation of new pockets of poverty; water shortages during the summer months as opposed to the abundance of water supply in the Israeli settlements; the destruction of Palestinian homes while new houses were built in the settlements; the non-release of prisoners tried for activities committed before Oslo; Israeli restrictions on building outside Areas A and B; and the establishment of Bantustan-like areas, controlled according to the whim of Israeli military rule and on occasion dictated by its symbiotic relationship with the settlers' movement. The settlers, for their part, did everything within their power to obstruct the spirit and word of the Oslo Agreement. The result was a relentless struggle, over land resources, with the settlers often receiving the tacit backing of the IDF and the civil administration in the West Bank (a majority of whose staff are themselves settlers).' ("From Oslo to Taba: What Went Wrong?")

In a later 2004 interview (http://www.justvision.org/portrait/812/interview), Pundak confirmed failings on both sides: 'After the Oslo Accords we were stingy on the issue of prisoners, the economy, and almost everything—not because we wanted to sabotage the process, but because from our point of view, all this might have led to a Palestinian state, which we did not dare to say out-loud—for example, partition of

Jerusalem, which is a must for any agreement. If we continue to say during negotiations that Jerusalem will always be under Israeli control, we are pushing aside Palestinian legitimate activities and sending the wrong message in regards to what we want to have. So to sum it up in a nut-shell, I think we screwed it up. All this without describing one inch of the legitimate criticism I have of the Palestinians: that they were slow, that they were terrible in not fighting terrorism seriously, that they were double talking and that Arafat is a terrible manager and doesn't really care about his own people, etc. And that his methods of negotiations were childish. But I say in spite of all my criticism against the Palestinians, and I have kilometers of criticism, still in the big picture, I think we screwed it up.'

6   The process—for at that time it was officially illegal for Israelis to meet with members of the PLO—is relayed somewhat as if it were an exciting spy story in Beilin's 1999 book, Touching Peace. He was preceded four years earlier by HananAshrawi's Oslo narrative, This Side of Peace; a year later, in 1996, Mahmoud Abbas published Through Secret Channels: The Road to Oslo : Senior PLO Leader Abu Mazen's Revealing Story of the Negotiations With Israel. Other negotiators wrote their own books (Ron Pundak published in Hebrew in 2013, Secret channel: Oslo – the full story; a year later, YairHirschfeld published in English, Track-Two Diplomacy toward an Israeli-Palestinian Solution, 1978-2014.

7   Said (2000) notes that the Taba ('Oslo II') interim agreement 'postpones still further dates for army re-deployment, which is now to be done in six-month intervals … Sixty-two new Israeli military bases are to be established on the West Bank … not one inch of East Jerusalem will be given up' (Said, p.15). The subsequent Wye River Memorandum finalized in October 1998 'to give Palestinians 10 percent more land, was never implemented by Netanyahu' and by May 1999 Netanyahu was succeeded, once more, by Ehud Barak, who 'does not seem inclined to visions of coexistence or of equality between Palestinians and Israeli Jews' (Said, p.xv). In short, the negotiations have led to no more than 'a series of municipal responsibilities in Bantustans controlled from the outside by Israel. What Israel has secured is official Palestinian consent to Israeli occupation, which continues in a streamlined and more economical form than before' (Said, p.14).

8   Said (2000, p. 312) retorted, 'Because the United States, the world's only superpower, has been the sponsor and the keeper of the "peace process", as it has come to be known, the arrangements agreed to by Yasir Arafat and three Israeli prime ministers (Rabin, Peres, Netanyahu) have become synonymous with "peace", the only game in town, and the real problems on the ground either papered over or ignored. To be critical of or dissatisfied with Oslo and its aftermath thus means to be against peace, and to be roughly in the same disagreeable camps as the "extremists" (Hamas and the settlers) of both sides, "haters of peace", as Bill Clinton called them.'

9   Israeli-Palestinian Joint Statement, 27 January 2001 [online]. Accessed at http://www.mideastweb.org/taba. htm on 19th September, 2011.

10   For an outline of the Parameters, see http://www.peacelobby.org/clinton_parameters.htm on the Jewish Peace Lobby website.

11 Mitchell was later to become a special envoy for the Middle East 'proximity talks' in January 2009, in the wake of the Operation Cast Lead Gaza War in 2008-2009. He resigned in disgruntlement in 2011 after two unproductive years.

12 For the text of the 14 reservations, see http://www.haaretz.com/print-edition/news/israel-s-road-map-reservations-1.8935

13 The Geneva Accord's homepage is http://www.geneva-accord.org/

14 The Elon Plan's website is at http://www.israelinitiative.com/

15 Right-wing Israeli political party founded by the late (assassinated) RehavamZe'evi, which later allied with the new Herut and Tkuma parties to form the National Union.

16 Alonlater 'resigned'/was dismissed due to his opposition to PM Sharon's Gaza disengagement process.

17 Jordanian citizenship had, in fact, been revoked in 1988 when King Hussein gave up ties to the West Bank.

18 See Khalid Amayreh's 2003 article, 'Against Israel Against God – Christian Zionists <http://english.aljazeera.net/Articles/News/ArabWorld/Features/Israel+and+Christian+Zionists.htm> and <http://www.rense.com/general41/aagi.htm>; Stephen Spector's Evangelicals and Israel: The Story of American Christian Zionism (Oxford University Press, 2008).

19 Israel's domestic secret service.

20 On the Israeli negotiating team headed by Yossi Beilin were Israel Labour Party members of Knesset (MKs) Avram Burg, AmramMitzna and YuliTamir, MK Haim Oron and several colleagues from Israeli political party Meretz, former MK Nehama Ronen, Brigadier General (reserve) GioraInbar, former chief of staff AmnonLipkin-Shahak and the writer Amos Oz; the Palestinian negotiating team headed by Yasser Abed-Rabbo included former PA ministers Nabil Kassis and Hisham Abdel Razeq and two leaders of the Fatah-affiliated Tanzim organization, Kadoura Fares and Mohammed Khourani.

21 Issues such as Jerusalem; an international presence at the volatile Al-Haram Al-Sharif /Temple Mount site in the Old City of Jerusalem; a corridor linking the West Bank and Gaza; security arrangements including air space, international borders and demilitarization; the establishment of an Inter-Religious Council for preservation and protection of Jerusalem's ancient sacred sites; designated roads allowing for travel between Israel and Palestine and vehicle tracking device installation; water; the environment; refugees; border crossing points, and the link to the Arab Peace Initiative.

22   The remarkably even-handed reports and summaries of the findings can be accessed at <http://www.ohchr. org/EN/HRBodies/HRC/CoIGazaConflict/Pages/ReportCoIGaza.aspx#report>

Chapter 10: The Yamba Dam: Conflict and consequences for a rural community

1   Japanese thermal hot-water bath.

2   Site visit by the author.

3   Site visit by the author.

Chapter 11: Language choice and political preferences in Ukraine: Can language unite the nation?

1   Source: http://2001.ukrcensus.gov.ua/eng/results/general/language/Poltava/

2   Source: http://2001.ukrcensus.gov.ua/eng/results/general/language/Kirovohrad/

3   Source: http://2001.ukrcensus.gov.ua/eng/results/general/language/Dnipropetrovsk/

4   Source: http://2001.ukrcensus.gov.ua/eng/results/general/language/Kherson/

5   Source: http://2001.ukrcensus.gov.ua/eng/results/general/language/Mykolaiv/

6   Source: http://2001.ukrcensus.gov.ua/eng/results/general/language/Kharkiv/

7   Source: http://2001.ukrcensus.gov.ua/eng/results/general/language/Odesa/

8   "The proportion of those whose mother tongue is Ukrainian totals 50.2% of the population of region, this is 0.9 percentage points more than in 1989. The percentage of those whose mother tongue is Russian totals 48.2% of the population, comparatively with the data of previous census this index has decreased by 0.6 percentage points. The percentage of other languages, specified like mother tongue, during the period that have passed since previous census has decreased by 0.3 percentage points and accounts for 1.6%." (Source: <http://2001.ukrcensus.gov.ua/eng/results/general/language/Zaporizhzhia/>)

9   "The proportion of those whose mother tongue is Ukrainian totals 24.1% of the population of Donetsk region, this is by 6.5 percentage points more than in 1989. The percentage of those whose mother tongue is Russian totals 74.9% of the population. Comparatively with the data of previous census this index has decreased by 7.2 percentage points." (Source: http://2001.ukrcensus.gov.ua/eng/results/general/language/Donetsk/)

10 "The proportion of those whose mother tongue is Ukrainian totals 30% of the population of region, this is 4.9 percentage points more than in 1989. The percentage of those whose mother tongue is Russian totals 68.8% of the population. Comparatively with the data of previous census this index has decreased by 4.9 percentage points. The percentage of other languages, specified as mother tongue, during the period that have passed since the previous census accounts for 0.03%." (Source: http://2001.ukrcensus.gov.ua/eng/results/general/language/Luhansk/)

11 "The analysis of the indicated native language of the population of Autonomous Republic of Crimea shows that 10.1% have indicated Ukrainian as their native language, 77.0% indicated Russian and 11.4% indicated Crimean-Tatar." (Source: http://2001.ukrcensus.gov.ua/eng/results/general/language/Crimea/)

Printed in the United States
By Bookmasters